# MY HITCH IN HELL

11/20/08

Dear Ann:
I hope you
find this story
inte...ting.

# My Hitch in Hell

## The Bataan Death March

**Lester I. Tenney**

POTOMAC BOOKS, INC.
Washington, D.C.

Paperback edition 2000, 2008
Copyright © 1995 by Potomac Books, Inc.

**Library of Congress Cataloging-in-Publication Data**

Tenney, Lester I.
My hitch in hell: the Bataan death march/Lester I. Tenney.
p. cm.
Includes index.
ISBN 978-1-57488-298-8
1. Tenney, Lester I. 2. World War, 1939–1945—Prisoners and prisons, Japanese. 3. World War, 1939–1945—Personal narratives, American. 4. Prisoners of war—Phillipines—Biography.
5. Prisoners of war—United States—Biography. I. Title.
D805.P6T47 1995
940.54'7252'095991—dc20

Paperback ISBN 978-1-57488-298-8          94-23594
                                                CIP

10 9 8 7 6 5 4 3

To the members of Company B, 192d Tank Battalion, both those living and those who died in the defense of their country

# ACKNOWLEDGMENTS

I would like to thank first Betty, my wife of thirty-four-plus years. She has put up with the idiosyncrasies and problems associated with my frustration, anger, past living conditions, and ill health, all brought on by my years as a prisoner of war.

I also want to thank my son, Glenn, for his strong support during this project. Since the late 1970s, he has urged me to get my thoughts down on paper or, better still, on my computer's hard drive. Also, my dear nephew, Si Tenenberg, encouraged me to get it done. He wanted to know more about me and my past experiences; he wanted to learn about my past through reading my history.

A special thanks goes to my two stepsons, Ed and Don Levi, who never pushed me to tell them what happened, always fearful that recalling some of those horrible events would create difficult emotional problems for me. I also want to thank, of course, my good friend and editor, Carol K. Weed, who saw my manuscript through completion.

My heart goes out to the families of my many friends who were a part of this experience but did not live long enough to return to freedom. I hereby acknowledge their tremendous contribution to *My Hitch in Hell* and to the part they played in our ultimate victory.

Last, I extend my thanks to the U.S. Department of Defense and the National Archives for some of the photos used in this book.

# CONTENTS

# FOREWORD

Lester I. Tenney spent his early twenties transiting, with intelligence and honor, one of the rockiest roads fate has ever dealt a generation of young Americans. A thoughtful Chicagoan of draft age just before World War II, he wanted to serve, but to serve with barracks buddies he felt comfortable with. So he took the trouble to visit the area's National Guard units like a freshman looking for a fraternity. He selected a Maywood, Illinois, outfit, Company B of the 192d Tank Battalion, and enlisted in October 1940, knowing and excited about the fact that the unit was soon going to be inducted into Federal service. He was going to get his year of military service over in a hurry and get on with business or college.

But history was already getting into gear in a way that few Americans expected. Lester's unit was federalized in November '40 and arrived in the Philippines exactly a year later. In less than three weeks, at 5:30 on a Sunday morning, a phone call came into their temporary headquarters near Clark Field. "Pearl Harbor has been bombed by the Japs; 'heads up,' they're heading your way!" By noon, the empire's bombs were enveloping them. American units in the Philippines were in mortal combat. And Company B would remain in combat and/or prison camp for nearly four solid years—spearheading the first American tank battle of World War II in a futile attempt to repel a massive Japanese amphibious invasion of the Philippines at Lingayen Gulf, holding the line in defense of the Bataan peninsula until their unit was surrendered by their commanding general in April '42, struggling through the Bataan Death March, and finally enduring brutal Japanese imprisonment in the Philippines and ultimately in Japan itself. This was a three-year and eight-month attrition path that saw only about one man in eight survive. The few that made it were on their last legs when they saw the mushroom cloud over Nagasaki, thirty miles from their camp. And those few, including Lester Tenney, stood and cheered as their lives were saved by America's nuclear bombs.

What kind of a guy gets through these things and winds up feeling good about himself? This has been my central interest since I traversed a similar, twice as long but less lethal track in North Vietnam (1964–1973). Specifically, what gets you through torture and isolation with self-respect intact? Let Lester Tenney show you in this book. He was brave without being foolhardy, honest to a fault with himself and his countrymen, had the self-discipline to curtail panic, possessed that enigmatic mixture of conscience and egoism called personal honor, and those gifts he calls "smarts": having an innate sense of knowing who you can trust, knowing who can take a joke and who can't, and knowing when it's prudent to be first in line, or last in line, or in the middle.

Lester and I were both imprisoned by Asian enemies who disregarded international law in both the proprieties of warfare and the treatment of their captives. In North Vietnamese prisons, though American deaths resulted in individual cases of government-prescribed and -supervised torture for military information of propaganda statements, and barbaric as the process was, the evolution at least proceeded from an external purpose. But in the Japanese prisons of World War II, Americans were subjected to recreational and unsupervised purposeless prisoner bashing. Killing, particularly of the weak and downfallen, was unbridled if not encouraged, and the result was vicious slaughter on a scale unmatched by any other enemy the United States has ever gone to war with. In Vietnam, the individual prisoner was pitted against an extortion machine. In Lester Tenney's prisons, he was pitted against the whims of uncontrolled, often fanatic, individuals.

In the letter element, Lester Tenney never went down for the count. More than once, it almost seemed that his ability to absorb punishment evoked in his tormentors sympathy if not admiration for his spirit. Time and again he would be caught in a compromising situation, be tortured for days, stoically resist (he claims his secret was holding on till he got so far out of it he couldn't grasp what the interrogators were asking), and wind up being dumped back in his camp, limp as a rag, unconscious for hours. Lester never begged for mercy. He knew that's what the Japanese wanted to hear, and saw with his own eyes instances of where coming across with what they wanted was rewarded with a bullet between the eyes.

But Lester was also cagey. In an enlightened move, he coaxed language instruction out of gregarious guards and learned to speak what he came to call "gutter" Japanese. Hemmed in in a workhouse prison in Japan, three miles from a once-abandoned coal mine in which he and the other Americans were forced to labor twelve hours a day a half mile beneath the surface, he organized and ran a clandestine free-market trading society. The major currency was Japanese cigarettes; the most heavily traded commodity was rice, but things like American toothpaste and shoes were also available from time to time. As Adam Smith predicted, this economy made everybody better off. Lester even provided for futures trading and bankruptcy protection. Through his acquired language capability he involved Japanese civilian mine supervisors and military guards in this enterprise. He was eventually found out, sentenced to death, and got out of it in a way that will amuse the reader.

Battered and beaten, this wonderful American left prison and Japan with torture injuries to an arm and a hip long overdue for surgery. Slowly, they were fixed up at home in Chicagoland, where as one would expect, he found both good and bad news.

But this courageous owner of a fighting heart bounced back to go on to better and better things—to become Lester I. Tenney, Ph.D., retired professor of finance at Arizona State University, and then to be much in demand as a motivational speaker.

It has been interesting to me to learn how similarly Dr. Tenney and I feel about our lessons learned in battle and behind bars. He says today, "I know without a doubt that my experiences during those trying four years shaped my thinking and my philosophies of life for these past fifty years."

I am glad I read this heroic story and proud to have been asked to write this foreword.

James B. Stockdale
Vice Admiral, U.S. Navy (Ret.)
Hoover Institution
Stanford University

# PREFACE

"In every battle there comes a time when one group of warriors must be sacrificed for the benefit of the whole. . . ," declared President Franklin D. Roosevelt during one of his fireside radio chats in March 1942. The battle he spoke of was the battle of the Philippines, and the warriors were those fighting American men and women on Bataan and Corregidor. The president's message was, he would provide no supplies, no reinforcements, no aircraft, no medicine, and no hope for the men and women fighting in the Philippines.

Up until April 9, 1942, we followed orders and fought the battle for Bataan and Corregidor. We even exceeded our top commanders' expectations about how long we could keep the Japanese at bay and gave the United States more time to mobilize and strengthen its fighting forces at home and overseas.

The Japanese high command had planned on capturing the Philippine Islands in just 55 days; however, the Allies' heroic armed forces in the Philippines held out for 148 days, almost three times longer than expected. Had our commanders so ordered, we would have continued to fight to the last man. But instead, with no food, no medical supplies, no reinforcements, no aircraft, and little ammunition left, we were ordered to surrender.

It was said best by Gen. Jonathan Mayhew Wainwright, on that last day of fighting in the Philippines: "There is a limit of human endurance and that limit has long since passed. Without prospect of relief I feel it is my duty to my country and to my gallant troops to end this useless effusion of blood and human sacrifice."

This was the first time in U.S. history that a whole army had to surrender to an enemy. The emotional and physical strain of this decision would last forever for those of us who were taken prisoner and later repatriated.

We survivors returned with our heads hung low. We had given up, surrendered; we were marked as cowards. We arrived back in the United States quietly, anonymously, without fanfare. There were no banners to welcome us home, no parades to march in, no speeches, and no acknowledgments of any kind. Our folks at home had so many heroes; they were busy welcoming winners, not losers. It was not the time to recognize those who had surrendered. More unfortunate still, many of us returned to find that family members had died and that wives and sweethearts had found other men to take our places. The telegrams, messages, and letters to my mother and dad and to Laura presented in this book are real and are reproduced exactly as originally written; they are an important part of my memorabilia.

The surrender was not something we were proud of, and it is only normal to keep quiet about those things we are ashamed of. But now, after all these years, I realized that I would be more ashamed of myself if I continued to keep quiet about the events that occurred on the infamous Bataan Death March, the physical and mental abuse, and the degrading and long-term physiological and psychological problems caused by our treatment while prisoners of war (POWs) of the Japanese. I no longer feel embarrassed that I surrendered, and I have finally decided to tell my story of what happened to that once-proud army on Bataan. However, this is not a rancorous book. This is not pleasant, but neither were the times. It is a realistic story of this man's fight for survival while keeping my ideals and faith intact.

Shortly after I came home in October 1945, my brother Bill began taking copious notes of everything I said regarding my experiences on Bataan. He questioned me about every detail, and he listened to my stories day after day and on many occasions right into the night. In addition, I was able to bring back dozens of pieces of paper with notes that I wrote while in prison camp. When I determined to write this book, I was able to reconstruct events by consulting these notes, together with hundreds of other items I received from my family and friends, and several hundred pages that I had written many years ago and by being willing to open the door to many painful, long-buried memories. Then, needing only the historical facts of the Philippine campaign, I began the long and tedious job of researching the files of the former War Department and the Department of the Army.

You may ask why I have decided to tell my story. I have four reasons. First, I find it difficult seeing the history of World War II dramatized and eulogized with little or no reflection on the Philippine campaign. During the fighting on Bataan, there was a saying going around that went something like this: "We're the Battling Bastards of Bataan/no mama, no papa, no Uncle Sam/and nobody else gives a damn." The Bataan Death March and its aftereffects took the lives of more than seventy-five thousand fighting men and women. Our ordeal, however, occurred in the early days of the war and was followed by many other important battles, both on land and at sea, to remember. Since the end of the war, the important Bataan campaign has been pushed into the background. Americans have been bombarded with information dealing with both the European and the Pacific theaters of operations, while at the same time they are largely ignorant about what really went on in the Philippine Islands.

Second, I still have nightmares of those events fifty years ago. The twelve days described as the "Bataan Death March" and the three and a half years I spent as a POW produced lifelong mental as well as physical scars. Although I still hurt, aging has made me a little more mellow. But regardless of the pain, I believe that the experiences of the past should not be forgotten. The quotation "Those who do not learn from history are doomed to repeat it" best describes my second reason for writing this book.

Third, I am angry. I feel I have been humiliated again by the Japanese, but this time I can say and do something about it without fear of retaliation, of a beating, or of other reprisals. Americans are not weak and lazy as several prominent Japanese businessmen and several Nippon government leaders attested in the late 1980s. In addition, Shigeto Nagano, a Japanese justice minister, recently described the atrocities committed by the Japanese in China and the Philippines in the 1930s and 1940s as "fabrications." He defended the Japanese wartime actions by saying they were attempts to free Asia from Western colonialism. This assertion was followed with a remark by Shin Sakurai, a cabinet member of the Liberal Democratic party and the minister of environmental affairs. Japan was not seeking to conquer Asia, he insisted; it was only trying to liberate the countries from Western influence. I cannot allow these attempts by government officials to justify the Japanese aggression and inhumane treatment of soldiers and civilians alike to go unchallenged nor unanswered.

My last reason for writing this book is to answer the multitude of questions I have been asked over the years regarding what happened on Bataan: "Was it really as bad as they said? Was it anything like the article I read? Did you actually see the incidents described in so-and-so's book?" My view of each scene, each horrendous experience, and each beating and humiliation was different than that of another person. Things happened so fast that a blink of an eye would bring with it another indelible memory. Camp 17, where I spent almost three years, was acknowledged to have the most brutal and inhumane commander and guards of any camp in all of Japan. This account of my experience will encompass my particular point of view and interpretation of the events that I saw. The events I witnessed and became a part of have never been properly described before.

These are my reasons for writing this book at this late date: I want the world to know just how we survivors feel, why we do what we do, why we say what we say, and why we live each day as if it is our last. I want my children and my grandchildren to know that war is horrible. Finally, I want them to respect all those who have given so much of themselves to defend the United States.

There is no doubt in my mind that the Japanese soldiers in this book were made the way they were by the war and therefore did not act as God would wish. I also believe any story of war is a story of hate; it makes no difference with whom one fights. I feel that our hatred surely destroys us spiritually just as the fighting destroys us bodily.

The tears shed here are for the dead, and my description of the horrors of war are for those who cannot stop hating. The hate shown in this book is intended to reflect man's inability to deal with reality, and of the love I describe herein, it alone kept me alive and sane.

There has been no collaboration on this book. I take full responsibility for any errors or omissions in recounting both historic events and narrative description. Some names have been changed to protect the respective individuals' privacy. While writing this book has been a trying experience for me, it nonetheless gave me new life to be able to contribute to the world's knowledge of what really happened on the Bataan Death March and of conditions in a Japanese prisoner of war camp.

# MY HITCH
# IN HELL

Main assault by
Company B of the
192d Tank Battalion

Agoo

Damortis
Rosario

*Lingayen*

*Gulf*

N

Dagupan

*South
China
Sea*

PHILIPPINES

*Luzon*

Mindoro

Samar

Palawan

*Panay*

Negros

*Sulu*

*Sea*

Mindanao

*Celebes
Sea*

L U Z O N

Tarlac

Cabanatuan
(Prison camp)

Camp O'Donnell
(Prison camp)

Capas

Clark Field

San Fernando

*SOUTH*

*CHINA*

*SEA*

Lubao

Hermosa

Mt. Natib

Orani

Abucay
Balanga
Pilar
Orion
Little Baguio
Limay
Lamao

**Bataan**

*Manila*

*Bay*

Manila

BATAAN DEATH MARCH

—— Travel on foot

--- Travel by rail

Bagac
Moron

**Peninsula**

0  5  10  15  20
MILES

Mariveles

Cabcaben

Cavite

Corregidor

120°

Jack Hopper

# CHAPTER 1

# A HITCH
# IN COMPANY B

At 12:25 P.M. on December 8, 1941, while bivouacked around Clark Field, the large U.S. air base in the Philippines, we heard the reassuring sound of planes overhead. We felt secure knowing that our air force was there to protect us and that we would not be the victims of a surprise attack like those bombed on Pearl Harbor only hours before (December 7, Hawaiian time). We looked up and saw fifty-four beautiful bombers in the sky—our planes coming back from a mission, we thought.

How wrong we were. The ground beneath us shook, and I will always remember the noise of those screeching bombs falling from the sky. Then came the explosions—first one, then what seemed like a hundred more— that sounded like thousands of large firecrackers going off at the same time. Some were direct hits on our planes, which were standing idle on the tarmac of Clark Field, while others exploded all around the airfield, killing or injuring hundreds of men who only a few hours ago were laughing and talking of the fun they were going to have once they got back home.

Craters opened up all over Clark Field from the high-altitude bombing. Then, without warning, in came the Japanese Zeros from the southeast, with the hot blazing sun as their backdrop. Just as we saw them, they began dropping their bomb loads. Then they swiftly turned and began strafing the entire airfield. Men ran for shelter from this barrage of bullets and shrapnel, but there was no place to hide. The bombing lasted for about fifteen minutes, while the strafing continued for what seemed like hours but was probably not more than thirty minutes. Despite all the available military intelligence about the Japanese plans and their preparations, plus our knowledge of the sneak

1

attack on Pearl Harbor that very morning, here we were, victims of another surprise attack that left our aircraft in shambles and our fighting force in utter disarray.

I was just twenty-one years old and thought I had my whole life in front of me. What a jolt this was to my dreams of a good life with a wonderful woman by my side and with a job that would pay me enough to do all those things I always wanted: to be happy, to raise a family, and to enjoy life. "Play the cards that were dealt you" was what I always said as a youngster, and it was my motto that December day.

It was easy to tell what *was* happening, but I did not know what was going to happen. Little did I know then that this uncertainty about the future would stay with me for nearly four miserable years. Perhaps it was not being able to look forward that made me think back eighteen months earlier.

I had dropped out of high school in my senior year. I thought I knew more than my teachers and continuing school was just a waste of my time. I had been attending Lane Tech, an all-boys' high school in Chicago, studying aeronautical engineering, a most sophisticated course for a high school. At eighteen I wanted to make my way in the business world. I did not want to wait for graduation. After all, going to college was not on my agenda, and I was dating a girl whose father wanted his daughter to marry someone who was successful in business or was in a profession.

A friend of mine was working in a factory that made various knick-knacks, mirrored wall supports, pipe stands, and hanging decorative plate holders. I got a job with the company selling these items to department stores. Luck was with me, and I made enough money in the first year to open my own little factory and make items that I created. As soon as I started to see my little business becoming successful, however, the government instituted a military draft of all young men eighteen and older. By this time I had reached the ripe old age of twenty, and I knew that I was a prime target to be one of the first persons drafted.

My jet-black hair, brown eyes, and dark complexion made people think my family came from Italy. In fact, the families of most of my Italian friends could not understand why I did not speak to them in Italian. Actually, my family is Jewish. My mother was born in Philadelphia and her parents came from Poland, while my father, whose parents came from Germany, was born in New York. The family name was Tenenberg, and my brother Bill used the name "Tenney" during the late thirties, when he wrestled under the name of "Wild Bill Tenney." Members of our family had been called Tenney for years, and during all my time in the service, I was known merely as Tenney. (I changed my name officially in September 1947, after finding out that many of my POW friends could not locate me in Chicago under the name of Tenney.)

I was young, healthy, and strong. I weighed about 185 pounds, was five feet ten inches tall, and was not afraid of a thing. By mid-1940, I saw the handwriting on the wall. There was no doubt in my mind that I would be chosen in the first draft, so I made plans to enter the service my way. I wanted to pick the outfit I would serve with and not be drafted and thrown into a group of strangers.

At about the same time, I read an article in a 1940 *Reader's Digest* that said ". . . the younger generation, that is, the war babies, now reaching maturity seem utterly incapable of taking on their responsibilities to the nation; they are aimless, soft and generally immature. . . ." I could not believe what I read. It sure was not talking about me, or was it? This article helped me make up my mind. I was going to volunteer and accept my responsibility to my family and my country. I was not soft and aimless, and I did not think I was immature.

In September 1940, I decided to volunteer instead of waiting to be drafted. I wanted to serve my one year and then to get on with my life. I had read that some National Guard units from the Chicago area would be mobilized that year. I realized I would have to live closely with those I served in the military; therefore, I wanted to have some choice in the fellows who would become my barracks buddies. Thus, I visited one National Guard unit after the other, but none seemed to satisfy my criteria. I did not even know what I was looking for, but I just did not feel comfortable with any of the groups I visited. Then one morning, after all my searching, I read a small article in the *Chicago Tribune* that contained the statement, "I am proud to serve my country in a time of need. The United States has been good to me and now I can pay back a little to America for all the good I have received." This quote was credited to Sgt. Richard E. Danca, 192d Tank Battalion, Company B of the Illinois National Guard from Maywood, Illinois.

This man with the positive attitude was what I had been searching for, people who felt proud to serve if called upon. My next step was to find out where and when this outfit met, and then to figure out how to get there.

Maywood was twenty-two miles from my home, but I was committed to go and find out if all the men in Company B felt the way Sergeant Danca did. So early one Thursday evening I set out for this small bedroom community west of Chicago. The trip took two transfers on the El (train) and two transfers on the bus. An hour and fifteen minutes later, I arrived at the door of the Maywood Armory, headquarters of the 192d Tank Battalion, Company B.

The Maywood Armory was more like a country club compared to the other National Guard units I visited. First I was greeted warmly with a "Hi, buddy! What's your name and where are you from?" Then I was invited to participate in a friendly game of pool. Aha, I thought, this is where they get me—big bets for a little unknown. But this was not the case; they were just being sociable.

Next came an invitation to bowl a game with some of the men. Impressed, I thought, gosh, a bowling alley at a National Guard outfit? Yep, true, this was like a country club. One of the men asked me to bowl a game with him. He introduced himself as Lewis Brittan and said he was also new here. Like me, he had just come by to take a look at the men in this outfit. "Just call me Lew," he offered.

Lew was about six feet tall and well-built, with dark black hair and a small, black pencil-stripe mustache. About two or three years my senior, Lew had a rare friendliness, and when he asked me to bowl, I could sense his warmth and sincerity. His voice and his facial expression showed that he was not just trying to be hospitable; he was interested in people and wanted to make friends. I immediately accepted his offer. Lew and I hit it off from that first moment. (We stayed together throughout the war, the march, and prison camp, and we came home together. In fact, we even went into business together while both of us worked on our degrees from the University of Miami. We remained friends until he died of a massive heart attack while sitting in his chair at home on September 23, 1990.)

While talking to many of the other men, I found out that they all shared the same philosophy as Sergeant Danca. They were willing to serve their country in a time of need. I knew right then and there that as long as I was going to enter the service, I wanted to serve with this group of men. It was a great group; the men all fought and responded as any good soldiers would. They played as if there was no tomorrow, they cared for one another, and they acted under pressure just as I had expected. (The few survivors in the early 1990s—14 out of 164—still care for each other and are concerned for each other's welfare.)

The word was out. All four companies of the 192d Tank Battalion were to be inducted into federal service on November 25, 1940. Company A was from Janesville, Wisconsin; Company B, our company, was from Maywood, Illinois; Company C was from Port Clinton, Ohio; and Company D was from Harrodsburg, Kentucky. (Company D was supposed to be transferred to the 194th Tank Battalion immediately after the war started and would have become that battalion's Company C.) Our destination was Fort Knox, Kentucky.

When the line formed for signing up, I was right up front. I wanted to be a part of this group. I was so proud that I was busting out all over. The man in front of me was asked for his date of birth, and after responding he was told, "Sorry, buddy, but you aren't twenty-one yet so you have to get your parents' consent before we can accept you." This news was a surprise to me. I thought eighteen was the legal age for joining up, and I would not be twenty-one until July 1.

When my turn came and I was asked, "In what year were you born?" I quickly said, "1919, sir." So on October 12, 1940, I became a proud member of Company B of the 192d Tank Battalion. Yes, I was going to get my year of military service over with in a hurry.

I was a proud American boy, and when I came home wearing my uniform, my folks were equally proud of me. I was the apple of the family's eye. All four of my brothers gave me words of encouragement and plenty of advice on how to keep out of trouble.

I was the baby of the family, and my brothers were older by ten to sixteen years. My mother and father had had their share of grief and had experienced and overcome heartache together years before. In 1918 my folks lived in Philadelphia, and on a cold December morning, while my dad was at work, Mom went shopping. My two sisters were home alone, and twelve-year-old Edith decided to light the gas stove for a little extra heat in the house. She lit a match and turned on the gas, but the match blew out, so she went to the cupboard for another. The gas from the stove had not been turned off and fumes filled the kitchen. When Edith struck the second match, the spark set off an explosion, and flames ignited her clothes. Ruth, the younger sister, was frightened beyond belief. Both girls ran outside. Edith rolled over in the snow to douse the flames while Ruth cried helplessly. Edith died on the way to the hospital. Ruth caught a cold on that dreadful day and died within a week.

The deaths of two daughters in one week gave my mother and father their first lesson in survival, personal fortitude, and the need for a positive attitude for their life. Their family doctor suggested that they try to have another child as soon as possible. I was born out of that catastrophe, and although I am sure Mom and Dad really wanted a little girl, they never showed any disappointment or remorse that their last child was a boy. My folks were wonderful people who faced life with the basic philosophy of "Enjoy your todays, and you will look forward to your tomorrows." I adopted their philosophy as my hitch in the service began.

The evening of November 25 came quickly. We all lined up in our sparkling clean uniforms, and with full packs on our backs, we stood at attention for roll call. Down the line came Capt. Theodore F. Wickord, looking every bit the part of a commanding officer. He was dressed in a spotless and well-pressed uniform. His five-foot ten-inch frame was nearly overshadowed by his proud, puffed-out chest, which seemed to shout, "I'm proud of my country and the service I am about to give." The captain was about thirty-two years old, and his hair was already starting to recede. Because of that mature touch, he had the appearance of an old hand at leading a bunch of soldiers. Actually, Captain Wickord was a supervisor with the local power company and only played soldier once a week with this National Guard unit.

The captain started asking each man in turn, "What do you want to be in this man's army?" Finally he came to me. I was one of the last men in the formation because my last name started with a "t." Little did I realize that Wickord was a man with great determination. He wanted to find a man for every job description in the outfit, and when he asked me about my job, I replied, "Tank driver, sir." The captain then said, "What's your second choice?" My response was a resounding, "Radio operator, sir." Then the captain said, "What's your third choice?" This question caught me off guard. At one time I had served an apprenticeship as a short order cook at a leading hotel in Chicago, so I joked, "Cook, sir." This answer was what he had been waiting for; 164 men were leaving that evening for Fort Knox, Kentucky, without one cook among us.

I was made the cook for our company until a few chosen men completed Cooks' and Bakers' School, a three-month course. Without an assistant except for fifteen KPs (kitchen police, or those assigned kitchen duty) for each meal, cooking was hard work and involved long hours. I cooked over coal-fired stoves that had to be started by 3:00 in the morning in order to be ready for breakfast at 6:00. As the only cook, I had to prepare three meals a day plus midnight guard meals every fourth day.

After we arrived at Fort Knox, our company was about ten men short of full strength, so ten new inductees from the Chicago area were assigned to our unit. These men were given kitchen duty during their first week. Their constant attendance in the kitchen and their willingness to do anything asked of them made my job as cook a little easier.

When the men who went to Cooks' and Bakers' School had graduated and returned to our company, I was relieved of my duty as cook and was given a ten-day leave to rest up and to choose whatever school I wanted to attend. With great anticipation and excitement, I went home—home not only to my mother and father but to Laura, the girl I loved and some-day would call my wife. On the train going home, I thought of how I met Laura.

It was at the Trianon Ballroom located in the south side of Chicago, when I was seventeen years old. During the late thirties, I loved dancing to the music of Kay Kyser, Tommy Dorsey, Paul Whiteman, and Benny Goodman, whose bands played the ballrooms in and around Chicago. On a particular Saturday night in June, four other fellows and I traveled the twenty-five miles to the Trianon to hear the music of Guy Lombardo. Luck was with me that night, for I met Laura, who had come to the Trianon Ballroom with three of her girlfriends to dance.

She was standing near the doorway as I entered. Laura was unusually beautiful. She was about five feet four inches tall, weighed about 115 pounds, and had a magnificent figure. Her slender waist, which I could span with my two hands, emphasized her ample breasts. Her clear blue eyes sparkled and lit up the entire room. Looking into Laura's eyes, fringed with long black lashes, made me wonder if she was an angel. Her light brown hair fell softly against her cheeks in the sleek, loose pageboy style of the day, and her smile was so friendly. She spoke with the gentleness of a true lady. I had never met a girl with so much charm and personality.

It was love at first sight for me; Laura told me afterward that it was love at second sight for her. I danced every dance with her that night. She was so beautiful, such a perfect lady, and so prim and proper in everything she did or said. I could not take my eyes off of her. The electrical charge from this meeting went through me at full throttle. When I left the ballroom with my friends, I told them, "I want nothing to do with any other girl from tonight on. I've found the girl I want to become my wife." After I got home I pinched myself to see if I was I dreaming. How lucky could one person be to find someone so enchantingly beautiful and to be so much in love? Laura was my first love, and in my excitement, I felt that I would never meet anyone who could compare with her.

During my leave, I saw Laura every glorious day. We talked about our future together, our plans and aspirations, our goals and dreams. We realized how much we meant to each other. When I had returned to Fort Knox, I had to clear Laura from my mind before I could decide which military school I wanted to attend. I opted for Radio Operators' School, a six-week course, and after graduation I was assigned as radio operator in the lead tank—the captain's tank, no less.

While attending Radio Operator's School, I did not have to pull any other duty, and because of Laura, I did not want to have any dates or fool around at dance halls or bars. Therefore, having a lot of free time I went to Louisville, Kentucky, which is about eighteen miles from Fort Knox, and got a part-time job at a Walgreen Drugstore as a soda jerk. I earned twenty-five cents an hour while keeping busy and tried to save a little extra cash for my future. At this time I was a private, making thirty dollars a month. So the extra cash came in mighty handy when I went on a leave.

As I completed Radio Operators' School, the newspapers reported that the United States was unhappy with Japan because of the war it instigated against China. The stories indicated that the Japanese soldiers were performing barbaric acts against the Chinese, both the civilian and military populations. The Japanese aggression against China started in 1931, but the full assault did not occur until early in 1937.

By April 1940 the Sino-Japanese war had depleted Japan's oil reserves to a catastrophic low. The U.S. government, realizing Japan's resources were dwindling fast and wanting to curtail any further Japanese aggression, imposed a complete iron embargo against Japan. Japan was being strangled, pushed into a corner. Then on September 27, 1940, Japan signed a military pact with Italy and Germany and condemned the United States for its interference. I had a feeling then that in just a matter of time we would be at war with Japan. The U.S. economic boycott of Japan continued until the surprise attacks on Pearl Harbor and the Philippine Islands.

Was it a coincidence that in September 1940, after the three-nation pact was signed, the U.S. military draft began? At this  time our armed forces began a concentrated effort to train men for combat.

For Mother's Day 1941, I wrote the following letter to my mother, expressing my love for her and my awareness of the possibility of war and of the need to fight to protect our country. I also wanted to acknowledge my mother's strengths and her influences on me: first, her positive attitude about life and, second, her conviction that the United States was the best place in the world to live. As I look back it is easy to see that I inherited her love of country and her positive outlook. That positive attitude was the most dominating influence in my survival.

May 7, 1941

My Dear Mother:

This year I'll not be home on Mother's Day which will be Sunday May 11, and I won't see that big smile of yours, while tears roll from your eyes. I'll not be there to wear my red carnation symbolizing my Mother is among the living, and mingle with those wearing a carnation of white, whose Mothers have gone beyond. So this year I give you this letter as my Mother's Day gift.

Seems funny, Mom, that when I think of you, I recall a lot of little things that bind us so close together. I remember the first time I wanted the car to drive all by myself, you interceded for me, and said you thought I was old enough to have it. I recall how you took me to the store to buy me my first long pants suit. Doesn't seem long ago that you caught me shaving. Of course I didn't really need it, but you only smiled. These and many other things come back to me now as I sit here and write you. Another thing I'll always remember is the look on your face when I left home for Fort Knox. You were torn between two desires. Your mind said you didn't want me to go, but your heart said I was doing what you had always taught me. That I should prepare myself as best I could for any eventuality. You also taught me it was right to help protect those unable to protect themselves, either as a person or their rights. That's what we thousands of boys are doing in the Army camps today, preparing ourselves to protect those people and those privileges we love, should the day ever come when someone might try to take them away from us.

When you get this letter, you will be but one of thousands of Mothers all over the United States who have letters from their sons on Mother's Day. Here at Fort Knox, almost every fellow I know is writing his Mother, if she is alive, and if she has passed on they will be thinking about her. I'm closing this letter now. I want you to know you are the most dominating influence in my life. You know my weaknesses and my strengths. My weaknesses you have tried to build up, and my strengths you have tried to guide in the right path. You smiled when I needed a smile and scolded when I had done wrong. For these things I'll be eternally grateful, and whatever I am, or might be, I owe to you.

Your ever loving and devoted son,

Lester

In early September 1941, the week before we left Fort Knox for maneuvers, Laura came to Kentucky to be with me. It was then we decided, in spite of everything, to get married. We were in love and did not think rationally. I had no profession to speak of and no future. And Laura's mother and father had made it clear from the start that they wanted her to marry someone with wealth or a man who at least had the opportunity to acquire it.

We had talked for hours about whether we should get married. Every reason why we should had at least two reasons why we should not. As so often happens, however, romance won out over common sense. That night I made love to her. I promised her that our life would be a good one and that we would succeed at whatever we attempted. The following morning I noticed that Laura was not herself. Then it came out: she felt guilty about what had happened. She asked me what we would do if she were pregnant. A nice girl just did not get pregnant out of wedlock and disgrace her entire family.

We made a decision. The following day I borrowed Lew's car, and we drove for an hour or two looking for a justice of the peace or anyone that could marry us and make our affair legal and honorable. Finally, in a little

town in the hills of Kentucky, I went inside the general store and asked if
there was an official in town that could marry us. Much to my surprise and
happiness, the store owner was a justice of the peace and said he could
help us.

No marriage ceremony as such, it was just a few words, simple and to
the point: "Will you take this woman to be your lawful wedded wife? . . ."
After taking our marriage vows, the justice handed me some very legal-
looking papers that I assumed included the wedding certificate. I put them
in my pocket, planning to put them in my footlocker for safekeeping. Then
the justice invited us to stay at his house that night. We accepted and were
shown to a small guest bedroom on the top floor of his home. The room
was furnished with old country-style furniture, made from boxes and scrap
lumber, but on our first night together as husband and wife, it seemed like
a castle to us. We thought it was a glorious way to end such a perfect day.

The next week the four tank companies of the 192d Tank Battalion
went on maneuvers at Camp Polk, Louisiana. Our battalion, the only
National Guard unit attached to the 1st Armored Division, performed at
an extraordinary pace. It seemed we did everything right. Under the
watchful eyes of the army's special investigative team, which included
Gen. George S. Patton, a brilliant officer who was an authority on tank
warfare, our battalion was declared the finest tank unit of all those on
maneuvers. In effect, we won the war games.

To this day I cannot figure out how we won the simulated war when all
we had were broomsticks for guns, markers for heavy tanks, and a few
tanks of 1930s vintage. In spite of all these flaws, we were chosen the tank
group to head overseas. Actually, unbeknownst to us, we had been selected weeks earlier as the tank group to fill Gen. Douglas MacArthur's plan
for defending the Philippine Islands, the plan known as War Plan Orange
III, or WPOIII for short.

MacArthur devised WPOIII in April 1941. Based on the assumption
that the war would only be between Japan and the United States, WPOIII
theorized that Manila would be abandoned and declared an "open" city
and that the U.S. forces would then withdraw to the Bataan peninsula,
where they could hold out until reinforcements arrived from Pearl Harbor.
Meanwhile, our offshore fortress, the island of Corregidor, along with our
ability to overlook all of Manila Bay would provide the firepower needed
for the delaying action that would eventually push the Japanese from the
shores of the Philippines.

By October 1941 the world situation changed, and a new plan was
devised that was to be implemented if the United States found itself at war
with Germany and Japan at the same time. According to the new plan,
Rainbow V, which was developed with the full cooperation and in consul-

tation with the British General Staff, Germany was considered the enemy to defeat before an all-out effort would be made against Japan. Rainbow V still called for the forces in the Philippines to adopt a defensive strategy similar to WPOIII.

While the war games were finishing, all four companies of the 192d Tank Battalion were gathered together in a special area of Camp Polk, where our commanding officer, Major Wickord (recently promoted from captain) and General Patton informed us of our honor of being the outstanding unit. They told us that we were going overseas, but they could not, or would not, tell us where. Then everyone in our tank unit was granted a ten-day furlough. Major Wickord said, "Go home, say your good-byes, get your life in order, because we set sail from Angel Island in a few weeks." Where is Angel Island? I wondered.

Within the next twenty-four hours, we lined up outside the medic's office and received inoculations for typhoid, tetanus, yellow fever, and diphtheria. In addition, of course, the army determined our blood types, just in case of an emergency. The 192d Tank Battalion was also issued brand-new tanks, so new that no one knew how to operate them. And because we needed so many, they were commandeered from other units then getting instructions on their use. All of our old tanks were traded to the tank units that were staying in the States. The new tanks accompanied us to the Philippines.

I enjoyed ten days with my new wife, planning and discussing our life together. I had a feeling then that this might be the last time, for a long time, that we would see each other. I was not alone in facing the problems that early marriage entailed under these conditions. Many of my buddies had married their childhood sweethearts; others planned on getting married to their girlfriends when they returned. A few did so, but many others never returned to fulfill their vows or enjoy the love of their family and friends.

The men who returned to Camp Polk from their furloughs were the younger men, without family obligations. The older men and those with children were not expected to go overseas with their unit, and special provisions were made for them. If they wanted to go with the company they could, but once under way, there was no turning back. A few of our men went absent without leave (AWOL). I guess they just did not want to go overseas. Two of the men who did not return after furlough were company cooks.

Those of us who did return started to load equipment aboard flatcars that were waiting at a siding by camp headquarters. We received new tanks, new half-tracks, and new command cars. Just about everything we loaded that day was new issue. We then packed all of our personal items into an olive green army duffel bag. I remember putting the folded papers from the justice of the peace into a letter-writing pad Laura had given me.

On October 20, 1941, we left Louisiana for Angel Island, which I found out was in San Francisco Bay, California. Our train traveled slowly through the countryside, and due to the extremely heavy load it was carrying, we had to stop frequently to check the cables and rods holding the equipment. Nighttime came, and we were given dinners of cold fried chicken, coleslaw, carrot salad with raisins, a large apple, and for dessert, a piece of chocolate cake—all wrapped and squeezed into a box six-by-eight-by-two-inches deep.

After eating our first meal aboard the train, we sat around in small groups, just reminiscing about what we had done during our furlough. I could feel the sadness of the entire group. No one said a word about the possibilities of war. Instead, we tried to pretend that we were going on an adventure. With very little to do on the train, most of us got into our bunks fairly early. I was tired and fell sound asleep almost at once.

I do not remember what time it was when I was abruptly awakened by Capt. Donald Hanes, our new company commander. He stood next to my bunk and violently shook me until I woke up. He said in a raspy voice, "Tenney, there're no cooks aboard. They all went AWOL. Can you get up and get breakfast ready for the men?" I knew this was not a question, but rather an order, so I got up and found my way to the chow car, about four cars to the rear. When I looked at my watch, it was 4:30 in the morning. All of a sudden I knew what I was going to do on this train ride—work.

Cooking on a troop train in 1941 was not a bed of roses. We cooked on stoves heated by coal. Washing pots and pans as well as the men's mess kits presented a problem all its own; water had to be boiled in forty-gallon pots. Coffee, a staple for the army, was still made the old-fashioned way, with ground coffee beans put into large kettles of boiling water that sat till the coffee looked and tasted done. When ready, we poured a little cold water over the coffee and the grounds would settle to the bottom, unless the train jerked at the wrong moment.

In preparing three meals a day, we worked from 4:00 in the morning straight through till 8:00 at night. We needed this much time for starting the fires, preparing the food, maneuvering around a room sixty feet long and only eight feet wide, and moving a line of 168 hungry soldiers through this maze without getting everyone and everything upset and agitated.

When we arrived at Angel Island, local longshoremen handled the unloading of the train and the loading of the ship. We were lined up for a set of examinations that many of the men hoped they would fail but with no such luck. Everyone passed with flying colors, and plans were under way for an early departure to destinations unknown.

I still remember that first night on Angel Island. I sat on my bunk and wrote a letter to my wife, Laura. I felt that this might be my last one to her for a long, long time. I poured my heart out to her, hoping she would understand my innermost feelings about what I believed would happen during the next few months. With tears in my eyes and a lump in my throat, I started the letter. I tried to express my feelings as best I could, realizing that whatever I wrote would not be taken seriously by anyone else in the world except Laura, who really cared.

October 26, 1941

My Dearest Laura:

I am sitting here on an old army cot, afraid to make a sudden move or the cot will collapse. But I must write you today because I may not have another opportunity for a long, long time. We just finished seeing our tanks and other equipment put aboard the "Hugh L. Scott" transport. We aren't sure just when we will be taking off, but the bet is it will be either tomorrow or the next day. Seems the rumor has it we will be heading for the Philippine Islands and getting ready to defend our military position there against the Japanese.

In spite of all of the partying, there is little or no real laughter here. This evening is one we will always remember. Sadness seems to be everywhere. Some of the fellows, I'm sure, are sad because they are leaving their recent wives, or their sweethearts who will eventually become their brides. I'm sad because I'm leaving you. I want you to know that you mean the world and all to me, and I'll always love you till the day I die. My life became more meaningful because of you. I'll be home before you know it, then we can start our life together—forever.

There is a lot of talk about war with Japan. Some say it is inevitable, that it will happen before this year is over. As we listen to the news broadcasts we are well aware of the pressure being applied to the Japanese to stop their war with China, but the feeling here is the Japs will not listen to us and won't be so afraid of our embargo of oil and the hold on all of their money won't alter their course of action. Not a happy thought, but we are being realistic and trying not to bury our heads in the sand. War is a real possibility, our being at the start of it is also a real possibility. None of us want to fight, but we will if pushed. One of our concerns today is the fact that we loaded new tanks for our future use, but we don't know how to operate them. Not drive them, they drive the same as any other tank, but the equipment inside: the radio, the machine guns, the cannon in the turret, all of these things are new to us and we haven't had any training or practice in the proper operation. Maybe when we get to the Philippines they'll teach us. I sure hope so.

Well, good night my dearest, try to keep thinking of me, think of all the things we will do when I come home and get out of the service. This may be my last letter for a while, so keep it close to your heart and remember, I love you, I want you or I don't want to live.

With great love as always,

Les

Laura saved this letter. She later gave it to my mother for her memory box, a shoe box filled with letters, newspaper clippings, and anything else that would remind her of her soldier son in the Philippines.

At about 8:00 P.M. on October 27, 1941, aboard the *Hugh. L. Scott,* formerly known as the *President Pierce,* we headed out of San Francisco Bay toward Hawaii and then on to the Philippines. The *Scott* traveled as a luxury cruise ship prior to being taken over by the U.S. government. When the government converted the ship to a troop carrier, it dispensed with the luxury accommodations. Most of the men slept on hammocks, three deep, in the hold of the ship. By the end of the first full day, I was just getting over my seasickness when I heard that the ship's chaplain was looking for an assistant—someone to run the games, check out game equipment, and oversee the other entertainment on board the ship.

I had nothing to do aboard ship, as I was given a no-work order by Captain Hanes. His theory was I had pulled duty on the train when all of the other men rested, so it was my turn to rest while all of the other men pulled duty. Sitting around doing nothing was not my style, so I volunteered for the job of assistant to the chaplain. Little did I know then what perks went with the job.

I was given my own two-room cabin to use as an office as well as my sleeping accommodations. I was allowed to choose a helper, and of course I chose my buddy, Lew Brittan. For the next month, our voyage on the troop ship was more like that of a cruise ship. Lew and I had all of the freedom and luxury one could expect. We printed a daily paper, assembled a ten-piece band, loaned out all types of games, and even ran some group games for all those aboard who wanted to participate.

Upon our arrival in Hawaii, Lew and I were given full liberty, along with a wallet full of money to buy interesting games for the men to use for the balance of the trip. By this time the rumor was we were heading for Manila in the Philippine Islands. To most of the men aboard our ship this sounded like a dream come true—to see the world and get paid for it. It was a chance to experience the romance, intrigue, and excitement of a country in the Far East, thousands of miles from home; a journey to a faraway land we would be able to tell our children about.

I was nervous about the upcoming trip. Just a few months before, in July 1941, the British had cut off all supplies of rubber to Japan, and the U.S. government had frozen all Japanese assets held in the United States. That meant all oil and other vital shipments to Japan were stopped at once, and Japan was left without funds to pay for the supplies it needed to continue its war with China. Of course, that was the idea behind both the embargo and the freezing of all assets—to stop Japan's war with China.

The more I read about Japan's economic problems, the more I worried about what consequences we would face because of our country's actions. I did not have to wait very long before I found out. From the time we left Hawaii till we arrived in the Philippines, we traveled in blackout conditions because we saw Japanese warships following us about two miles off our port side.

I wrote the following letter to my folks while I was in Honolulu, explaining to them my concerns about war with Japan. The letter, exactly as written, shows my apprehension regarding the United States' involvement with Japan.

November 9, 1941, from Honolulu

My Dear Mother and Father:

I hope and pray that this letter finds everyone in the best of health. Don't worry about me because I'm feeling OK. We believe we are going to the Philippines, we also are aware of the fact that we won't be home for a long while, some say two years, others say longer. Most of us are homesick already, and my coming from a lovely and warm family makes the being away even harder. But here I am 5,000 miles from home so I'll just smile and try to forget my worries and make the most of it. We had just docked at Honolulu and the scenery is really gorgeous, something out of a book. I may bring Laura here for a honeymoon some day.

As far as we know we are going to Manila, that's in the Philippine Islands, but there is the possibility that we may go on to Singapore to help out the Marines. I guess it all depends on the situation with Japan. Let's hope and pray that nothing comes of all this. It sure is hot down here. Nothing like it at home even in the summers. I went to the mainland this evening, and saw almost everything there is to be seen, including "Hell's Half Acre" and the Royal Hawaiian Hotel. Boy what a view from here, you can see in all directions, the beautiful water, the mountains and the land-scape for as far as you can see.

My job on the boat is the Chaplain's assistant (not bad for a Jewish boy). We sail in two more days for Manila. I'll send another letter once we arrive there. We are all very tense because when we leave here we are going to travel with a Navy escort and we will be traveling through some mighty dangerous waters. You see, we have to go right through some Japanese Islands. We were also told we would be traveling "blackout."

I don't know what else to write about. I'm always thinking about you. I'll never, in all my life forget you. You are the dearest parents a fellow could ever want, and I love both of you for it. There will never be anyone to take your place.

Your loyal, faithful and ever loving son,

Lester

P.S. Dad, Please take good care of Laura for me, look after her a little. Just in case anything should happen to me, please pay up my insurance, then if anything happens . . . well pay it up because the situation looks pretty bad. Keep your faith. I'll keep mine, you'll see, everything will work out for the best.

We received orders from stateside to avoid any contact with the Japanese ships we had seen. Those of us aboard the troop ship in November 1941 knew from what we had seen that there was a strong possibility of a confrontation with the Japanese in the not-too-distant future. Based on what we had read about the rape of Nanking, we thought we had a pretty good idea of what to expect in the coming months, but little did we dream of the full horror that lay ahead.

# CHAPTER 2

# SURPRISE ATTACK

We arrived in the Philippines on November 20, 1941, the newly proclaimed Thanksgiving Day, nicknamed "Franksgiving Day" because President Franklin D. Roosevelt moved it back one week to allow for more shopping days between Thanksgiving and Christmas. Instead of turkey that day, we enlisted men had hot dogs. (Our officers went to the Officers' Club and had turkey with all the trimmings.)

Unfortunately, no mail awaited us when we arrived; but after all, no one was supposed to know where we were going. Most of us were a little depressed when we found out there would be no mail call.

Our entire tank battalion was sent to Fort Stotsenburg, adjacent to Clark Field, where we were housed in tents about one thousand feet from the airfield. The tremendous military buildup in the Philippines of both men and equipment, over such a short period of time, caused a severe housing shortage and required hundreds of us to live in tents on the perimeter of Clark Field. This "tent city" arose overnight, with thirty or more tents in an area that only days before was a parade ground. Each tent was more like a tent-house, about twenty feet square, with a wooden floor and wooden supports. The canvas that was stretched over the basic form had a door and two window openings on each side. Six men were assigned to each tent.

Shortly after arriving at our new tent homes at Fort Stotsenburg, we discovered the relaxed way army personnel lived in the Philippines. To our amazement each tent-house had a houseboy, whose duties included shining shoes, making beds, and keeping everything shipshape. Within days of our arrival, we were propositioned by some of the local "businessmen" to buy Filipino-made knives for three pesos, to have sharkskin suits made to order for twenty pesos, and to have a good time with their "sisters" for only five pesos. The exchange rate at this time was one peso for fifty cents.

We had been in the islands a little more than two weeks when the war started, but we had not yet become accustomed to the heat and humidity. We also found the language and Filipino customs difficult to reconcile with our midwestern culture. Young boys selling the pleasures of their sisters; water buffalo, called carabao, roaming the roads and being considered a part of the Filipino family; and six or seven people living, eating, and sleeping in a one-room hut were hard for many of us Americans to accept. In addition, we could not distinguish a Filipino from a Japanese or Chinese person; the facial characteristics of all Asians appeared identical to our unaccustomed eyes. This later proved very distressful and challenging when we had to search for Japanese spies and infiltrators.

In spite of my frustration of being in unfamiliar surroundings and among people I could not understand, I was nevertheless having a good time. As a cook in the islands, I was supposed to work one day and have three days off—not a bad work schedule. This freedom gave me more time to explore the countryside. No matter where I went on the island, however, I always felt a twinge of insecurity that came from never really knowing which of the natives were my allies. Each time I saw someone with oriental features, I thought he or she was Japanese, which was silly because most of the Asians in the Philippines were Chinese.

On November 27, the Far East Air Command ordered two all-unit warnings and alerts—one during the day and the other at night—but the tank units never received the alerts. We could never figure out why.

Apparently, the Navy Department in Washington, D.C., broke a Japanese coded message giving November 29 as the date for hostilities to begin. Our leaders in Washington then sent Gen. Walter C. Short and Adm. Husband E. Kimmel in Hawaii a message that said, "This dispatch is to be considered a war warning. Negotiations with Japan looking toward stabilization of conditions in the Pacific have ceased and an aggressive move by Japan is expected within the next few days." This message, along with many other decoded Japanese messages, alerted our military high command that an aggressive move by Japan could be expected momentarily. When nothing unusual happened on the twenty-ninth or the following day, all caution was thrown to the wind. We went back to what we were doing before the warning—nothing.

On November 29, I was able to send the following postal telegraph message home:

ARRIVED MANILA SAFE WON'T BE ABLE TO WRITE FOR A WHILE TELL
LAURA I SEND MY LOVE HOPE EVERYONE FEELING FINE LOVE TO ALL -
LESTER FORT STOTSENBURG

By the end of November, the navy ordered all ships to leave Manila and move south, out of reach of the Japanese bombers. It seems everyone in authority knew that a confrontation with the Japanese was imminent. Yet in spite of all of this preplanning and knowledge, our ships in Pearl Harbor and our planes in the Philippines remained easy targets for the enemy.

On December 1, 1941, as reported in *U.S. Army in World War II*, 19,138 U.S. service personnel and 11,957 Philippine Scouts, for a total of 31,095 trained and equipped military people, defended the entire Philippines. Add to this an unknown number of Filipinos who were mobilized into the Philippine Army, but without training, guns, uniforms, or helmets. In addition to these meager, poorly trained and ill-equipped troops, we only had 35 B-17s, 18 B-18s, 107 P-40s, and a handful of other aircraft too old and outdated to mention. This fighting force, however, had the duty and responsibility to protect the Philippines against any aggressor—and Japan, in particular.

As early as December 1, many of our tanks went into battle position for the defense of Clark Field, a plan that was previously arranged; and some of the tanks were still there on December 7 when war broke out. On December 4, naval intelligence in Washington wanted to issue an attack warning, but the request was denied at a level higher than that of MacArthur. In spite of this, MacArthur still sent out patrols each night. They came back and reported sighting enemy bomber groups twenty miles to fifty miles out at sea. As soon as our planes spotted them, our pilots would turn away and head back to base.

As if this was not enough, we still did not have any training on the new tanks. While we were in Honolulu, our commander had tried to borrow two 37mm guns (the types mounted in our new tanks) and enough ammunition to practice from our transport deck while en route to the Philippines; but post ordnance in Hawaii refused this request. When our tank unit arrived in the Philippines, we asked for the use of a firing range so that we could become familiar with the weapons mounted in our new tanks. This request was also denied. Therefore, it was not until the Japanese bombers and Zeros came over Clark Field that we were able to get in our "practice." On-the-job training does not work very well under these conditions.

Due to the time difference, it was 3:00 A.M. on December 8 in Manila when at 8:00 A.M. Hawaii time, December 7, the Japanese struck the U.S. fleet at Pearl Harbor. General MacArthur, his staff officers, and all unit commanders were informed of the attack within minutes. At 5:00 A.M. the air force commander in the Philippines asked permission to load bombs on our planes and proceed to destroy the enemy on Formosa, a take-off point for the Japanese bombers and Zeros. If we could get to Formosa (now Taiwan) before any other Japanese aircraft could take off, we could direct a severe blow to the enemy, on their land, before they could deploy for the Philippines. The pilots and their crews were all hyped up, ready to rain retaliation on our new enemy, the Japanese; but our bomb group was told to wait for orders from MacArthur.

At about 5:30 in the morning of December 8, we were awakened and told the United States was at war with the Japanese. We were briefed on the disaster at Pearl Harbor and instructed to prepare for the landing of Japanese paratroopers at Clark Field. Our entire battalion—tanks, half-tracks, and other armored vehicles, as well as all personnel—were sent to Clark Field to repel an enemy landing.

At 11:30 A.M., six hours after we received word that we were at war, MacArthur finally approved the air raid on Formosa. The crews loaded the bombs—twenty-pounders, fifty-pounders, and one hundred–pound bombs—as fast as they could. When the planes were loaded, their commander authorized the pilots and crews to take a lunch break. Of course they left the planes loaded with tons of high explosives, all in a nice straight row, ready to take off as soon as the crews came back from lunch. Our pursuit planes, the P-40s, were out on a reconnaissance mission and were ordered to return at noon. The pilots taxied the P-40s in from the runway, lined them up like sitting ducks, and went to lunch. The radar man at Clark Field, an inexperienced operator, turned off his machine and also went to lunch.

Meanwhile, by 8:00 in the morning, we moved all of our tank equipment into position around the airfield. We were told to prepare for the landing of Japanese paratroopers. Everyone was on edge, because we did not know what was happening and, more important, we were still totally confused as to how to operate our tanks and their new cannons.

A typical conversation between tank radio operators went something like this. Tank One: "Where the hell are the shells for this damn cannon?" Tank Two: "We can't find them anyplace in this damn tank. Anybody got any ideas?" Tank One again: "We should have read the instruction book before leaving Camp Polk—I think it's too late now." Tank Three: "I asked the Captain. He said, 'How the hell am I to know!'" No one could fire a shell at that moment even if they had to.

Then it happened. At 12:35 in the afternoon of December 8, 1941 (December 7 in the United States), we heard the airplanes. As we looked up into the sky, we saw fifty-four bombers flying very high over Clark Field. Just as I was about to say, "They're not ours," the ground beneath us shook. The bombs fell. The war we feared was upon us.

During the raid the cannons on our tanks were silent. Our only retaliating fire came from the .30- and .50-caliber machine guns mounted in our tanks' turrets or the ones mounted on the back of our half-tracks. Then at last word came from Tank One: "Look under the radio operator's seat. You'll find fifty shells for the cannon—some are armor-piercing, others are for personnel. Let's get the bastards!" Then, just as we were at our low point of the day, a shout rang out from the tanks around us. "Look, a Zero in flames! Bardowski got him!"

They were talking about Zenon ("Bud") Bardowski, a Company B man. Bud was a big man, about six feet tall and two hundred pounds. He was as strong as a bull, with the personality and looks of a movie star. He was always friendly, always laughing, always happy; nothing seemed to bother Bud. He was manning the .30-caliber machine gun mounted on his half-track when he caught the Zero in his gun's sight. A burst of gunfire, a series of tracer bullets, and then—BAM!—he became the first man in the armored force to down a Japanese aircraft in World War II. Bud was one of those fellows who went over to Corregidor on April 9, the day of the surrender, and he was captured there and taken to Cabanatuan prison camp in mid-May 1942. (He survived and lives in Texas with his lovely and devoted wife. He is still happy-go-lucky—just a little older.)

The bombing and strafing of Fort Stotsenburg and Clark Field within hours of the raid on Pearl Harbor went virtually unnoticed by the average person in the United States. The attack occurred a little after noon, while all of our planes—the bombers and the P-40s—were lined up in a row on Clark Field, just waiting for disaster to strike. Finally, after what seemed like hours of bombing and strafing, everything became quiet, except for the cries and screams of the wounded lying intermingled with the dead all over the field. I will never forget the sights and sounds of that day. The history books associate Pearl Harbor with "the day of infamy," but for those of us in the Philippines it was our day of infamy also.

On December 12, I was able to send a Western Union message to my family that said,

DEAR FOLKS DON'T DESPAIR ALIVE AND WELL NOTIFY LAURA DON'T BELIEVE EVERYTHING YOU HEAR WITH LOVE - LESTER

I intended to soften the blow that the news of war with Japan would have on my folks. I wanted them to think things were better than they actually were.

Clark Field was bombed again on December 10 and 13. These attacks left more dead and injured, but we had so few airworthy aircraft that our equipment losses were minimal. On December 15, our tanks were ordered to leave Clark Field and proceed north on Highway 3 to Lingayen Gulf, where we were told the Japanese were planning a massive landing.

Before leaving for Lingayen, we were instructed to leave our personal possessions behind in our tents at Fort Stotsenburg. I had to abandon family pictures, Laura's home address, photos of Laura and me together, my binoculars, camera, and civilian clothing—none of which I would ever see again. As I think back to that day, I am so glad I had a photo of Laura in my wallet. Her image was my salvation for the next three and a half years.

Before our departure, as we began preparing our tanks for our first battle, our company clerk, Corporal Armada, asked if I wanted ten thousand dollars' worth of GI insurance. I did not understand what he was selling, but then he quickly explained that the government was making this insurance available to each enlisted man for very small monthly premiums. Without a moment's hesitation, I took it. Then he asked who I wanted to be the beneficiary. When I said, "My wife," he asked if I wanted her to receive a monthly allotment during the course of the war. Once again I answered with a resounding "Yes." When he asked for her address, I was stumped. It was with my other possessions in my footlocker in my tent at Fort Stotsenburg. Moreover, she was living with her folks, and Laura and I had decided not to tell them about our marriage until I came home. I knew if the checks were sent to her, Laura would have to answer a lot of questions by her mother and especially her father. So I gave Corporal Armada my parents' address, knowing that they would contact Laura and give her any mail intended for her. Once this insurance business was finished, our tanks left for Lingayen Gulf as ordered by General Wainwright.

General Wainwright, the leader of the forces on Bataan, knew nothing about the deployment and use of tanks in warfare but ordered our tank company to lead an attack on the Japanese forces believed to be in the area. We arrived at our predetermined destination, the town of Agoo, which is only five miles from Damortis and where our headquarters company reconnaissance group reported sighting only small arms and minimum personnel. Because we were not given enough time to do our own reconnaissance, we accepted the report from headquarters company as valid.

Our counterparts that day, the 26th Cavalry, Philippine Scouts, joined our platoon as we headed into battle. The Philippine Scouts were a strong, well-disciplined, highly professional, and courageous group of dedicated fighters. They were rough and tough cavalry men; we were proud to be in battle with them.

Back in October 1941, MacArthur had asked Gen. George C. Marshall to send an armored division to the Philippines for the islands' defense. What MacArthur got instead was two stripped-down National Guard tank battalions—the 192d and the 194th—with only 108 light tanks and 46 half-tracks. Worse, out of the 108 tanks available that day, only five were able to be fully gassed for the assault on the Japanese. Our ammunition was so old we were lucky to have one shell out of five explode, and only 10 percent of our hand grenades were usable. As for our rifles, they were World War I Springfields.

As our company prepared for our assault on the enemy, we found to our dismay that only enough fuel for five tanks had been delivered to our bivouac area from post ordnance. After carefully calculating the number of gallons needed for the assault and the return, or possible continued fighting or withdrawal, our commanding officer reluctantly ordered only five tanks to attack the Japanese forces at once. "Hit them at their landing site, and delay their advancement southward," were our instructions. So on December 22, with our tanks in excellent operating condition and loaded with ammunition and fuel, we went into our first tank battle. Actually, it was the first U.S. tank battle in World War II.

Five tanks, or one platoon, took off, and when they rounded the bend in the narrow, winding road, their occupants were amazed at what they saw—shocked would be a better description. As the tanks came down to the edge of the gulf, we ran smack into dozens of Japanese antitank guns, countless flamethrowers, about fifty tanks, and thousands of what appeared to be well-rested, well-fed, and well-equipped foot soldiers. In addition, dozens of artillery pieces were being put into place for the planned encounter with the Americans and Filipinos.

Lt. Ben Morin, who commanded the platoon from the lead tank, quickly realized that disaster was looking him straight in the face. He tried desperately to avoid the inevitable onslaught. To his right were the steep beginnings of mountains; to his left were rice paddies, filled with muddy water. Then it happened! A Japanese tank pulled right in front of him. Obeying Lieutenant Morin's foot commands, the driver made a hard turn, swerving to avoid a collision with the Japanese tank that was blocking the path. Morin's tank took a direct hit from a Japanese antitank gun. Lieutenant Morin had to maneuver his damaged tank out of the way of the barrage of gunfire coming at him from all sides. He could only turn left, into the rice paddies.

When a tank commander standing in the top of the tank wants to give commands to the driver, he does so by placing his foot on the shoulder of the tank driver. The left shoulder indicates turn left, and the right shoulder, turn right. A foot placed on the driver's head means stop. Last, if the foot pressure is very strong, it means the driver should make a hard turn in the indicated direction. In this case, I bet Morin practically stomped his driver with his left foot.

Morin's tank ended up mired in the ooze of the rice paddy. Its tracks would only spin around and around, without moving the tank an inch. It was stuck.

The other four tanks, realizing Morin's plight, tried to make a U-turn on the small winding road in order to fall back to the bivouac area. Just as the second tank began to turn, it was hit by armor-piercing shells. A shell went straight through the bow-gunner's turret and decapitated the gunner, Henry Deckert, who was wildly firing his machine gun toward the enemy at the time. The shell passed through the tank and out the rear, through the motor, taking with it many important parts. How that tank continued moving is beyond me, but the motor kept running, and the tank made it all the way back to our bivouac area. Only when it got there did it stop, immobilized.

Nick Fryziuk, the lead mechanic, worked on that tank for hours, using makeshift parts, tubes, gaskets, and rods, anything to get the tank to run again. All of our mechanics worked with Nick to get us through this ordeal.

Morin and his crew managed to escape the flamethrowers but did not return to our bivouac area that night. Their fate was unknown; they were taken prisoner, killed, or escaped into the jungle. For days all that we talked about was what happened to Morin and the crew. Then we heard the official announcement: they were declared "missing in action."

It was only after we arrived in Bataan in mid-January 1942 that we discovered that post ordnance had in its warehouse spare tank and half-track engines, tracks, guns, and other various useful parts. When Nick Fryziuk heard about this, he was furious. Our ordnance group had placed our tanks and the men's lives in unnecessary danger just because it decided that we would receive the spare parts only when we arrived in Bataan and not a day sooner. Post ordnance was also responsible for the safekeeping of gasoline and ammunition, and it began rationing these vital necessities from the first day of the war. Only after our units were safely back in Bataan, did they stop rationing gas and ammunition. Ironically, it was the Japanese who finally got all our spare parts, gasoline, and ammunition.

It turned out that first attack we made was not against "small arms and a small detachment of infantry," as we had been told, but instead against fifty thousand infantry, one hundred tanks, forty-six 15mm guns, twenty-eight 105mm cannons, thirty-two 75mm guns, and fifty-six ships with numerous 240mm cannons in the bay. As we began our strategic withdrawal from the fighting in and around Lingayen Gulf, the 26th Cavalry joined us in a last-ditch effort to delay the Japanese advances. As the Japanese began infiltrating our lines, we could hear the shouts of the gallant Filipino men of the 26th Cavalry, as they began charging directly into the enemy stronghold. But how long can a man and horse stand up to the modern weapons of war? These courageous men were being annihilated by the Japanese, for whether a man or horse fell, either meant death to the rider. After the guns took their toll, the survivors of the 26th Cavalry retreated along with the rest of us; it was the only sane thing to do at the time.

After the four surviving tanks made it back to our bivouac area, and the mechanics repaired the one that was so badly damaged, our tank company moved out of Agoo and began the withdrawal strategy of the War Plan Orange III. Our mission then was to control and protect the withdrawal of our troops into Bataan by providing cover for all our forces.

First to leave was our infantry, then our artillery, and last to leave before us was the Corps of Engineers, whose job it was to blow up any bridges after we crossed them. Only after all other U.S. forces had gone in front of us was it our turn. Then after we crossed a bridge, it would be blown by the engineers, who by that time were safely on the other side. The purpose of this strategy was twofold—first, to delay the enemy's advance as much as possible and, second, to ensure the safe withdrawal of all of our troops.

Our tanks, M3s, weighed about thirteen tons, and the bridges in the Philippines were not built to sustain such a heavy load. During our strategic withdrawal back to Bataan, we had to cross a dozen or more very precarious bridges. Each crossing was painfully slow and cautious. The enemy aircraft following us were able to bomb and strafe our positions without any interference from us. We were too busy getting across the bridge to worry about their harassment. We knew the Japanese did not want to destroy the very bridge that tomorrow they would want to use. So once on a bridge, we felt relatively safe inside our tanks.

Due to the poor road and bridge construction and maintenance, and the fact that our tanks could not maneuver around the countryside at will, it became embarrassingly apparent throughout the operation that our tank commander had to reevaluate certain tank missions imposed by USAFFE (United States Armed Forces in the Far East). The greater possibility that there would be certain and irreplaceable losses jeopardized the overall tank mission MacArthur established.

Another problem still facing the U.S. forces was our lack of training on the new tanks. Although the commanding general at Fort Stotsenburg made every effort to familiarize the officers under his command with our tanks, an American officer approached a Japanese light tank, mistaking it for a U.S. vehicle, and began discussing the battle at Lingayen. A few days later, U.S. tanks were erroneously reported as enemy tanks, and heavy mortar and anti-tank shells were fired upon them. The problems relating to tank recognition and tank deployment were greatly magnified when the officers and men of the Philippine Army became involved in the decision-making process.

After a comprehensive battalion-by-battalion, tank-with-infantry training and awareness, all troops became familiar with the looks, configuration, and the practical strategic uses of our tanks. However, our tank group received this training on tanks and their effectiveness only after we arrived on the Bataan peninsula in mid-January.

We entered Bataan as we crossed the Pilar-Bagac Road. On the west side of the peninsula was Bagac, with a well-traveled road leading to the Japanese-held town of Moron. The possibility of an enemy landing on this side was considered remote due to the region's high cliffs and marshy terrain. On the east side was Pilar, a town situated on the main road leading into Bataan proper where the coastal cities and beaches were located. Across the bay from Pilar was the bustling capital of the Philippine Islands, the large city of Manila. There was real concern that the Japanese would try beach landings using barges loaded with troops and equipment. The fear on the east coast was that the Japanese, if they made a successful landing, could then march right down the highway leading from Pilar directly into the center of Bataan.

On January 16, 1942, a tank company of the 194th Tank Battalion was sent to the west coast by order of General Wainwright. Wainwright requested a platoon to assist in opening, and keeping open, the Moron highway. Our infantry would then be able to deny the Japanese forces entry past the town of Moron. Once again, General Wainwright had proposed moving two or three tanks along the western beach and across a coastal creek to surprise and retake the town of Moron. Our tank group commander, prior to sending any tanks, sent out a small reconnaissance group to determine the enemy's position and strength.

The group returned quickly; it spotted antitank guns on the beach leading into the town of Moron. It also reported unfit terrain—terrain that was mucky, soft, and likely bad enough to bog down our tanks. The group tank commander then informed General Wainwright that to accomplish Wainwright's proposed mission would take a full company of tanks, with the real possibility of losing at least one full platoon. With this news, the project was abandoned.

Why, we will never know, but the following day three tanks, along with a company of infantry, were ordered to move forward and confront the enemy. When they reached the first bend in the road, they encountered fire from an antitank gun. The commander of the lead tank fired a burst from his machine gun in the turret and followed it with a high-explosive shell from the 37mm cannon, silencing the antitank gun. The Japanese and their equipment were strewn all over the road, and before the tanks could advance, the crews had to clear the road.

The three tanks then proceeded about a quarter of a mile up the road at which point land mines imbedded in the road exploded and badly disabled two of the tanks, thus blocking the road again. The crew of the remaining intact tank, along with crew members from the disabled tanks, hooked cables from one tank to the other and then to the tank still in operating condition, and towed the two disabled tanks to safety. Luck was with the men that day, for the Japanese had decided to wait at the town of Moron for the assault to begin, thereby giving the crew of the disabled tanks time to seek cover as well as to save the tanks themselves.

Here was another instance in which an entire tank company should have been used instead of one platoon. Unfortunately, once again men were being ordered into battle by non-tank officers, who knew nothing about the damage a land mine could do to the tracks of a tank. Once the tracks are blown off their sprockets, a tank can only go in a circle.

On January 25, the last day of troop withdrawal, we were issued the following written instruction from USAFFE headquarters.

> Tanks will execute maximum delay, staying in position and firing at visible enemy until further delay will jeopardize withdrawal. If a tank becomes immobilized, it will fight until the close approach of the enemy, then it should be destroyed; the crew previously taking positions outside shall continue the fight with the salvaged and personal weapons. Consideration of personal safety or expediency will not interfere with accomplishing the greatest possible delay of the enemy.

The order was very clear: protecting the complete and successful withdrawal of all U.S. and Filipino forces, as well as civilians, was our first order of business. Reading in between the lines the message said death was better than an early withdrawal on our part.

As I mentioned earlier, given that we had arrived in the Philippines only a few weeks before hostilities began and that most of us American soldiers came from traditional midwestern Caucasian homes, we found distinguishing the Filipinos and the Chinese from the Japanese people very difficult. As a result, the constant infiltration of Japanese soldiers and civilians and the threat that Japanese sympathizers would give our position away caused us great anxiety. Our safety was in jeopardy. During our withdrawal, we found ourselves shooting indiscriminately into Filipino huts and stores if the occupants did not answer our command to come out.

We were suspicious of every Asian we saw. When we moved into a new area and found people milling around, seemingly unafraid, we became nervous and cautious. We would demand satisfactory identification from each person. Lacking such reassurance, we would spray the buildings with gunfire from our Thompson submachine guns, thus taking what we felt were necessary precautions against potential enemy spies.

There were many times when we in fact did locate and eliminate some of these enemy sympathizers. On one such occasion, as our tank entered a town we saw three men running away from a large area that had been cleared of foliage and undergrowth. As we approached, we found a twenty-foot arrow made out of white sheeting material on the ground and pointing in the direction from which we had just come. On our march into this village, we had been bombed by enemy aircraft and precision shelling by Japanese artillery. Now we knew why they had their guns aimed so perfectly and how their aircraft was able to locate us in the middle of the jungle so easily. We were set up by spies or Japanese infiltrators. Some of the villagers were our enemies, and we wanted to know who they were.

Our tank crew decided that with only four of us, we could not safely enter and search each of the four homes. Instead, when no one would admit who the guilty people were or where the three men were hiding, we proceeded to spray round after round of bullets into each of the homes in this small community. We knew we had to find these enemy spies, or we would face the same bulldog attack each day of our withdrawal into Bataan. When we finished shooting, we felt emotionally drained and guilty. We sat down and almost cried. Did we kill anyone in these buildings? Was anyone wounded by our gunfire? We never knew the results of our attack. We felt that had there been people inside they would have answered our previous commands to come out. Did we act without concern for the people inside, if any? I do not think so. Our fear of being killed made necessary what might seem a brutal act.

Maybe we realized how close we came to being killed, or maybe we realized we had to take the good with the bad, and this was bad. During the next few weeks, we stayed alert, always watching, questioning when necessary, and never letting our guard down. After all, our lives were at stake. We went in and out of a dozen or more villages while on our withdrawal into Bataan, and each time we became more cautious. Never willing to take a chance, we always wanted the comfort of knowing who our allies were and wanted to eliminate our enemies.

By the end of January, our tank unit was assigned to patrol and keep the enemy at bay on the East Coast Road and to protect the coastline facing the fallen city of Manila from enemy infiltration. Knowing that our tanks could play havoc with any landing force caused the Japanese to reconsider potential infiltration through our well-protected lines. A Japanese field officer admitted this fact to the tank group commander in a conference the day after the surrender of Bataan, April 9, 1942. The Japanese field officer left no doubt that if the tanks had not been covering the coastline Bataan would have succumbed much earlier.

Before long, the food supply for U.S. troops on Bataan was not only getting low, but it was beginning to be tasteless as well. About that time, I learned about the food being served aboard the USS *Canopus*. From the first day of fighting to the last, the men aboard the *Canopus*, anchored off the tip of Mariveles, ate well. A submarine tender, the *Canopus* supplied the submarines in the Philippines with such necessities as food, ammunition, and gasoline. If a GI was lucky, he could wrangle an invitation aboard the *Canopus* for an evening meal. And what a meal it was rumored to be. While the men fighting on Bataan ate their measly ration of under-cooked rice, a small piece of meat, and maybe a spoonful of sugar, a meal on the *Canopus* could very well be fried chicken, mashed potatoes, carrots and peas, hot strong coffee, and for dessert a piece of freshly baked chocolate cake à la mode.

During a brief rest stop near Mariveles, I came into contact with a *Canopus* crew member. I inquired what I would have to do to get an invitation for dinner some evening. He asked me, in so many words, "What do you have to trade for a good meal?" It seemed that the men serving aboard the *Canopus* were interested in Japanese souvenirs: rifles, sidearms, flags, or just about anything that would be a memento to take home when the war ended. Once I found out what they wanted, the rest was easy.

I went back to my tank and informed the rest of my crew of my discovery. With just a little extra work and for a few Japanese trinkets, we could be eating a meal fit for a king. Our goal then was to volunteer for an assignment that would take us close to the front line. Another thought crossed my mind: how about going back to the Pilar-Bagac Road where we had just finished winning a very important skirmish with the Japanese? No doubt the area had many of the souvenirs the men on the *Canopus* wanted.

After waiting all day for orders as to where our next battle would be, I contacted my good friend Lew. With his help, we obtained a jeep and driver and drove the few miles back to our last battlefield. There, not more than twenty feet from the road, was a flag of the rising sun. About four feet wide and three feet long, it looked brand-new, without a mark on it. Then, about two feet from the flag, we found a sniper's rifle, which came apart in the middle, thus allowing the carrier to move about without the disturbance associated with a full-scale rifle. We hurriedly picked up the two items, jumped into the jeep, and headed for our bivouac area, singing "Happy Days Are Here Again."

That afternoon, after our little mission, I went to the *Canopus*, found my new friend, and negotiated dinner that night for Lew and me and dinner the next night for my whole tank crew, all four of us. The first night we had roast beef, all the trimmings and chocolate cake with ice cream. The following night we had the special fried chicken, once again with all the trimmings, and cherry pie à la mode.

I was able to obtain enough Japanese items to have dinner aboard ship three more times. In fact, the last time was just a week before the surrender of Bataan. On the day we surrendered in April, the crew of the *Canopus* set sail for Corregidor and halfway there scuttled the ship. Along with the ship went forty cherry pies. (I met the ship's baker at one of our POW reunions, and he told me it was one of the saddest days of his life when he had to scuttle those pies.) An old saying goes, "The Navy eats well." How true, how true.

February and March were periods of extremely high and very unusual fatalities. Lt. Edward G. Winger, a most courageous and warm individual, became the victim of the enemy's first use of oil and flamethrowers. Lieutenant Winger was blinded by this terrible new weapon and jammed his tank between two large trees, where it had to be abandoned.

In another tragedy, after running directly into one of those flamethrowers, a tank caught fire, burning the crew. The Japanese, instead of allowing the men to come out and surrender, dug foxholes all around the tank and threw the dirt and sand directly into the tank through the top turret entrance. By burying the men in the tank, the Japanese were able to plan a surprise attack on our rescue tank and crew.

The Japanese hid in holes beneath the tank, and as soon as our rescue effort started, they began firing at us. Luckily, being under the tank did not allow them clean shots, and the rescue team was able to reboard the tank. Within minutes the team eliminated the small Japanese contingent under it. After towing the tank back to the bivouac area, we were able to give our buddies a decent burial. Two had died from burns, and two were suffocated by the dirt and sand.

By the end of March, our daily food ration seldom contained as much as eight hundred calories. So many men were sick with dengue fever and malaria that we had to set up emergency dispensaries in the field because many of the sick could not be moved to the base hospital.

Our tank company had been constantly working either on the front lines or in the forward position, and we were always far from our rear echelon and kitchens. Our food, what little there was, was cold, bland, and more geared to the Filipino than to the Caucasian taste. In fact, besides our contingent of fighting men, our forces on Bataan were also feeding the approximately twenty-eight thousand Filipino civilians who had fled the advancing Japanese army and followed us into Bataan, hoping for safety and food. Although these civilians came of their own free will, they still had to be fed, and the food came from our already meager supply.

It was not just the lack of food that disturbed us. An additional concern was the fact that our entire battalion was issued only ten gallons of gas per day for all purposes except going into battle.

By April 1, one thousand men a day entered our hospital wards with one or more disabling sicknesses. Two days later, our medics estimated that between 75 percent and 80 percent of our frontline troops were ill. Coincidentally, on this date the Japanese carried out the biggest attack of the war. April 3 was the anniversary of the ascension to the throne of Emperor Jimmu, the first occupant of the Imperial throne, and it was important to the Japanese that the all-out offensive start on this momentous day.

At 9:00 in the morning at our last outpost—the last line of defense along the Orion-Bagac line—U.S. observers noted more than nineteen artillery batteries, ten mortar batteries, and countless tanks, all ready to strike. Within minutes the assault began. The artillery barrage was fortified by aerial bombardment of our front lines, and the Japanese tanks advanced slowly but surely into the center of our troops. The enemy's objective was to capture Mount Samat, only a few kilometers from the rear of our front line. With a ground force numbering close to thirty thousand men, and with sixty twin-engine bombers constantly bombarding our front lines, the enemy achieved its goal.

Company B had to take over more and more of the beach defense as the Filipinos' ineffectiveness increased and the enemy's activities and threats became more intense. Gasoline was once again in short supply. In fact, 92-octane gas, the lowest rating gas that the tanks could use for safe operation, was no longer available. Putting gas with an octane rating of 85 into our tanks meant that we could not be sure how our engines would respond under extreme circumstances. Also, because we were no longer in direct combat with Japanese armored vehicles, our ordnance department converted our 37mm armor-piercing shells into high-explosive shells.

We defenders on Bataan were killed or wounded at an alarming rate. The dispirited U.S. and Filipino troops were tired, sick, and starving. Continued resistance was virtually impossible. Each nightfall we survivors counted our losses and began to appreciate our luck—lucky is how we felt—to be alive. We all knew the war was slowly coming to an end for us.

During the next few days, fighting was ineffectual in spite of the casualties inflicted on the enemy. On April 7, with our orders to hold the line at all costs, the Japanese infantry charged our position in such large numbers that they literally used their dead and dying soldiers as stepping-stones to cross the imaginary front line.

According to the Shinto religion, the Japanese believed that the emper-
or was a god, or a divine being, and that if a soldier died for the emperor,
the solider would enjoy an afterlife of eternal bliss. During this deadly battle, we realized that the Japanese soldiers were not fighting just to defeat
us but were fighting in order to die for the emperor, a concept that was difficult for us to accept. In contrast to the Japanese, the Germans, who
indeed wanted to win, also wanted to live. The Germans fought as bravely
and as well as the Japanese, but this fanatical willingness to die was rarely
witnessed by those Americans fighting the German soldiers.

The continued firing of our machine guns caused the barrels to become
so red-hot they could no longer fire, forcing us to retreat yet another few
hundred yards. It was another day of being pushed back another half a
kilometer, and not many kilometers were left. The handwriting was on the
wall: this slaughter could not go on much longer. Our tanks were bombed
on and off the trails; we were severely punished without an opportunity to
fight back. Our stamina was gone, our food was gone, our health was deteriorating, and our ammunition and gas had just about run out. We were
helpless. The Filipino soldiers, who could try to slip back into their barrios
and resume a more normal life, were in fact moving toward the line of
least resistance, or the road leading out of Bataan.

After four months of fighting the enemy, of being on short rations, and
of surviving everything from malaria to gunshot wounds with little or no
medical treatment, we heard the news: the Japanese had finally cracked
our last defense. We were now only about two miles from the water's edge
with no place to go and without the means to fight. We were going to
surrender. No, we did not surrender as individuals, but instead we were
surrendered as an entire army by our commanding officer. Fighting for
another day would only mean thousands more would die. Surrender was
the only way to save as many men and women as possible.

We troops felt let down, even betrayed. If we had been supplied with
enough ammunition and guns, troops and equipment, and food and medical supplies, we believed that we would have been able to repel the
Japanese. Instead, we were facing a degrading surrender and the brutality
that was surely to go along with it.

We were scared and wondered what was going to happen to us. At 6:40
on the evening of April 8, 1942, Gen. Edward P. King acknowledged the
situation as very critical. Apparently, he knew our battle on Bataan was
coming to a fast, bloody, and dangerous end. General King paced back and
forth at Bataan forces headquarters, his mind only on the event that he
alone knew would put all of his fighting forces in great danger. But it had
to be done, and he had to do it: he must face the enemy and surrender.

General King sent the following message to the commanders of the tank units:

> You will make plans, to be communicated to company commanders only, and be prepared to destroy within one hour after receipt by radio, or other means, of the code word CRASH, all tanks and combat vehicles, arms, ammunition, gas and radios, reserving sufficient trucks to move our forces to the rear echelons as soon as everything is accomplished.

By 10:30 that night, General King made an announcement to the three general officers present. He said that further resistance would result in the massacre of the six thousand sick and wounded and the twenty-eight thousand Filipino refugees now congested in and around the front lines. General King believed that fighting on was useless and that the forces could hold out, at the longest, one more day. At midnight General King, with eyes puffed from holding back the tears, declared that the following morning at daybreak he was going to take a white flag across the front line on Bataan. That, he said, was his responsibility.

When our tank commander asked if any help was on the way, General King said sadly, "No"—nothing now and nothing in the future. All of this was unknown to most of the men on Bataan, but we did know that we could not go on, that the situation was hopeless. Then, at ten minutes to midnight on April 8, ordnance was instructed to begin destroying all equipment and supplies under their jurisdiction. That night and into the morning I had the radio in our tank tuned to General King's command post frequency, and at 7:00 in the morning, we heard the words, loud and clear: "CRASH, CRASH, CRASH."

I passed the message on to Capt. Robert S. Sorensen. He just gulped down a sob of distress and ordered us to destroy everything in sight. We did what we were supposed to do. First, we lined up the tanks one behind the other and then fired rounds of 37mm shells from one tank into the engine and body of the tank in front. Then we threw away our guns and ammunition. We were "naked" soldiers at the mercy of the enemy. That was what the Japanese had ordered, and General King had no choice but to agree to their terms.

There was not a dry eye among us. Our world had collapsed, we were beaten, and we had lost the war for the United States. God, how could we live with ourselves again after a defeat like this? We let our country, our families, and our friends down. We felt like cowards. I failed Laura. I had told her I would be home soon and asked her to wait till I returned before telling her family about us. I felt my being there would ease the verbal abuse she was sure to get from her father. I worried, What was she going to do now? How would she take this news when she heard about it? Would she think I was a coward? All I could think about was Laura.

The more I thought about my beloved wife the more I was determined to get home in one piece. My initial plan was not to get involved in any unnecessary actions or confrontations with the Japanese. In addition, not knowing the Japanese, I decided that after being taken prisoner I would neither rush to be first to do anything nor be the last one to respond to their wishes. I reasoned that being first might result in my doing something wrong and being last could signify I was a laggard. The goal I established for myself was to live and to get home all in one piece. Everything I did from that day forward had to lead to my accomplishing that primary goal. I wanted to be back with Laura, to hold her in my arms, and to tell her how much I missed her. I had to get back. That was all there was to it.

As soon as we finished destroying all of our equipment, we went back to our bivouac area for further instructions. Our commanding officer, Captain Sorensen, told us that we had a few options available. First, we could take off for Corregidor, which meant we would have to find a boat that would take us, and once there we would have to face the possibility of the eventual surrender of that fortress. Second, we could try to escape into the jungle and hope that we would be able to survive without being captured. Finally, we could all stay together and surrender as a unit. Captain Sorensen then said, "We fought together; let's surrender together." I chose to surrender with the men from Company B. I started out with these men, and I wanted to be with them at the climax of our war effort.

In Western civilizations, capture has always been viewed as being better than death, and surrender was looked upon as one of the misfortunes of war. True, luck does play a large part in survival, and our bad luck was that we were being captured by people from a civilization that believed death was preferable to surrender.

# CHAPTER 3

# THE FALL OF BATAAN

On April 8, at about nine o'clock in the evening, the ground began to shake. Our legs felt like rubber stilts as we started to rock back and forth. Without realizing it, we were in the middle of a most unusual phenomenon for the Philippines—an earthquake. Every man felt the earth tremble, as if God was telling us, "I'm unhappy with what is happening." The explosions from destroying all our equipment, guns, and ammunition were overshadowed by the devastating effects of nature. To many of us it was the last straw of defeat, like the coming of the end of the world. All we wanted to know was, How much more pain—not just the physical, but the mental pain of anxiety, frustration, and uncertainty—could we be expected to endure?

At 9:30 the following morning, all hell broke loose once again, but this time it was man-made. Japanese planes rained bombs all over Bataan. After the planes dropped their bomb loads, they then began a systematic strafing of all of the men, remaining equipment, and installations they were able to locate.

We all ran scared. We were on a battlefield with no way to defend ourselves. Oh God, we thought, this is the end and what a way to have to go. Is this what General King bargained for? It couldn't be! What was going wrong? What happened to our supposed surrender? That was the question on the mind of every American and Filipino on Bataan that hour. We were being annihilated; it was the beginning of the Bataan massacre.

As the bombs started to drop, a few of my buddies and I looked for a safe haven, any place to get out of the way of the flying shrapnel. Not too far away we saw a very primitive Filipino baking oven that native women used to bake breads and babinkas, a sweet cake. The oven was nothing more

than a mound of dirt and hardened clay about four feet high and six feet
in diameter. It had a small opening at one end that three of us were able to
climb into. Once inside we cursed the Japanese for not honoring the surrender, and we vowed to get even for this attack. After about fifteen minutes, the bombing stopped. We were ready to leave our shelter when we
heard a blast of gunfire, followed by hundreds of other shots coming from
the Japanese planes circling over Bataan. This strafing continued for
another twenty-five minutes, while those of us in the shelter wondered
what was going on. We also wondered where our other friends were. Did
they find shelter from the Zeros' barrage of bombs and bullets?

Finally, after another hour or so, we decided to come out and see what
had happened. We found huge bomb craters within ten feet of where we
had taken shelter. Then we noticed that within one hundred feet of our
oven there were dozens of other ovens just like ours. As we began hollering the names of some of our friends, other fellows started to emerge from
their hiding places. All in all, about thirty of us had taken refuge in the
ovens. We gathered in a circle and began discussing what was going on
and what we were going to do. We realized for the first time the possibility
of our not being taken prisoner but instead of our being slaughtered like
animals.

Good common sense would have dictated some form of strategy, but fear
of the unknown once again overwhelmed us. What was going to happen?
Were we going to be taken prisoner and then killed, or would we never be
taken prisoner, just killed in this field? Emotions ran high. With wide-open
eyes, goose bumps in spite of the high temperature, and voices now only a
whisper, as if someone close by was listening, we planned our next move.
We decided that if the bombing and strafing continued past noon we
would all head for Mariveles, a bustling barrio on the water's edge and
only three miles from the island fortress of Corregidor. From there we
would try to obtain a boat to take us to Corregidor or one of the other
thousand islands surrounding Bataan. We were not going to stick around
and be slaughtered. We would make a run for safety.

At noon, however, the bombing and strafing stopped just as quickly as it
started. We did not know why or what was happening. Years later we
found out that the Japanese high command would not accept General
King's surrender of only Bataan; they wanted the surrender of all of the
Philippines, including the garrison on Corregidor. General King explained
that the fortress island of Corregidor was under the command of General
Wainwright, and King did not have authority over Corregidor's men. After
much waiting, the surrender of just Bataan was finally accepted.

On April 9, 1942, General MacArthur, from his headquarters in Australia, paid tribute to the defenders of Bataan.

No army has ever done so much with so little. Nothing became it more than in its last hour of trial and agony. To the weeping mothers of its dead, I only say that the sacrifice and halo of Jesus of Nazareth has descended upon their sons and that God will take them unto Himself.

This tribute was not heard by the defenders of Bataan. Instead it was heard by their mothers, fathers, brothers, sisters, wives, and sweethearts, who were anxiously awaiting word about the fate of their loved ones. The anxiety and the untold heartache that the folks at home had to endure during those last days of fighting on Bataan are another story all its own.

All the men in our company returned to the bivouac area after the bombing stopped that fateful morning. Upon reflection, at last we fully appreciated the true meaning and the consequences of President Roosevelt's fireside chat that we had heard in March while preparing for an encounter with the Japanese. We had been sitting in our tanks, listening to a shortwave broadcast directly from the States, as President Roosevelt began his talk. He first explained exactly where the Philippine Islands were located and then told his listeners that Singapore and all of the Asian islands close to Japan were under enemy rule. President Roosevelt then said, "Take out your maps; look at the problem facing our forces in the Far East. In every war there must be some sacrifices made of a few for the benefit of the war effort at large." He went on to explain that what would appear to be a decision that would place our fighting forces in jeopardy was not his intent. He then said, "But in this war, as you can see from the location of the Japanese forces, getting supplies and reinforcements to the Philippines is next to impossible."

On that day in March, we had understood that the sacrifice he was referring to meant losing the war in the Philippines for the benefit of the total offensive. In spite of realizing who the sacrificial lambs would be and knowing that we were waging a losing battle, we continued to defend the islands and to face an end that would mean either death on the battlefield or capture by the Japanese.

The fighting forces on Bataan had followed General King's orders. We completely destroyed all of our arms, ammunition, equipment, and even some of the money our company had on hand for payroll. In fact, I was in charge of getting rid of about two hundred thousand dollars in U.S. currency. I thought of the things that I could buy with that much money. It was mind-boggling. The temptation of having that much money at one time was too great for me. I decided to bury the full amount in a place where I would be able to find it when I came back in a few months. (That is how long I expected the war to last.) After all, Captain Sorensen had merely stated, "Don't let the Japs get the money," so I decided to do it my way.

I found a large mango tree with a most unusual root system. I carved my tank company's name and my initials in its trunk and then dug a hole at the base of the tree about two feet deep. I placed the metal box containing the paper money in the hole, put a few rocks on top of it, and then filled the hole with dirt and debris from around the area. Before I left, I hastily drew a map showing how many feet the tree was from the edge of the road and how many feet from the kilometer post marker, and I included a description of the tree and its root system. I was well prepared to locate the treasure and to live a beautiful life forever after. I thought about what I did over and over again. Was it wrong? Was it right? I did not know or care; I just felt I was "obeying orders." Of course, my definition was a loose one, to satisfy myself.

The surrender we had feared had come. While waiting for the Japanese actions to be better defined, our captain asked us once again if we would stay together and surrender as a unit, the way General King had promised the enemy. Most of the men agreed, but a few felt that if they went to Corregidor they would have a better chance of survival and certainly would get some food.

Corregidor was a small island fortress about three miles out in the bay from Manila. Because of its location, with the tip of Bataan on one side and Manila Bay on the other, we expected it to be able to withstand and counter any enemy attack. In addition, there were fortified bunkers and tunnels dug all over the small island. (Malinta Tunnel was the most noteworthy. From there General MacArthur controlled the military operation for the entire Philippines' defense, and later General Wainwright grudgingly offered the surrender of the entire Philippine garrison.) Surely, we thought, these tunnels would prevent any damage or destruction from enemy bombardment. Last, Corregidor had twenty-nine heavy-duty gun batteries, with fifty-nine large cannons strategically placed for the defense of the Philippines.

The men on Bataan had been getting halved food rations since the middle of February, and many of us had contracted malaria and dysentery and suffered their associated pains, cramps, and fevers. Taking these factors into consideration, some of the men thought Corregidor, the "impregnable" fortress, was the place to be. They found out differently on May 6, 1942, the day General Wainwright was forced to surrender the beleaguered garrison at Corregidor along with the balance of all U.S. and Philippine forces fighting on any islands of the Philippines.

Meanwhile, immediately after the fall of Bataan, my family and, of course, Laura received hundreds of letters and phone calls from friends and relatives all over the country. All were trying to give my loved ones hope— hope that I was alive and well and that I would soon come home. Just at that time, a warm, meaningful letter arrived from the governor of Illinois. It made my family feel proud of their contribution to our country's defense.

STATE OF ILLINOIS
EXECUTIVE CHAMBERS
SPRINGFIELD

Dwight H. Green                                              April 21, 1942
Governor

Mr. Gus Tenenberg
1200 Sherwin Ave.
Chicago, Illinois

Dear Mr. Tenenberg:

Illinois is extremely proud of her sons in the armed services. Of none is she more proud and grateful to than those members of Company B, 192nd Tank Battalion of Maywood, who so bravely defended Bataan. The heroic stand of these stalwart Americans against insurmountable odds has written a chapter in our national life which will be inspiration to all future generations.

May I take this opportunity to extend official recognition to you from the State of Illinois for the patriotic service which your son has given to his State and country, and to join you in the prayer that he is unharmed.

Sincerely yours,

Governor

Although the surrender of Bataan occurred on April 9, 1942, the U.S. government did not communicate with my family until May 7, 1943, thirteen months later. During this long period, my family knew nothing of my whereabouts or my physical condition. Cold and callous, the letter did little to ease the pain of their not knowing.

WAR DEPARTMENT
THE ADJUTANT GENERALS OFFICE
WASHINGTON, D.C.

IN REPLY
REFER TO
AG 201 Tenenberg, Lester I.

(5-7-42) PC-3                                                 May 7, 1943

Mr. Gus Tenenberg
1412 Chase Avenue
Chicago, Illinois

Dear Mr. Tenenberg:

The records of the War Department show your son, Sergeant Lester I. Tenenberg, 20 600 429 Infantry, as missing in action, in the Philippine Islands since May 7, 1942, presumed either dead or a prisoner of the Japanese.

All available information concerning your son has been carefully considered and under the provisions of Public Law 490, 77th Congress, as amended, an official determination has been made continuing him on the records of the War Department in a missing status. The law cited provides that pay and allowances are to be credited to the missing person's account and payment of allotments to authorized allottees are to be continued during the absence of such persons in a missing status.

I fully appreciate your concern and deep interest. You will, without further request on your part, receive immediate notification of any change in your son's status. I regret that the far-flung operations of the present war, the ebb and flow of combat over great distances in isolated areas, and the characteristics of our enemies impose upon some of us the heavy burden of uncertainty with respect to the safety of our loved ones.

Very truly yours,

J.A. ULIO
Major General

The timetable for a total Philippine victory had been established by the Japanese high command in Tokyo. The responsibility of this quick victory was originally given to Gen. Masaharu Homma, who was expected to conquer the Philippines no later than January 22, 1942. The defensive and strategic action, the determination, and the fighting skills of the U.S. and Philippine forces on Bataan gave the United States an extra seventy-six days, from January 22 to April 9, to fortify Australia and to provide the Allies with a base of operations within the Pacific theater. Australia, otherwise, would have been a sure, albeit costly, victory for the Japanese, because most of Australia's servicemen were then fighting for the British in Africa. The Australian home front was manned mostly by the sick, the elderly, and the women of the land.

If Gen. Tomoyuki Yamashita, after taking military command of Singapore on February 12, 1942, had detoured around the Philippines and gone straight to Australia, the war may have had a different outcome. But General Yamashita was sent to the Philippines to end the bloody defense of the islands and to do what General Homma was unable to do: obtain the capitulation of the Philippines.

Our heroic defense thwarted this Japanese strategic military planning, cost Japan at least an additional twenty thousand ground troops, and caused General Homma to lose face with the officers in Tokyo's high command. Little did the Japanese realize that the main enemy of the Bataan defenders was not Japan's military might, but the lack of medical supplies, starvation, and the misery, pain, and suffering brought about by such diseases as malaria, dysentery, scurvy, and gangrene. These newly combined enemies of our fighting forces presented a much worse effect on our troops than the physical onslaught of the Japanese.

According to War Department records, during World War II there were 16 million Americans in uniform, of whom 291,000 died. Of this total, 55,000 personnel died while defending the Philippines. The war's unfortunate and sad statistics show that of the total number of deaths to the total number of those in the service, the ratio was 1 to 55—that is, one died for every fifty-five that lived. In examining just the statistics from the Philippine defense, the ratio was 2 to 1: there were two deaths for every survivor of the Philippines' defense. The actual number of deaths that occurred specifically during the fighting in the Philippines, from the Bataan Death March, or from incarceration in POW camps may never be accurately known, because the surrender and the holocaust that followed were never accurately recorded from each of these events. In spite of not knowing specifics, the deaths that occurred in the defense of the Philippines represented 17 percent of all the deaths in World War II.

# CHAPTER 4

# THE MARCH

Knowing the war was over for us and that it was only a matter of time before we would become formal prisoners of the Japanese, our emotions ran high the night of April 9. Bob Martin, Jim Bashleban, Orrie T. Mulholland, and I sat around our bunks, whispering about our concerns and about what our families would think of us when they found out we had surrendered.

I started to talk about Laura and all she meant to me. There was no doubt in my mind, I told them, that I would return home. I tried to explain how I was going to be decisive, and that my first priority would be to make it back all in one piece. I finally said, "You can do anything you set your mind on doing; you just have to set goals and priorities." My words must have had some meaning to these friends of mine, for all three came home.

The men who stayed together that night in our company's bivouac area were abruptly awakened the following morning by loud voices obviously speaking Japanese. The Japs had come for us. They stormed our area carrying handguns and machine guns; they were ready for business. My knees began shaking, my hands felt cold and clammy, and sweat broke out on my neck and forehead. We were all scared beyond anything imaginable. What was going to happen now? Were we going to be shot? Was this what happens to soldiers that surrender? I began recalling some of the stories I had heard about how some of our men who were captured early in the war were treated. Then, as a terrifying afterthought, I realized that at that moment we were facing the same enemy who only days before we were trying to kill. And, of course, if I knew that, so did these fighting Japanese soldiers who were just now coming up the path to us. Their mission, we were praying, was to take us prisoner.

Within seconds, dozens of Japanese soldiers came into our area, some asking politely for cigarettes while others pounded our heads with bamboo sticks whose ends were loaded with sand. These rough soldiers did not ask for a thing; they just took whatever they wanted. They ransacked our bodies and our sleeping area. They were belligerent, loud, and determined to act like the winners of a tough battle (which they were). Once again we were frightened by what was happening and fearful that our future treatment was going to be worse.

The first Japanese soldier I came into contact with used sign language to ask if I had a cigarette. Fingers together, he moved his arm to his mouth, and inhaled, making it easy to see what he meant. I had to tell him I did not have any cigarettes. He smiled and then a second later hit me in the face with the butt of his gun. Blood spurted from my nose and from a deep gash on my cheekbone. He laughed and said something that made all of his buddies laugh, too. He walked away from me and went to the GI on my right. He used the same sign language, and this time my buddy had cigarettes and offered him one. The Japanese soldier took the whole pack, and then he and his friends began beating my friend with rifle butts and cane-length pieces of bamboo until he could not stand. Then they left, laughing, laughing at the defeated and weak Americans.

My God, what was next? I wondered how I would stand up to this type of punishment for a prolonged period. If we had known earlier just how we would be treated and for how long, I think we would have fought on Bataan to the last man, taking as many of the enemy with us as possible, rather than endure the torture, hunger, beatings, and inhumane atrocities we were to undergo during the next three and a half years.

Unfortunately for us, the Japanese plan for evacuating their captive prisoners was based on three assumptions, all of which proved to be without merit. First, the Japanese assumed that only twenty-five thousand to thirty-five thousand military people were on Bataan. The correct number may never be known for scores of men were killed the day before the surrender and more escaped into the jungle or attempted to reach Corregidor. Besides the Allied personnel, almost twenty-five thousand Filipino civilians also sought the shelter and expected safety of the Bataan peninsula. Therefore, the number of people in Bataan at the time of the surrender was closer to 105,000. The number that actually started the infamous Bataan Death March has been estimated at 65,000 Filipino servicemen, 28,000 civilians, and 12,000 Americans—considerably more than the Japanese had estimated.

Second, the Japanese assumed that the enemy forces were in good physical condition and capable of a sustained march without much food or
water. The reality was just the opposite. We men on Bataan had had our
rations cut to as few as eight hundred calories a day during the past forty-
five days. We ate rice and a small spoonful of C rations (an emergency military field ration of food intended for use under combat conditions and
consisting of specially prepared and packaged meats). In some cases we
augmented our meals with a snake or a monkey or two, or possibly even an
iguana. For all of the men on the front lines, we only had two meals a day.
This starvation diet brought along with it scurvy, pellagra, beriberi, and of
course the diminished ability to fight off the malaria bug or any other sickness. We were anything but ready to march, with or without water and
food. Those of us able to walk should have been in the hospital, and those
men in the hospital looked as if they were dead.

Finally, the Japanese thought that all details of our evacuation were
planned to perfection and that they knew what had to be done and how to
do it. In fact, the individual Japanese units did not know what they were
supposed to do. No sooner had one group of Japanese lined us up and told
us to start walking than another group would tell us to wait. All of these
orders were issued in Japanese, and if we did not respond immediately, we
would be hit, spat upon, shoved, or in some cases shot for not obeying
orders. Once again, they obviously wanted to "get even," wanted revenge,
and wanted to show us they were superior. In some situations, however,
the guards were simply ignorant of the outside world and thought that
everyone understood Japanese. They became irritated by our slowness to
respond and our inability to understand their commands and vented their
frustration on us.

So, contrary to the Japanese plans, when the march began from Mariveles there was confusion everywhere. Cars, trucks, horses, and field artillery filled the road, all going in different directions. The Japanese were
moving all of their heavy equipment and guns into Bataan for the assault
on Corregidor. Figuring out how they could achieve total victory in the
Philippines with all of the enemy service personnel in the way was a major
problem to the Japanese. Confusion reigned, and it seemed that no specific
officer was in charge, which made the task of maintaining control almost
impossible.

It is also interesting at this point to note that the men captured on
Corregidor never made the Bataan Death March. Instead, after the fall of
Corregidor on May 6, 1942, the captives were taken by boat to Manila and
from there trucked to Cabanatuan, their first prison camp. Another significant difference between the prisoners from Bataan and those from Corregidor was their overall health condition. None of the men from Corregidor

had to suffer the brutalities of the march or our first prison camp, Camp O'Donnell. We men from Bataan were half dead by the time we arrived at the camp. Without any hesitancy I can say that fully 100 percent of the men who arrived at that first camp had at least one, and most of the men had two or three, of these health problems: malaria, dysentery, malnutrition, hunger, dehydration, pneumonia, beriberi, or diphtheria. In addition, almost all of us were beaten and tortured beyond the body's normal endurance on the march. Then of course we all suffered psychological damage after our surrendering and then helplessly watching our buddies being killed right in front of us, powerless to stop the slaughter and always fearful that we would be next.

By contrast, the prisoners taken from Corregidor ate well until the last days of fighting. The main quartermaster, with full control of all supplies, was headquartered on Corregidor. As the war continued from December to April, transporting large amounts of food or other supplies to the Bataan peninsula became more hazardous and difficult; therefore, food on Corregidor was plentiful. Thus, while the men on Bataan had fourteen to seventeen ounces of food per day, those on Corregidor had forty-eight to fifty-five ounces per day. Furthermore, those who were not wounded during the fighting on Corregidor were in pretty good health. Malaria did only mild damage to those on Corregidor, but it struck 99 percent of us on Bataan, whose jungles were known to have the heaviest infestation of malaria-carrying mosquitoes in the world.

Ultimately, none of the assumptions the Japanese made about the forces on the Philippines were realistic or based on solid intelligence. In the opinion of many, the assumptions, which were discussed at the end of the war at the war crimes trials, were made to justify the treatment meted out to the men on the march. The Japanese had no way of knowing the real situation on Bataan, and they did not really care. At their courts-martial, many high-ranking Japanese officers who served in the Philippines said about the same thing: "I didn't really know the situation or condition of the Americans and the Filipinos."

Actually, after looking at a map of the Philippine Islands and especially of Bataan, it is easy to see that the Japanese could have saved themselves a great deal of trouble. Had the Japanese just kept a small force of fighting men along the Pilar-Bagac line, we would have been our own prisoners of war, under our own command. In fact, we often said, "If they leave us alone now, we will be the first POWs with guns and ammunition, taking orders from our own officers." The bottom line was we had no place to go. Going north we would have come into contact with the enemy. Going south, east, or west, we would have ended up in the water. If the Japanese had just left us alone, we would have starved and would eventually have been forced to surrender. This strategy would have allowed the Japanese a two-month head start on their conquest of Australia and their dreams of ruling the entire Southeast Asia territory. The Japanese ego, however, insisted upon a clearly defined defeat of the U.S. forces in the Philippines. They were then faced with the problems of dealing with almost eighty thousand disorganized and diseased military prisoners, as well as twenty-five thousand civilians.

That morning of April 10, the Japanese marched us to the main road, a distance of about half a mile. During this short march, the Japanese soldiers hollered and prodded us with their bayonets to walk faster. Once at the main road, we waited for three hours, standing, sitting, or resting any way we could; but talking was not allowed.

Down the road, we saw a cloud of dust from which a group of walking and shuffling U.S. and Filipino soldiers emerged. When they passed us, we were told to join them and to start walking. For our group the Bataan Death March began at kilometer marker 167, about two miles east of Mariveles. It had originated at the tip of Bataan in the barrio of Mariveles, where many of the U.S. and Filipino soldiers had congregated and where the Japanese had made their main landing on the Bataan peninsula.

If only we had heeded General King's message to save some vehicles for moving our forces to another location, if we had not destroyed all of our trucks, maybe we would have been able to ride to prison camp. For some unknown reason, or just being in the right place at the right time, a few of the American prisoners ended up riding all the way to our first prison camp, Camp O'Donnell. We walked.

The road we marched on was about twenty feet wide and constructed of rock covered with crushed stone, then a layer of finely crushed rock, and a final coat of sand. The sand, when put down, was intended to make the road hard enough for small automobiles, Filipino carts pulled by carabao, and of course, pedestrians. By the time the march started, the road had already been overused, not only by all of our heavy trucks but also by our tanks and half-tracks whose metal and hard rubber tracks made the road a shambles for driving, much less for walking. The entire road was now nothing more than potholes, soft sand, rocks, and loose gravel. Walking on this terrain for short distances would have been bad enough, but walking for any long distance or for any extended period of time was going to be a painful and difficult experience.

We started our march in columns of fours, with about ten columns in a group. By the end of the first mile we were walking, not marching, and not in columns at all but as stragglers. What was at first an organized group of about forty men was now a mass of men walking or limping as best they could. We had no idea what our final destination was. Many of us felt that we were headed for death. It was just at this time that I decided if I were to survive it would be necessary to have a plan of survival. I thought back to the night before, before we were captured, when I determined that I had to really believe that I was going to survive and get home. To do so I had to set attainable goals, like making it to the next bend in the road or to the herd of carabao in the distance. And of course I had to dream, for it was my dream that kept me going.

After watching everyone being stripped of just about everything we owned, I placed my picture of Laura in my sock, on the ankle side of my boot. She gave me inspiration for my dream, and I reasoned that without a dream, no dream could ever come true and my resolve would weaken. I did not want the enemy to take away the very thing I was dreaming about, the reason why I had to live, to see Laura again, and to make my dream become a reality.

We did not march very far before we found out what kind of treatment was in store for us. After the first shock of being taken prisoner wore off, we realized that how we were outfitted when we were taken from our bivouac area was how we were going to spend the balance of our march. For instance, those who left without a canteen had no means of getting water, even if it was available. Those who left without a cap or headpiece walked in the broiling hot sun and midday temperatures well above one hundred degrees without any head protection. They also suffered the pain of stinging rain during those periods when it would pour down in buckets and the wind-blown dust made seeing difficult.

After the first few hours of marching, however, the men who did have a few extra items with them started discarding them along the road. Some of the men carried knapsacks loaded with a variety of gear: toothbrushes, toothpaste, shaving cream and razors, blankets, and pup tents. The road out of Bataan was strewn with a sampling of these various articles, thrown away at random after the first few miles.

The Japanese guards also began hollering at us in Japanese, which we did not understand. Because we did not respond to their commands as fast as they thought we should, they started beating us with sticks that they picked up from the side of the road. They were trying to get us to walk faster or to walk at a slow trot would be a better description. It made no difference to the guards that we could not understand what they were saying; they just continued repeating the same words over and over again. It dawned on me then that our guards were not the brightest members of the Japanese army. In fact, I concluded, they were most probably the poorest educated and could not connect the fact that we did not respond with our inability to understand what they were saying.

After four or five hours of this constant harassment and beating and of being forced to march in their poor physical condition, many of my fellow prisoners just could not go another step without rest; but the guards did not allow us to rest under any circumstances. One man in my group, Hank, finally limped over to the side of the road and fell in the brush. Within seconds a guard ran over to him. Some of us passing our fallen friend hollered as loud as we could, "Get up, get up!" It was too late. With his bayonet aimed at Hank's body and while screaming something in Japanese at the top of his voice, the guard bayoneted the exhausted American soldier. After five or six jabs, Hank struggled to get up. With blood trickling down the front of his shirt, he hobbled back into the line of marching prisoners and joined a different group of prisoners who were marching by at that particular moment.

Hank survived, but not for long. That evening I was told by another friend of ours that Hank had passed out while walking, fell to the road, and was shot by one of the guards. I could not cry; it seemed I was all cried out. All I had left were just memories, memories of a fine young man who did nothing wrong but who was in the wrong place at the wrong time. Nothing could be clearer: taking a rest while on the march was impossible, that is, if we wanted to live. But what would we do when we had to defecate? Or urinate? We sadly and quickly found out. In order to live, we had to go in our pants.

On the second day of the march, I saw a Japanese truck coming down the road. In the back of the truck were guards with long pieces of rope that they whipped toward us marching men. They tried to hit any prisoner who was not marching fast enough. They snapped a rope at one of the marchers on the outside of the column, caught him around his neck, and then pulled him toward the back of the truck. They dragged him for at least one hundred yards down the road. His body just twisted and turned; he rolled this way and that way, bumping along the gravel road until he was able to free himself from the whip. By then he looked like a side of beef. As he crawled on his hands and knees and slowly raised his bleeding body off of the road, he screamed at them, "You bastards! I'll get even with you for this. I'll live to pee on your graves." In spite of his physical condition, the welled-up anger gave him new strength. He pulled himself up to his full height and began marching with a new spirit.

Also on that second day, when we stopped at the Cabcaben barrio, I watched a Japanese soldier finish eating rice from his *bento* box (mess kit) and fish from a can he had just opened. He had about two spoonfuls of fish left in the can, and as he turned in my direction, he looked me in the eye and pushed the can toward me. He must have seen a pitifully hungry-looking soldier, staring, not at him, but at his can of fish. I had not eaten in almost two days, and I was hungry, tired, and demoralized. Without a moment's hesitation, I took the can. Using a piece of tree bark I found on the side of the road, I scooped out just enough for a good taste. I then turned to my buddy Bob Martin, took one look at his face as he sat there staring at me, and gave him the makeshift spoon and the can of fish. From that moment on, Bob and I were close friends.

Always happy-go-lucky, nothing ever seemed to bother Bob. Maybe the word *nonchalant* would better describe him. Although only five foot seven inches tall, he was a big man when it came to giving of himself, and nothing was ever too much to ask of Bob. His smiling face always made people feel warm and friendly, and his brown hair and green eyes complemented his effervescent personality. Whether wearing his dress uniform hat or his fatigue cap, Bob always perched it jauntily on the back of his head; it was one of his trademarks.

Watching Bob keeping up his own spirits while at the same time trying to make the rest of us on the march feel better made all of us realize that Bob Martin was someone special. Bob and I shared many experiences together on the march and throughout the war. As of this writing, I am glad to be able to say he is alive and well, and we are still very close friends.

I also clearly remember a good-looking and clean-shaven lieutenant from the 194th Tank Battalion, a man about twenty-eight years old with blond wavy hair. He was a large man, about six feet tall, and I guess before the war he had weighed at least 200 pounds but now, on the march, was closer to 150. He appeared to be quite strong but he walked slowly, carrying a large bundle—first under his arms, then as we walked farther, over his shoulder. Then he tried walking with the bundle on his head. None of us knew what was in the bundle, but we assumed it was the usual type of gear any good soldier would take with him for emergency purposes.

Our group was walking a little faster than the lieutenant, and as I got closer to him, I saw his eyes were bloodshot and glassy, almost as if he did not know where he was. As I passed him, I asked if he needed any help; I got no answer. Then, as I looked toward him again, I realized he was not walking but staggering, first to the left, then to the right. He was not going to make it, that I knew, and I felt awful not being able to help someone who obviously needed help and was going to die. If any of us had stopped for him, we would have had to accept whatever punishment the guard near us felt appropriate.

As the march continued, he fell farther and farther back, hardly able to walk. We had tried to persuade him to throw away unnecessary items, for his pack was too heavy a burden for him under these conditions. He refused and, after stumbling along for several hundred feet, fell to the ground. The Japanese guard overseeing our marching group stopped and looked at the fallen figure. He yelled something in Japanese and without a moment's hesitation shoved his bayonet into the young officer's chest. Then with a mighty scream, the guard yelled what we interpreted to mean, "Get up." Of course it was too late. That bayonet had finished the job the march started, and another good U.S. soldier had died in the service of his country. I could not help but think, There but for the grace of God go I. As I witnessed one after another of these atrocities, I became more and more convinced that what was going to happen to me was, to a great extent, going to be up to me.

While walking forward, we looked back at the sickening scene. There the lieutenant lay in the middle of the road. Within minutes we heard the rumble of trucks coming down the road; the Japanese were moving some of their fighting men in position against Corregidor. Making no attempt to avoid the fallen body, they ran over the dead man, leaving only the mangled remains of what once was a human being.

No sympathy, no concern for us as humans, no burials—the Japanese were treating us like animals. We had no doubt as to how we would be treated as prisoners of war.

We had thought that the first few hours of captivity would probably be the most dangerous, but the horrors we witnessed continued well after the surrender. For the Japanese, their sweet taste of victory should have overshadowed the bitterness associated with their strenuous fighting on Bataan, but it was obvious to us that the Japanese soldiers were committing acts of revenge. Many of them had witnessed the death of close friends only days before, and they wanted to get even with those who killed their comrades. Emotions ran high during the battle, and now their elated feelings of victory, coupled with their vengeful reactions associated with close physical contact with their enemy, made many of the Japanese soldiers barbarians. The warrior philosophy associated with the traditional Bushido code was reawakened when the victorious Japanese achieved the surrender of the forces on Bataan. All Japanese soldiers were indoctrinated to believe that surrender was the coward's way out, and a soldier who was captured was expected to commit hara-kari at the first possible opportunity.

Our ignorance of the Japanese language, their customs, and their military discipline contributed heavily to our casualties on the Bataan Death March. While few of us spoke Japanese, we were aware that many Japanese soldiers spoke a little English but did not dare reveal this ability in front of their comrades, for fear of being accused of having pro-American sympathies.

On the march the guards seemed to have most of their fun with prisoners who seemed to be weak. Later, in the prison camps in Japan, the guards and civilian workers seemed to seek out those prisoners who appeared to be big or strong for punishment. Many times the Japanese guards would boast, "Americans are big but weak; Japanese are small but strong." They had a severe psychological hang-up about being small.

The guards also forced us to go without water on the march, making it one of the most difficult and painful physical experiences I had ever encountered. My stomach ached, my throat became raw, and my arms and legs did not want to move. Words cannot properly explain the mental and physical abuse the body takes when in need of liquid. By the third day, marching without food and water caused us to start daydreaming about food and drinks we had consumed in the past. Simple things like hamburgers covered with cheese and smothered with onions, milkshakes, a beer or even a Coke made our mouths water. Our minds played tricks on us, but eventually we came back to reality—to hunger and thirst and not knowing where or when our next meal or drink would come from. Still, we were forced to push on and to keep going, one foot in front of the other, with our bodies going in the direction of our feet.

Although there were many free-flowing artesian wells located in and around Bataan, the Japanese had no set policy on giving water to us prisoners. Some of the guards would let a few men go to a well for water but would deny others the same benefit. One day our tongues were thick with the dust kicked up from the constantly passing trucks, and our throats were parched. We saw water flowing from an artesian well, and after a long, hard look at the water being wasted and given the fact that there was no guard right at our side, a marching buddy, Frank, and I ran toward the well to drink what we could and to fill our canteens for future use. We reached the well and started to swallow water as fast as we could. First I took some, then Frank took a turn, then I drank again, and then Frank. We took turns until some other marchers saw us at the well.

Within a few minutes, another ten to fifteen prisoners ran to the well for water. At just that time a Japanese guard came over to the well and started to laugh at us. The first five of us drank our fill, and when the sixth man began drinking, the guard suddenly pushed his bayonet down into the man's neck and back. The American prisoner fell to his knees, gasped for breath, and then fell over on his face. He died without ever knowing what happened—killed, murdered, slaughtered for no apparent reason.

All of us at the well ran as fast as we could to get back into the marching line. Fear filled each of us. My heart pounded like a jackhammer, my eyes popped opened to twice their normal size, and I could not help but think once again, There but for the grace of God go I. Tears streamed down my cheeks as I thought about this young man, murdered and cut down in the prime of his life by a maniac who felt that killing was a game.

About two hours later, we passed a carabao wallow about fifty feet off the road. After one look at the water, I could see it was not fit to drink; green scum floated on top and two carabao were in the water cooling themselves off. The men were dying of thirst, however, and ready to do anything for a drop of water. Not only were we thirsty, but many of us had malaria and were burning up with fever. In addition, most of the men on the march had severe dysentery and felt that water would heal all of their problems. One of the men motioned to a nearby guard and in sign language asked if he could get some of the water. The guard started to laugh and made a hand movement that indicated it was OK.

In a matter of minutes dozens of half-crazed men ran toward the carabao-occupied water. The men pushed the green scum away and started splashing the infested water all over themselves and drinking it. Some thought that using a handkerchief to filter the filthy water was going to make it safer to drink. How foolish they were! Nothing could have filtered that dirty scum-laden, bacteria-infested water, swarming with blowflies, to make it fit for human consumption.

Only a few minutes went by before a Japanese officer ran to the wallow and began hollering at the Americans in the water. Once again, none of us understood him, yet he continued to shout. He did not use any sign language to indicate there was trouble, but the fellows in the water ran back into line to continue the march. Then the unbelievable happened. The officer, with a big broad smile on his face, began prancing around the area where the Americans were lined up and ordered the guards to search our ranks for any men who had water-soaked clothes. The guards picked them out of our group of marching men and lined them up on the side of the road. Then the officer ordered the guards to shoot all of them. What a horrible massacre! And those of us forced to watch had to stand by helplessly. We knew if we attempted to interfere with the orders of the Japanese officer we also would be shot.

These past few horror-filled days helped me to evaluate my chance for survival. What would my priorities be? How would I deal with these overzealous conquerors of Bataan if they came for me? How would I be able to stay alive on what seemed to be a never-ending march to nowhere?

Hope is what kept most of us survivors alive on the death march. Hope that the starvation, the disease, and the agonizing effort to put one foot in front of the other would end when we got to wherever we were going. Some of us heard rumors that we would be exchanged for Japanese prisoners and that we would be taken care of in a U.S. hospital or other facilities. Others hoped that our capture was a brief bad dream and that we would soon be on our way home. Those were the optimists. Everyone, however, hoped at least for a destination where food and fresh water would revive us and where a shelter would protect us from the sweltering tropic sun and the stinging, slashing precipitation made up of rain and gritty sand.

Again, the one thing that kept me going was my determination to make it to that banana grove or mango tree or whatever I could see down the road. I had to have a goal, a place to march to. Most of the time we walked without thinking of where we were going, with our heads down, dejected. We're real failures, I thought to myself, but I must go on.

Many of the men on the march were just too weak and had too many illnesses to continue. If they stopped on the side of the road to defecate, they would be beaten within an inch of their lives or killed. Of course, with the small amount of food we were getting, we did not worry very much about having a bowel movement. Those men who had a bad case of dysentery, however, never knew when they would have to defecate.

On the fourth day of the march, I was lucky enough to be walking with two of my tank buddies, Walter Cigoi and Bob Bronge. Cigoi looked like a typical southern Italian. He was over six feet tall, with jet-black hair, a heavy beard that always seemed to need shaving, and a full head of wavy hair that made his strong, handsome, elongated face look sinister. His dark brown eyes were sunken a little, almost as if he had just awakened, but they seemed to dance from left to right, then back to the left again. Wally was very soft-spoken and never raised his voice, even when irritated or angry. From the day of the surrender, though, he was notably on edge about what was taking place.

Bronge, on the other hand, looked like he was from the northern part of Italy. With blond hair, bright blue eyes, and a firm, strong body, he had a loud voice that could be heard a block away. The life of the party, Bronge always had something funny to say and was liked by everyone; he was included in all get-togethers. Bronge stood just short of six feet and was built like a bear, with strong arms and a barrel chest that portrayed power. Everyone in Company B liked both Bronge and Cigoi. They were known throughout the entire battalion as the "Meatball Twins."

I was walking with Bronge and Cigoi when a Japanese officer came riding by on horseback. He was waving his samurai sword from side to side, apparently trying to cut off the head of anyone he could. I was on the outside of the column when he rode past, and although I ducked the main thrust of the sword, the end of the blade hit my left shoulder, missing my head and neck by inches. It left a large gash that had to have stitches if I were to continue on this march and continue living.

As the Japanese officer rode off, Bronge and Cigoi called for a medic to fall back to our position. The medic sewed up the cut with thread, which was all he had with him, and for the next two miles or so, my two friends carried me so that I would not have to fall out of line. We all knew that falling out of line meant certain death.

Cigoi and Bronge saved my life; I only wish I could have saved theirs. Military records show that Bronge died in Cabanatuan Prison Camp on July 31, 1942, of dysentery, and Cigoi died of the same disease in Formosa on November 3, 1942. Upon coming home, it was very difficult for me to see both of my friends' families and to answer questions about how their sons acted as soldiers and how they died. The emotional meetings with their parents left an indelible mark on my mind and heart that I will never be able to erase.

Each day on the march we trudged along like zombies. We walked from 6:30 in the morning till 8:00 or 9:00 at night. Most of the days we would get a few minutes' rest when the Japanese changed guards; otherwise it was hit and miss regarding a rest period. The guards were always fresh, for they only walked for about three miles and were relieved for the next three or four miles. This constant changing of the guards kept us always on edge because we never knew what the new group would want us to do or not to do. Moreover, the new guards were always trying to impress their fellow soldiers and, of course, the officers. In addition, being well-rested, they were able to walk at a faster pace than we were. Thus, we were fearful and apprehensive every hour of the march. I also made sure that I never again walked on the outside of the column of marching men.

Due to the poor road conditions, our deteriorating health, the lack of food and water, and our overall defeatist attitudes, we were able to walk only about a mile, or two at the most, for every hour on the march. With the added constant screaming and the beatings by the Japanese guards, we could merely trudge along the road at a snail's pace. I would wonder, where were they taking us? If they were going to kill us, why not do it where we could be buried along the side of the road and no one would ever know the difference? Walking with a destination in mind would have been much easier. If the Japanese had only told us to walk for seventy miles before we could rest or that we were going to a prison camp so we could work for them, it would have been better than walking for what appeared to be eternity.

Once again, we had not eaten in days, and we were nearly going out of our minds from thirst. We were all slowly becoming completely dehydrated, and we realized that we would die soon without water. The Japanese, we were told, planned on feeding us once we arrived in the town of Balanga, which was thirty-five miles from where we were taken prisoner. Under normal conditions, for a well-rested, properly trained, and adequately fed army, a march of this distance could be made in about nineteen hours. We prisoners were not in the condition necessary for a march of this type, or any type. We were tired, worn out, and in need of prolonged rest and medical attention. Also, the heat of the day seemed to suck any energy we had left.

Finally, on the fourth day, as we entered the town of Balanga, Filipino civilians stood along the sides of the road, throwing various food items to us: rice cakes, animal sugar cakes, small pieces of fried chicken, and pieces of sugar cane. At that moment, the sugar cane was more important to us than anything else. By peeling the bark off with our teeth and chewing the pulp, we were able to get enough liquid to satisfy our thirst and get the energy and nourishment found in its natural sugars. These Filipinos' gestures lifted our sunken spirits to a new high.

Suddenly, we heard shots ring out from somewhere in the middle of our marching group. Within seconds, the people along the side of the road scattered in all directions, for the Japanese soldiers were shooting at them for offering food to us prisoners. Two of the Filipinos started to run across the field, heading for a water hole. Three of the guards turned, aimed at the running Filipinos, and fired round after round in their general direction. The Japanese guards were not very good marksmen, so they just continued firing until the two men fell to the ground. The guards then ran over to the fallen men and began hollering at and kicking them, first in their backs, then directly in their heads. Next, the Japanese guards fired several shots at point-blank range into the men's prostrate bodies.

The guards watching over our marching group made us stop and watch the proceedings. Watching this made me feel woozy. I almost started to vomit, but there was nothing in my stomach to come up, so I just stood there with my eyes fixed in the direction of the slaughter. Then I tried to wipe away the scene from my mind as fast as I could. I knew what was happening; I did not have to watch it any longer to have another indelible memory of Japanese barbarism. Once again, in the blink of an eye, more innocent people were slain by the conquering Japanese.

During the shooting and hollering, the Filipino civilians were running to get as far away as possible. Many of the Filipino prisoners on the march with us broke away and ran with their countrymen. Their goal was to enter the barrio, change clothes, and become just another civilian. Because it was starting to get dark, the escapees had a good chance of succeeding.

We continued marching into the center of town, and when nighttime finally came we were herded into a large warehouse. About 75 feet wide by 160 feet long, the building was used for storing grain, rice, sugar, and other agricultural products. Those men who could not find room inside the building were herded back outside into a large open area. I ended up inside the building. When the warehouse was filled to capacity, the guards pushed and shoved another couple hundred men inside. We were so tightly packed together that we sprawled on each other. When one of us had to urinate, he just did it in his pants, knowing that the following day the heat from the sun would dry them out. Those who had to defecate found their way back to one of the corners of the building and did it there. That night, the human waste covering the floor from those who had dysentery caused many others to contract this killing disease.

The stench, the sounds of dying men, and the whines and groans of those too sick to move to the back of the building became so unbearable that I put small pieces of cloth into my ears in a feeble attempt to drown out some of the noise. Nothing could be done about the smell. The air inside became putrid from the odors that accompanied the abnormal body functions associated with dysentery and the urine-soaked clothes the dirty men were wearing. The Japanese guards, also unable to bear the horrible smell, closed the doors to the warehouse, put a padlock on them, and kept watch from outside.

Getting accustomed after a few hours to both the noise and the smell, I allowed my mind to drift away from this nightmare and back home to Laura. Was she aware of what was happening? How was she standing up to the news of our capture? Or did she think I was killed? Did she think I was a coward? Did she still love me and want me as much as I wanted her? After I pondered all these questions, I began daydreaming about our life together. Oh, I thought, when would this nightmare come to an end? Then sometime in the middle of the night, I shook my head, got rid of the cobwebs, and began facing reality.

The following morning when the guards unlocked the doors, we staggered to the door of the warehouse totally dazed. We exited the dark and dreary warehouse with the quickness of scared animals. We lunged to get away from the smell of death that permeated the air around us. That morning, at least twenty-five men were carried out and thrown in the field behind the building. I was mesmerized by what I had seen. All I could do was cry and say to myself, "Oh God, please have mercy on their poor souls." I felt they deserved more than being left to the elements. Would it have been so hard to have allowed some of us to bury those poor men who died so miserably during the night?

In the courtyard of the warehouse, we saw a group of Japanese guards milling around. Within minutes, we were herded in their direction. There, to our surprise, in the center of all this activity we found three large kitchen pots, each containing rice. Those men without a mess kit received one ball of rice about three inches in diameter. Those with a mess kit were given one large scoop of rice equivalent to the rice balls. At the far end of the field, another group of guards was rationing out hot tea. A man who had no container would borrow a friend's canteen or cup just long enough to obtain his ration of this most welcome liquid.

After the hunger of these last four days, we relished the food, however sparse. The Japanese reminded us how lucky we were that they had provided so much food and tea for us. As soon as we received our rations, they ordered us back on the road leading out of Balanga. The Japanese guards began laughing at us, and their grins and acknowledging nods showed that they were having fun taking advantage of us. We were pushed back into a marching column heading north. The march, obviously, was going to continue. But where were we going and when would it end?

On many nights the Japanese guards would just stop the marchers and yell for them to sleep right on the rocky, dirty, dusty road, strewn with items discarded by the marchers and of course reeking with human waste. However, after the ordeal in the warehouse the previous night, my first choice would be to sleep outside even though the guards would roam around at all hours, prodding and kicking us and generally not allowing us more than a few minutes' uninterrupted rest.

During the first four days of the march, not only did we have to contend with the guards' physical abuse but we had to endure constant psychological torture that sapped our strength. Of course, the lack of food and water did not make things any better. There were also times during this ordeal that we suffered the pangs of loneliness. I thought back to when I was ten years old and I went to camp. That first night I had cried myself to sleep because I was so lonely and had lost the sense of security I had while at home. Now, many years later and ten thousand miles from home, I had the same feelings of alienation that I had had as a child. During the grueling, lonely hours of marching down that long road, my thoughts often turned to my past happy home life and to Laura. For what seemed like an eternity, but was actually only four days, I kept saying, "This is a bad dream; it can't be for real." When my spirits were low, I would think of Laura being there to comfort me and to tell me everything would be all right. In my thoughts, my family gave me hope, my friends showed me compassion, and my loved ones gave me the warmth and understanding I needed.

On the march we were always ready for a good rumor. We told each other, "When we reach Balanga, we will be taken by ship to Manila and then traded for Japanese prisoners. We'll be home soon," or "We'll be fed as soon as we get to the next barrio." In spite of persistent contradictory evidence, we lived on these rumors for the entire twelve days of the march.

On that fifth day of the march, I witnessed one of the most sadistic and inhumane incidents on the entire march, and I did see some of the worst. We had just stopped for a brief rest while waiting for another group to catch up with us. When the other group finally arrived, the guard ordered us to stand up and start walking. One of the men had a very bad case of malaria and had barely made it to the rest area. He was burning up with fever and severely disoriented. When ordered to stand up, he could not do it. Without a minute's hesitation, the guard hit him over the head with the

butt of his gun, knocked him down to the ground, and then called for two
nearby prisoners to start digging a hole to bury the fallen prisoner. The two
men started digging, and when the hole was about a foot deep, the guard
ordered the two men to place the sick man in the hole and bury him alive.
The two men shook their heads; they could not do that.

Once again without warning, and without any effort to settle the problem any other way, the guard shot the bigger of the two prisoners. He then
pulled two more men from the line and ordered them to dig another hole
to bury the murdered man. The Japanese guard got his point across. They
dug the second hole, placed the two bodies in the holes, and threw dirt
over them. The first man, still alive, started screaming as the dirt was
thrown on him.

A group of about five or six of us witnessed this slaughter of innocent,
unarmed men. As for me, I turned away and hid my face in my hands so
that the Japanese could not see me throw up. It was one of many experiences I will never forget, one that made me sick for days. I asked myself
over and over again, "Is this what I'm staying alive for? To be executed
tomorrow or the next day, or the next? How will I be able to continue to
endure these cruelties?" The strength of my resolve was once again challenged. After wiping away the tears and the vomit, with my eyes focused
along the winding road in front of us, I sought another landmark to use as
my objective. I had to have a goal; I had to go on.

Under normal conditions, in the real world, only two possible courses of
action are open to us: either we can try to make our lives conform to our
beliefs, or we can modify our beliefs to conform to our lives. Although true
contentment may depend a great deal on which path we choose, under
the conditions I faced on the march, I quickly found that in order to survive emotionally and physically I had to choose a little of each. Therefore,
to survive I had to modify my beliefs to conform to what the Japanese
wanted and at the same time try to make my life conform to my beliefs.
For example, if the Japanese guards forced me to assist in burying a man
who might still be alive, I quickly realized that although obeying the
guards' commands did not conform to my beliefs, I still had to make my
life conform to their demands in order to continue living. Had I insisted on
conforming to my beliefs and on not burying a man who may still be
breathing, then I too would have been killed, as were so many other prisoners, for disobeying a Japanese order. By altering my beliefs, I rationalized,
I could increase my chances of being around later to help others. When a
man is able to be successful without compromising his morals, it is a blessing, a blessing I had to forgo in order to survive.

I could not forget or understand the guards' actions. I had observed that
the Japanese soldiers were well disciplined and obeyed their officers with-

out question. I thought the officers would have known the Japanese army regulations pertaining to the handling of prisoners of war. These regulations can be found in Japanese Army Instruction Number 22, issued in February 1904. Chapter 1, article 2 states, "Prisoners of war shall be treated with a spirit of goodwill and shall never be subjected to cruelties or humiliation." The Japanese guards in the Philippines did not adhere in any way to these written instructions of their emperor. In fact, the Japanese interpreters told us on more than one occasion, "You are lower than dogs. You will eat only when we choose to feed you; you will rest only when we want you to rest; we will beat you any time a guard feels the need to teach you a lesson."

These Japanese army regulations were not followed at any time—not on the march or in any of our prison camps or on any of the work details. Obviously, these regulations were just words—not meant to be taken seriously—intended to influence world support and to show that the Japanese were "humane and caring" people. We found out the hard way that the Japanese guards were just the opposite. They seemed to revel in watching men being tortured, in the mistaken belief that they were superior and could do anything they wanted to us.

Immediately after witnessing the execution-style burial, my mind turned to the positive side for survival. What, I wondered, can I do to overcome the total despair I felt when I was forced to witness these brutalities? Or, for that matter, forced to participate in the very march itself? What can I do to better prepare myself for survival?

First, I had to become determined and convince myself of what I can do. Second, I had to keep a positive attitude, and I had to realize that I could do anything the Japanese wanted me to do. Then, I quickly understood the importance of having the "smarts," or knowing when to do or not do certain things, such as when to walk faster and to become a part of another column of men. I vowed to walk with determination, my head high, shoulders back, and chest out. This posture would make me feel righteous, and the guards did not harass or belittle the men who looked healthy and in control of themselves.

We walked for several more days and often right into the night as well. Only twice were we offered food and water, and then very little of each. The four- or five-mile march from the town of Lubao became another nightmare. We did not know why we were being hurried the way we were. The guards yelled more and louder than ever before. We prisoners were subjected to constant hitting, pushing, and prodding every few minutes by a different guard.

At one point on this section of the march, we were ordered to double time, or run, and try to keep up with a fresh group of guards. As we passed a group of Japanese soldiers, our guards ordered us to stop. When we looked over to where the group of soldiers were, we saw an American soldier kneeling in front of a Japanese officer. The officer had his samurai sword out of the scabbard, and he was prancing around the other soldiers, showing off his skills in moving around the kneeling American while swinging his sword in every direction. Up went the blade, then with great artistry and a loud "Banzai," the officer brought the blade down. We heard a dull thud, and the American was decapitated. The Japanese officer then kicked the body of the American soldier over into the field, and all of the Japanese soldiers laughed merrily and walked away. As I witnessed this tragedy and as the sword came down, my body twitched, and I clasped my hands in front of me, as if in prayer. I could hardly breathe. I could not believe this killing, just for pure sport, was happening again.

I have relived this scene hundreds of times since that day; I will never be able to get that scene out of my mind. At the time, however, despite my horror, I was determined to go on. I knew I had to survive this ordeal in order to let the world know what had happened.

It took two more days to reach the barrio of Orani, a distance of about fifteen miles. During these two days we again went without food or drinking water. Along the route, we witnessed more of the same kind of treatment we had seen the first four days. The Japanese were trying very hard to humiliate the Americans any way they could in front of the Filipinos, as if to prove Japanese superiority. Each time they killed or tortured an American, they would seek out some of the Filipinos on the sides of the road and force them to watch. Men, women, and children—there were no exceptions—all had to do whatever they were commanded by the guards. The Filipino people watched in stunned silence the many atrocities. They did what they had to do; but they watched with tears in their eyes and a prayer on their lips.

While marching through the town of Orani, we came to a group of Japanese standing on the side of the road. They would scream at us, "Hayaku, hayaku" (faster, faster). Before long we were almost running. Then as we passed the guards, the Filipinos standing on the edge of the road threw us balls of rice. If we caught one, we ate it on the run. If it dropped on the ground, then that meal was gone forever. Luckily most of us were willing to share, so no man went without some of the tidings our Filipino friends threw to us during the days on the march. Unfortunately, once we arrived at our first camp, there was no longer an opportunity to share. We each received only a small ration of rice for our early meal and another for our evening meal, with nothing more to share, no Filipinos throwing food at us, and no food growing on the side of the road that was easy picking. Our spirit of comradeship deteriorated. While I tried on many occasions to talk some of my tank buddies into eating their rice and not trading it for a cigarette, other prisoners preyed on sickly men and tried to convince them to trade away their life for a cigarette that supposedly would make them feel well again. It became a dog-eat-dog existence.

Finally, exhausted and barely able to stand, we were forced to continue the double-time march until we entered the city of San Fernando, about two kilometers away. What now, we wondered? Which one of us would be the next to die? How much more of this can our bodies endure?

Upon our arrival in San Fernando, the largest town on the march, we found a bustling little city scarcely touched by the soldiers and equipment associated with war. We Americans, on our withdrawal to Bataan, had not stopped in San Fernando long and neither had the Japanese in their hurry to locate and annihilate us. Some fairly large factories were located in this capital city of the Pampanga province. We noticed many Japanese soldiers milling around town in groups of four or five, all of them armed and all having a good time at the expense of the Filipinos.

We marched to the local railroad station, where we were told to rest. In the distance we could just see a group of boxcars being pulled by an old engine. We sat for about an hour along the railroad tracks before the train finally chugged its way into the little station. We were going to Manila, we heard, to be traded for Japanese prisoners. We would be home soon, we reasoned. We found out soon enough that these were all rumors, just rumors.

We were herded onto small railway boxcars. Cars that would normally hold ten animals, or perhaps twenty-five or thirty people, were jammed with eighty to one hundred men. We had to take turns just to sit down because there was not enough room for all of us to sit at the same time. Even sticking our feet out of the car did not leave enough room for the rest of the men. Some of the men were unable to breathe and were so tightly packed in the middle of the car that they suffocated while trying to get a breath of fresh air. The lucky ones were those who were able to get to the outside door and breathe some of the air that seeped in. We all stood shoulder to shoulder for most of the five-hour ride to Capas, the town near our final destination, a POW camp.

I was one of the lucky ones. I got a place at the door, and I was able to sit down with my legs dangling out. Enjoying fresh air with a little breeze and resting without a bayonet at my back provided such a relief. But then along came one of the guards, swinging a large canelike piece of bamboo. He swung the bamboo toward my feet and hit me just above the kneecap. I was taken by surprise, and I yelled out in pain—exactly what I do not remember, but it was not complimentary toward the Japanese guard who hit me. Then, without warning, he grabbed the handle of the sliding boxcar door and slammed it shut, once again striking my legs. My pain proved not in vain, however; my legs stopped the door from closing all the way. Because of this small opening, we were able to get a little fresh air, and while the train was moving, a significant breeze flowed into our boxcar.

As the train slowly rolled along with its cargo of thousands of diseased and dying soldiers, Filipinos stood along the track and threw rice balls wrapped in banana leaves, rice cakes made with sugar and spices, and pieces of cooked chicken to us in the boxcars. When I saw the Filipinos throwing food toward us, I shoved the door open another couple of feet, allowing us to retrieve much of the food. Little did they know at the time that their actions and generosity saved many of us from starvation. Their show of concern helped us get through another stage of this living hell.

Finally, the train stopped, and for the next ten minutes we stayed where we were. No one said a word; the quiet of the day was broken only by the moans of dying men. At this point, we still did not know what was going to happen to us. Were we going to be executed and placed in a mass grave out here in the country where no one would witness this? We were all afraid of the quiet. Even the Japanese guards said nothing. I barely heard a whispered prayer from within the boxcar. Oh God, I thought, please give us a chance. Do not let us die like animals in this remote section of the Philippines where we would never be found.

Only the living finally got off this train; the dead, we were instructed, were to remain inside the boxcars. Those men who could jumped out of the cars while the others slowly sat down at the edge of the door and slid off. I slowly jumped out of the boxcar, and as I tried to start walking, I fell on the side of the tracks. I realized that my cramped legs would not cooperate with my brain. I did not get up as fast as one of the guards thought I should, so he started beating me with the butt of his rifle on my back, legs, and neck. At one point, he made a thrusting movement toward me with his bayonet, a threat meaning death if I did not move. I got the message, and I got going.

We started to march again, not knowing where or for how long. All we knew was that we were being herded like cattle into a slaughtering bin. I felt like my body was burning up when I got out of the boxcar. After walking about two miles, I started to feel faint. I began wobbling back and forth across the column of marching men, and before long I dropped to my knees from sheer exhaustion and fever. Luck was with me once again, however, and I found myself being carried by my two friends, Cigoi and Bronge. They carried me for about a mile before I got my strength back and was able to make it on my own. How often in one person's lifetime will he be saved by the same people twice and within only a few days?

The columns of haggard, half-dead men—our dirty bodies drained of almost all fluids, our clothes tattered and torn, our faces unshaven—

continued down the road. Along this narrow, unfinished road we admired the beautiful and tall, full mango trees and other rich green foliage. Then, every so often, we would see the body of a fellow American sprawled near the side of the road, the rich green foliage near his body splattered with dark brown blood.

Mobuhiko Jimbo, author of *Dawn of the Philippines*, was a Japanese soldier who served in the Philippines during the Philippine campaign. In his book, he states that on the day Bataan surrendered all of the Japanese troops were told that at least seventy thousand prisoners were in the hands of the Japanese Imperial Army.

The following Japanese order, issued in Manila, explains in detail the reasons for many of the atrocities suffered by the prisoners who were forced to march out of Bataan.

> Every troop which fought against our Army on Bataan should be wiped out thoroughly, whether he surrendered or not, and any American captive who is unable to continue marching all the way to the concentration camp should be put to death in the area 200 meters off the highway.

This order may be the justification the guards used during the march to kill any American who dropped out of the marching line for any reason. Once General Yamashita accepted the surrender of Bataan, his only interest was not in our welfare but in the final capitulation of all fighting forces in the Philippines. Then he could direct all energy and supplies toward Corregidor. Without a shadow of doubt, I am convinced that the slaughter of our surrendering troops was premeditated and authorized by someone with considerable authority, someone in the Japanese military high command in the Philippines.

Meanwhile, what ended up as the last day on the march nearly ended my life as well. My feet had swollen to about twice their normal size, and I had trouble keeping up with my column. I found out later that this problem plagued many of the men.

We had just been turned over to a group of well-rested Japanese guards, who got a kick out of yelling, pushing, and clubbing those of us who could hardly continue walking. The weak were their chosen prey. One of my walking buddies, seeing my swollen feet, suggested that I cut the sides of my boots. This seemed like a good idea, so not only did I cut the sides of my boots, but I also removed the shoestrings to allow for continued swelling. By this time I was so weak, hot, and tired that I seriously doubted whether my fever would permit me to continue any farther. As my health problems threatened to overwhelm me, I quickly realized that I had to continue and that I had to make it to wherever they were taking me. Then, like a miracle, my fever seemed to disappear. After what seemed a lifetime, but was in reality an excruciating eight miles, we finally saw the faint outline of barbed wire and typical Philippine huts in the distance. I felt as if the end of this forced march might at last be in sight.

# CHAPTER 5

# OUR FIRST CAMP

Half-starved, barely able to walk, and sick with malaria and dysentery, we entered an old, abandoned Philippine Army camp. Known as Camp O'Donnell, it was named in honor of the original landowner, a Spaniard. Unfortunately for us, the camp was never completed and it looked as bad as we felt. It had several nipa-thatched that built on stilts, the custom in the Philippines, except these huts were on rickety stilts and looked like they were ready to collapse at any moment. Many of the buildings did not have roofs, and although it was in the middle of a lush jungle, this camp was treeless. It looked as if no one would be able to live there for long.

From what we could see there were weeds growing everywhere, even in the huts. Like most of the huts in this part of the world, windows were nothing more than openings, and the rat- and insect-infested dwellings reeked of decay. Forty men were to be crowded into each one, which was only intended to house sixteen. The one thing that seemed to have survived the years was the rusty barbed wire that encircled the camp.

The soldiers pushed and beat us unmercifully and indiscriminately. There was no reason for this action. All they wanted us to do was get in a line, march into the compound, and stand at attention. We could have accomplished this simple order without the physical abuse that was doled out to most of the men, me included. Because I was limping as I entered the camp, the guards began hitting me with their rifle butts. One of the guards who was stationed in the camp had taken his military belt off and was swinging it wildly toward me. The belt ripped into my back and across my buttocks, and I felt blood gushing down my back and legs. Then, with a mighty snap, his belt caught me squarely in the face. The shock of the blow and the stinging pain so clouded my mind that I almost tore after the guard in retaliation. Luckily, I caught myself before I did anything foolish. I wiped away the blood on my face and pressed the tail of my shirt to my cheek, hoping to stop the bleeding before I got hit again. This proved a point to me: the Japanese did not bother beating the healthy men, only those they viewed as weak or sick.

We were then pushed into an open marching field and told to place all of our possessions—everything we had in our pockets, on our body, or in a pack if we were carrying one—on the ground in front of us. The officers and their soldiers began walking up and down the rows of men, looking for that telltale item that only the Japs knew would mean death for its possessor. All of a sudden we heard the crack sound of a rifle being fired. Quickly the word passed around the POWs that if anyone had anything Japanese, or any Japanese propaganda material, "to get rid of it fast." The guards reasoned that the only way any of us would have anything Japanese would be that we took it off a dead Japanese soldier. However, when the Japanese arrived at our bivouac area on Bataan and asked for cigarettes, occasionally one would give a prisoner some money and sort of pay for what he took. Unfortunately, such Japanese generosity got one of our buddies killed, because he had a Japanese coin on the ground in front of him. When the camp guards found it, no questions were asked, and the prisoner was taken around the side of the camp and shot.

If a prisoner had one of the "surrender certificates" that had been dropped from Japanese planes flying over Filipino territory, he was also pulled from the group and shot. The Japanese reasoned that he had had an opportunity to surrender and receive good treatment but he chose not to take advantage of the offer. Any of us who had anything like this chewed and swallowed it or pushed it up his anus as far as it would go. It was one more strain on our physically destroyed bodies.

As I started to place all my items in front of me, I noticed one of the surrender certificates fall onto the ground. I was panic-stricken. What could I do to avoid being shot by our captors? I took four or five deep breaths, surreptitiously put the paper into my mouth, and chewed it as fast as I could. After two or three chews and a mighty gulp, I managed to swallow the incriminating document.

Next, we were told to stand at attention while the Japanese camp commander lectured us on what we were to do and say as prisoners of war. Captain Tsuneyoshi—a man of about thirty-five years old, five feet eight inches tall, and 160 pounds—stood on a raised platform directly in front of the group of prisoners, about three thousand of us at that time. Through an interpreter, he began by telling us that we were cowards and that we should have committed suicide, as any Japanese soldier would have done if capture were imminent. He called us "lower than dogs" and hollered and screamed that Americans had been enemies of the Japanese for more than one hundred years. Nothing we Americans could ever do would change that feeling; we would have to pay for the way the Japanese people had been treated by the Americans. Then he said, "We will never be friends with the piggish Americans."

By this time the commander was hysterical, waving his arms and throwing punches at the air. He was in a frantic frenzy. He began to huff and puff as the heat of the day started to get the best of him. With his sword hanging on the left side of his belt and medals draping his uniform, he was obviously an officer who had seen action on Bataan. He then said we would soon find out that our dead comrades were the lucky ones. Oh, how right he was.

We were then instructed on what we were expected to do and how we were supposed to act. First, we were always to salute and bow to a Japanese soldier no matter where he was and as long as we could see him. Second, any time a Japanese soldier talked to us we were always to stand at attention and say, "*Hai*" (yes sir). He told us that those who did not follow the rules would be severely punished or killed, whichever the Japanese soldier decided at the time. The intensity of the commander's screams made believers out of us. He also told us that the Japanese had never ratified the Geneva Convention agreement on the handling of prisoners of war; therefore, we could be treated any way the Japanese soldiers wanted to treat us.

This speech went on for nearly two hours and ended about 3:00 P.M., the hottest time of day. We had to stand at attention during the whole tirade. At least a dozen men fell to the ground, victims of heatstroke. They stayed on the ground until the commander's speech was over. Only then were we allowed to pick the men up and give them aid.

After the camp commander finished his performance, the soldiers looked over our personal items and took whatever they wanted—our watches, rings, photographs of our wives or sweethearts, and just about anything they fancied. Fortunately, my treasured picture of Laura was still safe in my sock, next to my boot. We were then led to the nipa huts and allowed to roam inside the camp and choose our own huts.

I keep using the word *men*, as if there were no women on Bataan. That was not the case. Although no women were on the march or in Camp O'Donnell, many women were stationed on Bataan and Corregidor; in most cases they were active-duty nurses with the U.S. Army or Navy. In addition, there were many wives of both civilian and military personnel. All of the women and most of the civilian men captured by the Japanese in the Philippines were interned at the University of Santo Tomás in Manila.

Almost without exception every man in Camp O'Donnell had something physically wrong with him. Dysentery was by far our worst enemy because it not only affected the victims, but the stench of the men's feces and vomit sickened all of those around them. In addition, dysentery was so contagious and conditions so crowded, that everyone seemed to have the runs associated with dysentery.

The American medics established one of the nipa huts as a hospital ward, and another was aptly labeled the "Zero," or "Z," ward (meaning no place left to go). The hospital ward was full of men who were too sick to stand. They had one or a combination of malaria, dysentery, beriberi, malnutrition, pneumonia, and various other diseases common to men so deprived of such bare necessities as food and water. Most of the men in the hospital ward were eventually transferred to the Z ward. Reserved for dying men with no hope of recovery, the Z ward's patients were the living dead. We simply delayed burying them until they stopped breathing.

Some of the men who were not confined to either the hospital or the Z ward were still so sick and exhausted that they collapsed and fell asleep in their own excrement. Usually their next stop was "Boot Hill," our cemetery. Those who survived did so because they refused to let themselves become filthy animals. During the day, the healthier ones would walk around and try to help those who had lost their sense of direction or their desire to live. In spite of being sick ourselves, we would not succumb to self pity. At night those who could, would go out to the slit trench—the community latrine—and sleep beside it. That way when we felt the urge to defecate, which was quite often, all we had to do was roll over a little and go. Insects buzzed and climbed all over the stinking mess, but we had to live that way because the Japanese refused to help us improve our sanitary conditions or to provide us with any medication to control either the dysentery or the malaria. Death was running a merry-go-round and we men were the riders, going around and around and never knowing when it would stop to take us off.

While sitting outdoors near the slit trench one evening, my buddy Bob Martin pointed to the large yellow globe in the sky and said, "Look at that majestic moon. Just think, it's the same moon being seen back in Maywood. I wonder what our families are doing tonight, what they are thinking of?" That thought was going through the minds of all the men. What was happening at home? What did our families know about us and our trip with death? Some day that glowing moon would shine down on us at home, and we would be able to appreciate fully the glory of seeing a full moon once again. With that thought, hope returned, and my determination to cope with adversities became the dominant factor of my life.

Before long the realities of life set in. We heard the moans and cries of our companions. Some we knew, some were strangers, but all suffered as brothers. Through the huts' "window" openings, we spied shadows moving up and down. Someone inside was probably stealing the few possessions of the dead and dying. "Hell can't be worse than this," mumbled Bob. "But we'll live through it, won't we, Ten-Spot?"

"We won't die, Bob," I reassured him. "The Lord only takes the good." Then as an afterthought, I said, "We must survive. Someone has to tell our friends and families of the inhumane treatment, the unsanitary conditions, the torture, and murder of their loved ones by the Japanese barbarians calling themselves soldiers. We must live to be able to tell what is happening here."

As we discussed the treatment we could expect, Bob declared, "It would be better to die in the jungle than to live here in this degradation. We have to get out of here as soon as possible." But how? That was the question. When? That was another question. And we did not have an answer for either.

The Japanese did not bother to count or identify any of us in Camp O'Donnell, however. In fact, the idea of someone escaping was not even a remote possibility in their minds. After all, we were of a different race than the people of the Philippines and the Japanese. So, the guards reasoned, where could we hide without being detected or turned in?

In the meantime, we established many types of work details in camp. We gathered wood and water for cooking and for our medics to treat the sick. We also had to bury the dead many times each day. There was always something to do but not enough able-bodied men to do all the chores. American servicemen were dying at the rate of fifty or more a day. There were five times more Filipinos than Americans, but they were dying at a slower rate of 150 a day. No doubt the Filipinos were better able to cope with the sicknesses associated with their Philippine environment than we Americans were. How many of the sixty-five thousand Filipinos and twelve thousand U.S. servicemen would survive this ordeal? Only time and God would know.

After watching the burial detail for the first few days, it turned into a waiting game. We wondered, Who's next? Two men would carry out a dead man on Monday, and by the end of the week, one of the two grave diggers would be carried out. I did not like those odds, and I knew that if I stayed in the camp long enough, the odds would get even worse. I had to do something, and quickly, to prevent my contributing to these sad statistics. The odor of death permeated the entire camp. Death was everywhere— from the physical act of a person dying to the mental anguish of knowing death was ever threatening.

When we buried the dead, we could only dig graves about three feet deep, because ground water seeped into the holes if we dug any deeper. In most cases the dead would be buried naked because the living needed their clothes. On many occasions, we would bury a man only to find his body floating up to the top of the grave before we had a chance to pour dirt on it. By leaning on a pole that held down the dead man's body, one of us could force it down long enough for the other men to cover it with dirt. If they were available, we always tried to place the man's dog tags on a hurriedly built cross at the head of his grave, hoping that someday someone would find them who could notify his next of kin. All of us on the burial detail would then say a short prayer for the man we had just buried. The Twenty-third Psalm became a very popular part of the burial ceremony. "The Lord is my shepherd; I shall not want. He maketh me to lie down in green pastures. . . ." After a burial, we would look at each other and wonder, What prayer will they say for me? Which of us will be next?

The single most important event of each day was waiting in line for a canteen of water. Sometimes we stood in line for hours. Once I saw a man drop to the ground after waiting in line for more than three hours. We called for the medics, and when they arrived, they said he was dead. He had died in line just waiting for a drink of water. What barbarians our captors were. In spite of the unusually high number of men dying daily, the Japanese still refused to provide us with any type of medical relief or access to adequate amounts of water.

On the fourth day in camp, I volunteered for a water detail that involved bringing water from a pond back to camp for the men. Although there was spring water in the camp, it was only enough for our drinking needs. We needed the pond water for cooking and general cleaning.

All of those who volunteered—only the healthiest volunteered—for the water detail were chosen. The detail left camp with only one guard. I knew that if ever there was a time to escape, it was while working on the water detail. I never gave any thought to where I would go or, for that matter, how I would fare in the jungle alone. I did not know the language and I knew little of the area's geography. But I had seen enough of death and dying, of torture and beatings. I wanted to live, not die, and I knew I could not live long in Camp O'Donnell.

Without food, water, and medical attention, my fever from malaria hit 102 degrees on a daily basis, and my bowels were being torn inside out from dysentery. I thought my probability of survival in camp was nearly zero.

If I was going to escape, I would have to do it soon. The rumor from a few of our officers was that the Japanese were planning on instituting a numbering system for all POWs. The system would work this way: each man in a barracks or on a work detail would get a number, and then if one of the men did not answer morning or evening roll call, the guards would execute the men with the five numbers before and after the missing man's number. We would end up being watchdogs for each other.

That night before falling asleep in my usual spot near the latrine, I realized my dysentery had vanished, almost like an omen. In spite of my two recent brushes with death while on the march—when Bronge and Cigoi carried me through the malaria seizure and while I got the stitches in my shoulder after my encounter with a Japanese samurai sword—I felt a surge of new life. I felt better just knowing I was going to take charge of my survival. I was determined not to die like so many of my friends, nor did I want to go through the constant mental anguish of being in the wrong place at the wrong time. I had come this far, and I was not going to give up now. I no longer allowed myself to see the signs of death, but instead I developed a stubborn, unquenchable thirst for life. I was going to make it, I told myself.

Before dawn I was awakened by boots kicking my back and side and a bayonet jabbing my chest. The guard started to laugh after he screamed at me in Japanese. As I got up, I saw my fellow POWs stumbling out of their huts to use the latrines. Maybe that was what the guard was trying to tell me: get out of the way. Otherwise, I might have ended up reeking with the odor of urine and feces like the ground near the latrine.

As I got up and looked around, I was horrified to see the bodies of those men who had died during the night being stacked like firewood around the base of one of the huts. The corpses were being placed in one central area so that the burial detail could proceed without too much delay. I turned my face away from the bodies being brought out. I just could not look at the gray faces and sunken eyes that still seemed to plead for help. Which of my friends did not make it last night? Tears filled my eyes as I thought of what was happening. These were my friends; they had families back home waiting for them. Why them? Why was I saved from this end?

Although the first few days in camp were nothing but utter confusion, at last I was able to look seriously for my good friends Cigoi, Bronge, and Lew Brittan. By the fourth day, there were forty thousand men already in camp, and three hundred more arrived every hour. Slowly I got my mind back in gear. I wandered around the camp, looking all the men over and hoping to see a familiar face. Finally, after walking all over camp, I located someone who said he had not seen Cigoi or Bronge but knew that Lew was in the hospital ward. It did not take me long to locate the building, and inside I found Lew, fidgeting with his clothes, sitting in a corner, and staring blankly as if his mind was a million miles away. When I saw him, I knew instantly that in order for him to live, I had to get him out of that ward. I saw emaciated, half-dead men being helped to stand up by other dying men to give the mandatory salute as the guards entered. Lew, just a shadow of himself, was able to stand up on his own. That made me feel better, made me feel that Lew could make it.

With a lump in my throat, I implored, "Lew, the first thing you have to do is get out of this stinking sick bay. Take every opportunity, use every ounce of energy to go outside. At least outside there will be fresh air. Volunteer for a work detail no matter how weak you are. There will always be someone to help you; we are all in the same boat here." Then in order to bring a little humor to my serious appeal, I said, "Lew, my Hasidic grandfather used to say that according to Jewish law it is forbidden to despair. I'm sure that goes for Catholics, Protestants, and all the religions that believe in God. After all, there is only one God for all of us. So you see, Lew, you're not allowed to despair."

Then Lew and I went outside for breakfast, if that is what it could be called. It was *lugao*, rice cooked with much too much water for a sort of hot porridge. Lew did not want to eat, protesting that he could not keep anything down. While we were talking, he offered to trade his ration of rice for a cigarette with a guy walking by. "Lew," I yelled, "you can't do that! You have to eat to stay alive." I pleaded, using all the reasoning and excuses possible to no avail. Then I insisted, "Lew, for God's sake, eat; otherwise, we won't be able to get even with these bastards, and if you won't eat then I won't eat. We'll go down together if that's what you want."

He looked at me and a slight smile crossed his face. Lew said, "You win. I'll try making the most of a bad situation. Where's my mess kit?" His dark eyes flashed a "thank you," not just for making him eat, but for my friendship and caring for him as a person.

I saw firsthand the consequences of not being willing to eat. Many men, too sick to move and too weak to care, traded their small ration of rice for one cigarette. All they wanted was one more drag, one more taste and smell of tobacco. That was what they traded their lives for. Tobacco, the deadly addictive drug, caused many prisoners to die. During the first few days, only their will to live kept these men alive. Those who traded their rice for cigarettes today were not alive for any tomorrows.

After breakfast, the guards did not do a roll call or assign numbers to the men. Time was still on my side. We lined up outside for work details, and once again I volunteered for the water detail. I saw Lew standing nearby and told him my plan. "Could you make it, Lew?" I asked. "Could you just make it to the stream where we get the water, about one mile down the road?"

"No," he said, "you go and may God be with you. I'll do as you say. Don't worry; you have given me a reason for living. I'll be ready for a work detail in a few days. You go, do what you have to do."

Again that day only one guard accompanied us on the water detail. We made three trips from the stream back to the camp, each time carrying two five-gallon containers filled with water. I was confident that the water detail would be my ticket out of the rat hole and to survival. I would make my break the next chance I had.

That night Lew approached me and said, "Les, you don't have a snow-ball's chance in hell in those unfamiliar jungles, not knowing the language or which way to turn once you're out of here."

I answered with the best assurances I could muster. I said, "Look, Lew, over sixty thousand Americans and Filipinos started the march at Mariveles and less than half got here. Many died or were killed, but some must have run away into the hills, and I intend to find some of these guerrillas and join them."

Seeing that it was useless to argue any further, Lew removed his belt buckle and handed it to me. I saw a small compass on the inside of the buckle. A motorcycle reconnaissance man from headquarters company, Lew was a man dedicated to his job and always well prepared. He said to me, "Take this. It'll help you out in the jungle."

I refused the offer, saying, "You keep it, Lew. I'll need more than a compass to stay alive." I realized that if I did not find someone to guide me through the jungle the compass itself would not be of much help.

# CHAPTER 6

# LIFE WITH THE GUERRILLAS

On my sixth day in Camp O'Donnell I made my break for freedom. Occurrences during the past few days made going *now* a necessity. First, the death rate of both the Filipinos and the Americans had reached more than 250 per day. Those who did not have malaria or dysentery one day were certain to have a life-threatening sickness by the next.

Second, men were being herded into forced work details regardless of their health or physical condition. We did not know what we were going to do or where we would be working. I wondered why we were chosen to do this work and how we were going to be expected to do the work set out for us. All I knew was that what I had seen thus far I did not like. If the future was going to be anything like these past three weeks since our surrender, I did not want any part of it.

Third, and maybe most important, the Japanese still had not issued the prisoners group numbers or any other type of identification. One of the doctors had told me that some of the men sent out on work details were placed in groups of ten and told that if any one of them escaped the remaining members of that group would be beheaded. On other work details, I was told, the guards assigned a number to each man. If one escaped, the guards would then kill the men with the five numbers above and below the escapee's number. No person or group inside Camp O'Donnell had been given a number at this time, but the doctor expected such a numbering system would be implemented any day.

The reason I am emphasizing the numbering system is that many men were killed when a man in their numbering order escaped. I was opposed to anyone trying to escape once we had been assigned numbers for there was a great possibility that innocent fellows would be shot, beheaded, or bayoneted because of the action of one self-centered, non-caring person. I was forced to witness several beheadings after someone escaped or attempted to escape from either camp or a work detail. I will never forget it. So I am setting the record straight right now: no one in Camp O'Donnell at this time had been given any type of identification or number. The Japanese would have no way of knowing whether a prisoner had escaped; therefore, no one else was likely to be punished for another man's actions.

The following morning the guards began hollering for men to go on the water detail. They needed another group of prisoners who were physically able to make the one-mile march to the creek and who were strong enough to carry two five-gallon cans filled with water back to the camp. I wanted Bob Martin to go with me, but he was unable to make the walk to the creek and back let alone escape through the jungle. Not many men volunteered for this detail. In fact, on a few occasions either our officers or the Japanese guards would have to pick the men to go. I was waiting for this detail and hoping that only one guard would accompany us and that the guard would as usual not count the number of men on the detail. I was in luck that morning: only one guard was assigned to look after the twenty-five men who had volunteered for the detail. This detail seemed to be made for me and my plan. So, filled with determination I moved into the water detail's line of volunteers.

The guard in charge was short—about five feet six inches—with a stocky build and clean-shaven head. Bowlegged, he set a rapid pace. He looked innocent enough with his steel-rimmed eyeglasses placed halfway down his nose. If he did not like the looks of one of the volunteers, he pushed him out of line. I could hardly control my excitement while we waited for the detail to begin. The five minutes of waiting seemed like an hour. Some of the men who volunteered stepped back out of line, and others stepped in. Confusion reigned everywhere while we waited for the detail to start.

When we finally got to the creek the men spread out over its entire length, about 150 feet, and waded about four feet into the water. Some of the men on that detail volunteered just to cool off, to clean off a little bit, and in general to refresh themselves in the water. Because of the number of men on the detail, the guard decided that we would make three roundtrips to the creek.

My waiting paid off. It was starting to get dark as the last trip began. This "overtime" by the guard was my chance. Everyone was tired, including the guard. At one point, I had tried to hold my breath underwater. I had seen this done as a kid in a Tarzan movie many years before, and it seemed like an easy way to fool the guard. This was my original plan of escape, but I found that I could not hold my breath for as long as I thought was necessary. So I began thinking of another way. With the protective covering of darkness coming, I realized I could easily slip into the surrounding jungle and hide in the tall grass behind a large mango tree. I then thought of an excuse I could offer if I got caught. My plan was simple: if caught I would explain that I had to have a bowel movement, and because I had dysentery, I left the area to avoiding spreading the sickness to others. While all these things were going through my mind, darkness fell. I then moved to my protected position.

Nighttime came and no one missed me. The guard called for all the men once again to start carrying their cans of water to the camp. From the grassy area I watched the work detail trudge back to camp for a meager ration of rice, our so-called dinner. After what I estimated to be an hour or so, I started to stand up and suddenly felt a strong hand on my shoulder, pressing deep into my flesh. I was instantly afraid. I broke out in a sweat, my heart pounded like a trip-hammer, and nausea filled my throat. What was going to happen to me now? They caught me, and my excuse was not going to be believed. I slowly turned my head in panic, and I knew there was no retreating from my plan. With a deep sigh of fear, I was ready to face my fate. Then I heard a voice behind me say, "Don't worry, I'm an American. I've been watching you for the past hour. I'm going to help you get some medical attention and some food. Come with me!"

I turned around quickly, still leery, and saw a massive-looking, bearded man staring at me. I soon found out I was in the good hands of an American guerrilla. He told me his name was Ray. I never did bother to ask him his family name; what difference would it make? Ray was about thirty years old. He was dressed in old army fatigues and a cap that looked like it had been around for a dozen or so years. His beard was at least two inches long and covered most of his face. As he explained later, "This is the best darn camouflage a guy could have in this jungle." He had a hoarse voice, as if he had a bad case of bronchitis. I guess his time in the jungle made him very suspicious and cautious, because he did not say much until we had moved a good couple of hundred yards away from the pond.

Ray explained that he had been helping many of the men on the march and from Camp O'Donnell join the behind-the-lines fighting force. Its purpose was to become a thorn in the enemy's side by keeping the Japanese constantly busy protecting themselves and to psychologically erode their "better-than-thou" attitude. When Ray spoke about this mission, his voice reverberated, and he shook visibly. I could see how much he hated the Japanese, and I wanted to know what they had done to him, but I decided not to ask.

As I found out later, one of the first rules of conduct within a guerrilla band is that no one asks personal questions. After all, there were many reasons for joining a guerrilla group. Some men had escaped during the march, some had become separated from their outfits during a battle, and a fair number were simply AWOL, having fled from what they considered an intolerable situation or even to avoid the consequences of an illegal act.

Finally, after walking about a mile, Ray allowed me to stop for a short rest. Things out here were so different than at O'Donnell that I fell to the ground, laughing and crying at the same time. Nothing, I thought, could be worse than our sufferings on the march. Anything would be better than the stench of O'Donnell, seeing men dying by the hundreds day after day, and then being buried with dozens of other corpses, in a single hole, like animals. God, I was glad to be out in the jungle, away from the pain and agony of being a prisoner of the Japanese.

Ray told me that we would have to walk through a mango grove, a pineapple field, and a herd of wild carabao to get to the bivouac area his guerrilla group was using. Ray said that each band of guerrillas had their own area of command and their own area of combat readiness. In other words, each had responsibility for annoying the Japanese in certain areas. Every man within each group was expected to torment the enemy.

When we started to walk again, I admired the moon shining through the trees. What a beautiful sight, I thought. We stopped for the night in a well-camouflaged area, hidden by tall grasses, big trees, and heavy shrubs. We were not too far from a stream and a path that the natives used while traveling through this jungle. Paths were always near water because the natives always traveled with their carabao. Because this swampy area was full of leeches, mosquitoes, red ants, and snakes, we did not expect the Japanese to come even close.

The weird sounds of the night were actually music to my ears. I was hearing them as a free man without being slapped around, starved, deprived of medicine, or forced to do the dirty work of any Japanese soldiers. Yes, at that very moment I felt that if I had to die in this war then it was better to die a free man than to have to live under the subhuman conditions in a germ-laden, stinking nipa hut of Camp O'Donnell. Or was it?

I kept thinking that for me it was an easy choice, but then I considered how my folks would take it. Laura would then be a very young widow. How would she react when word reached her of my death? Then I started to think about all of those friends I left behind at O'Donnell and what was going to happen to them. Is there anything—even any small thing—I can do now as a free man to help them? I wondered.

Maybe if I had stayed at the camp I would have died in captivity. Then I would have joined that stack of corpses that were stripped of everything they owned and dumped into a shallow mass grave. Maybe my hand would be sticking out, maybe a foot, or maybe a pole would have to be jammed into me so that I would not float to the top of a water-filled hole. Would I get a prayer? Only a handful of the Japanese guards allowed us to say a prayer for the dead at the burial site. In most cases, the detail carrying the dead bodies would say a silent prayer as they lifted the poor, malnourished skeleton of a body that was once a vibrant happy man into the grave. All of these thoughts kept going through my mind as I lay in the open field a free man once again.

That night before we settled down for some shut-eye, my newfound friend Ray opened his musette bag and took out two cans of Spam, one for each of us. I quickly forgot that Spam was one of those foods GIs joked about. I could not remember when I had my last taste of real food, and Spam was real food to me. I devoured the contents of the can but was not greedy enough to ask for more. I was happy with what I got. Then to my amazement, Ray pulled out of the bag a bottle of fluid that looked like wine. A few minutes later, by golly, it even tasted like wine. Then with a smile on my face, I stretched out on the grass and fell sound asleep.

Early the following morning we began our trek up the mountains to the area where I would be questioned and then indoctrinated into the life of a guerrilla. Ray explained that there was a Filipino barrio there, and I would meet about six or seven other Americans who had also escaped or were cut off from their own troops during the fighting on Bataan. In fact, that was how the guerrillas got started. Men who were trapped, out of touch with their own units, and unable to move through the jungle found friends in the Filipino communities who were willing to help Americans.

When we started to withdraw, we came into contact with many Filipinos, most of whom were pro-American and willing to do anything they could to win back their country. To counteract this pro-American loyalty, the Japanese tried to convince the Filipinos that they belonged to the same race as the Japanese, and the Filipinos should not protect or befriend Caucasians. The pro-American Filipinos were considered traitors by the Japanese, who were just as brutal to the Filipinos as they were to us Americans.

Along with Filipino soldiers, the U.S. soldiers continued to fight the Japanese but in a different manner. The guerrilla activity in the Philippines was not a surprise to General MacArthur. Prior to the start of the war, MacArthur tried to form a guerrilla resistance unit in northern Luzon as a means of ambushing the Japanese if and when a war with them was declared. I wondered if I might run into some of my old buddies in one of the guerrilla groups.

We finally arrived at the barrio headquarters of the guerrilla band that I was to join. After being questioned I was fed all the rice I wanted, broiled chicken, and barbecued pork—a meal fit for a king. Once again my thoughts went to my friends at O'Donnell. I wondered what they were doing, whether Lew went out on a work detail, and if any of my buddies from Company B died in the last two days. In spite of eating a magnificent meal, I was crying between bites. I could not really be happy with my friends still prisoners. I was mixed up and did not know how to react to this newfound freedom.

The officer in charge, a lieutenant who said to call him Riley, informed me that the other men of my detail were going out first thing the next morning to contact a Japanese unit that was traveling on one of the roads leading from Manila. The Japanese were carrying their supplies inland, and it was our job to see that these supplies never reached their destination. I was reminded once again that our role as guerrillas was "to be a thorn in the enemy's side." I was told, however, that until I recovered physically I was not to go out on any detail searching for the Japanese.

Lieutenant Riley was a big man of at least two hundred pounds and a good six feet two inches tall. With his almost bald head and a full beard, this man was awesome. Yet his voice sounded calm, and his tone was reassuring. He enunciated every word with pure artistic talent. Riley was a proud man of Irish descent, and when he wanted to sound comical, he would use an Irish brogue to emphasize a point. Everyone in his detail respected him, for he made a point of never asking his men to do anything that he was not ready to do first.

Virtually every man in our group, I discovered, had some dark past experience hanging over his head. I began to understand why the men did not ask each other personal questions. One of the men confided in me that he had walked away from his lookout position the day before the surrender. He said it was useless to continue fighting, but his commanding officer did not realize the situation and wanted his men to be ready to charge the Japanese front line. I am sure one of the other men in our group was half crazy. He cried at the drop of a hat, and on a few occasions, in his sleep, he started screaming in a foreign language. One of the mornings after being awakened by this screaming I asked Ray what was going on with this guy. Ray just shrugged his shoulders and said, "Don't ask."

By my fourth day, under the watchful eyes of Lieutenant Riley, I had gained both weight and a sense of what was expected of me. My first detail consisted of twelve Filipinos and two other Americans. Each of us had a .45-caliber automatic pistol, a large bolo knife, and a Thompson submachine gun with two extra loaded drums. We took off about 7:30 in the morning, and an hour and a half later, we found the road over which the Japanese were expected to drive their loaded trucks. We arrived well ahead of the Japanese convoy and were instructed on where and how to rig explosives along the side of and on the road. Once the explosives were set, we took up positions about one hundred feet forward of the expected vehicles' destruction.

We did not have to wait too long. Within fifteen minutes, we heard the strain of the trucks' motors and knew they were getting closer to our hidden explosives. Soon the convoy of three trucks rounded the bend in the road. On each truck we could see four guards plus two men in the cab. The bed of the trucks were all open, revealing an assortment of much-needed supplies and, more important to us, no other Japanese soldiers. As I watched from my hiding place beside the road, my legs felt wobbly, my arms were heavy, and my knees seemed to knock at a constant tempo. Waiting, I realized, was almost as bad as the fight itself.

Then, within a split second, I heard the explosions, loud and resonant. I sprang from my hiding place into action. With a pistol in my right hand and a hand grenade in my left, I was ready for any Japanese survivors of the blast. The explosions sounded just like the Japanese bombs over Clark Field only a few months before. All three of the trucks rolled over from the impact, and the Japanese guards riding on or in the trucks were hurled twenty feet in the air and landed only a few feet from where we were crouched. None were alive when we reached them, and their cargo was strewn all over the road.

As we looked at the bodies, the trucks, and the blown-apart supplies, we did not speak a word. We were not sure whether another contingent of soldiers was bringing up the rear. We moved back into our positions immediately, waiting for whatever was to come. Then we received orders from the lieutenant: all was clear, mission accomplished. We returned to our bivouac area, carrying those salvageable supplies that we so badly needed.

Once back at our staging area in the small barrio of Dinalupihan, I marveled at the ease with which we were able to accomplish our mission. The whole event took less than five hours. I felt good about being a part of this effort to destroy the enemy. If only Lew or Bob knew what was going on outside of prison camp, they too would be excited. At last I had my opportunity to "get even," to repay those Japanese bastards with the same type of treatment they had been giving us. Show no mercy was our motto; "Give them hell" was what we said.

In these few weeks after the surrender, the activities of the guerrilla bands were mostly retaliatory in nature. We wanted to avenge all of the atrocities we had witnessed. Sitting still and waiting for the next assignment were more stressful than going out and confronting the enemy. Staying out of sight of low-flying enemy aircraft was the more sensible approach.

Some of the local citizens gave the guerrilla group I was attached to a few hundred books that were taken from the local library. They reasoned that the Japanese did not want the Filipinos reading American books.

During lulls in our activities, I read whatever books were available. My favorite was the *Pocket Book of Verse,* which for some reason the Japanese allowed me to keep, and I still have and treasure this book that made many of my wartime days seem shorter.

A book on the power of positive thinking was another one I liked. After all, I was the living proof of the benefit of a positive attitude. Due to the nature of our missions, and the start-and-stop time requirements, I found a way to read faster than ever before. I was not skimming; I was speed-reading. During the next few days, I read a book on philosophy, one on history, another on the power of money, and last, a book dealing with different business opportunities. Reading was a great way of keeping busy when we were not getting ready for another assignment. During these inactive periods, I also ate better and more food and gained a much-needed ten pounds.

We were forbidden by the officer in charge to keep any written notes of names, places, or any other evidence that could identify us as guerrillas operating behind enemy lines. Not having records of these events proved a lifesaver for me only a few weeks later.

The psychological power of knowing one is not completely isolated from his fighting forces goes a long way in achieving the necessary support for civilian resistance to an occupying force. The Filipino people never lost faith so long as they felt that they were not forgotten. On a day-to-day basis, one or more guerrilla bands would engage the Japanese militarily in one way or another. This constant reminder that the Americans were still involved with the war effort made the Filipino civilians feel they could, and should, continue to fight for their beliefs.

Inevitably there were some men, both Filipinos and Americans, in my guerrilla band who did nothing all day long and soon found themselves in arguments with other members of our group over the smallest of details. Others played around with the local female population and drank whatever alcoholic beverages they could find. I knew these misfits were not going to be worth much if we had to go out on a surprise mission.

I was with the guerrillas for only two weeks. In that time, however, we picked up four Americans who were found wandering in the mountains, and we had five skirmishes with the Japanese, all of which we won hands-down. We did not suffer a single loss; not one of our group was even wounded. In fact, during my time in the hills, only one man was injured; but he fell and broke his leg while trying to catch a couple of wild chickens.

By my tenth day with the guerrillas, I was used to the trials and tribulations of the group. Then the following day word came from another guerrilla band that the Japanese were planning an all-out offensive against the guerrillas. Word was circulating around the various barrios that the Japanese were offering hefty rewards for information about the whereabouts of any guerrilla bands or any individual fighting with the guerrillas. One of the rewards was a sack of rice. We knew the Japanese were shipping most of the rice harvested in the Philippines to their fighting forces around the Pacific theater of operations and the rest to Japan. For the near-starving Filipinos, a sack of rice was a greatly tempting reward for turning in an American.

With the reward posted prominently in all the cities and barrios of the Philippines, we were told to be very careful in our contact with the locals. Many times before or after a raid on the Japanese, the guerrillas would have to stay in a local village overnight. Most of the villagers were seriously malnourished and only shadows of their former selves. We were constantly concerned that, in a moment of anxiety for their children, one of them might turn us in for the reward. We would not blame them. After all, they and their children were suffering severely.

On our next mission we arrived at our destination earlier than expected. As we approached the barrio, we heard women screaming and the sound of rifle fire. We took cover at the top of a ridge and looked down at the village. We were aghast at what we saw. Tied to each nipa hut leg was a Filipino woman with her clothes torn almost totally off, and we watched in horror as Japanese soldiers inserted something into each woman's vagina. These women screamed, begging for mercy, crying for someone to stop this torture, but the Japanese merely laughed louder and harder. They were getting quite a kick out of their terrible game.

Some of the guards began fondling the women's breasts while other guards hit the ones who were screaming with pieces of bamboo loaded with sand and gravel. This weapon, if swung with enough force, could rupture or tear apart any part of the human body, and that was exactly what the Japanese soldiers were doing. One woman looked as if she was bleeding all over; from some areas her blood was literally squirting out, sort of like a fountain.

Watching this brutal, savage treatment of innocent victims was more than I could take. Just as I was about to turn my face away, I saw a few of the soldiers light the fuses that were protruding from the women's vaginas. Within twenty seconds, I heard the explosions.

God, what a horrible sight: the women were blown apart, and their huts were reduced to rubble. Through the smoke, children screamed and cried out for their mothers. And during all of this carnage, other Japanese soldiers, who had just come out of their hiding places, horsed around and laughed at their assault on these innocent people. Barbarians, one and all.

We counted about forty Japanese soldiers and only five of us. In addition, we saw another fifty or sixty civilians in the barrio who had been forced to watch this execution. We wanted to attack the Japanese soldiers, but with all those civilians nearby, it would have only meant more destruction and killings. The people had had enough of that for this day. We decided against any reprisal at this time, and we did say *at this time*. Then we heard the voice of the interpreter, loud and clear: "That was for not answering our questions about guerrilla activities in your village. Next time you fail to answer we will eliminate the whole barrio." With that, the Japanese soldiers got in their trucks and drove off. I was still trembling with disbelief and disgust. My rage at the brutality and at being helpless to stop it is impossible to describe.

When we were sure the Japanese had gone, we came out of our little bunker and started to tend to those who were injured during the melee. We saw that almost half of the little homes in the barrio were totally destroyed. Helping to put people's lives back together is one thing, but putting their bodies back together after this massacre was quite another. As we searched for the wounded, we found the most gruesome sight awaiting us on the barrio's streets: large and small parts of arms, legs, and torsos were scattered all over.

Those people able to walk unaided did so with great difficulty. Our small guerrilla band sewed up dozens of wounds and applied emergency tourniquets wherever needed. Then we placed the most seriously injured in the bed of a truck and had one of the men from the barrio drive them to the closest town with a doctor and hospital.

By the time we finished these simple medical procedures and directed a clean-up crew to start clearing the debris and to make plans to rebuilding the destroyed huts, it was already dark. The barrio's leaders thanked us and insisted that we stay for dinner and sleep there that night. We rarely traveled after dark, so we accepted their hospitality.

Once we decided to stay in the barrio, we could only hope that the people there would not hate us for what the Japanese did to them. Unfortunately, we were wrong. While most of the people accepted us, the ten-year-old son of one of the women killed that afternoon told us we were to blame for his mother's death. He cried and screamed at us for what had happened to his mother. He did not hold the Japanese who did the killing responsible; he blamed us.

One of the regulations set forth by the leaders of the guerrilla band was that when we stayed in a village we were always to split up. Each member of the group was supposed to sleep at the home of a different family. That way, the odds were that only one of us would be captured or injured in a confrontation. I was assigned to one of the huts on the outskirts of the barrio that night. None of us needed a blanket, pillow, or a change of clothes; we just slept in the clothes we were wearing.

I did not fall asleep that night as quickly as usual. Instead, I lay awake thinking of the horrible tragedy I had witnessed that day. I guess it was about one o'clock in the morning when I finally fell asleep, and at half past five I was awakened by a sharp pain in my left leg. In fact, when I touched the spot that hurt so much I felt a warm wetness flowing from it.

Then as I became fully awake I saw a Japanese soldier standing over me who had just pulled his bayonet from my leg. That was what I felt, what had caused me the initial pain. The quiet of this little village was broken as the soldier began screaming at me. At first, I thought he was hollering for me to stand at once. Then, as quickly as he started he stopped, turned to a few of his soldier friends, and showed them my blood on his bayonet. Then they all began to laugh loudly, sounding almost like a donkey braying. As I started to get up, he kicked me in the chest.

As I tried to rise again, I realized that getting up on my own would be very painful, if not impossible. A Filipino standing next to me helped me get up, and as I did, the guard kicked me again, this time in the leg he had bayoneted. The pain was horrible, but I bit my lip and refused to give him the satisfaction of hearing me moan, cry, or scream. I finally got to my feet, stood as erect as I could, and saluted the entire contingent of guards standing around me.

The simple instructions my guerrilla friends had given me immediately came to mind. If captured, show military respect. Give your name, rank, and serial number. Say you are not and never were a guerrilla; that you have no idea where any other Americans are; and that you have been in the jungle for months because your outfit got split up. In other words, pretend you know nothing, and deny you were ever a guerrilla. Our guerrilla leader felt that because it was only recently that the surrender took place, maybe the Japanese would buy the excuse that we were lost from our units. All of these instructions came to my mind in a flash.

I quickly applied everything I was taught. I stood at rigid military attention, looked the Japanese officer squarely in the eye, and said, "My military number is 20-600-429." I realized also that I should not use the word *hai*—the sole acceptable response to a Japanese soldier, regardless of rank—for the only way an American would know to say *hai* was if he had been incarcerated at Camp O'Donnell, and if he had been there, they would know he must have escaped.

Before I could do or say another thing, I was hit across my face with the scabbard of the officer's samurai sword. The blow did its damage. It shut me up and cut a five-inch gash on my right cheek.

At just about that time, the man who helped me get up whispered in my ear, "The boy got a sack of rice for turning you in." I knew who the boy was, and I just could not blame him. He was an emotional wreck. Seeing his mother tortured and beaten, molested, and then murdered was too much for most adults to deal with, let alone a child. I gave no further thought to what caused my capture; I focused only on how to cope with the situation as best I could.

The Japanese then grabbed me by my hair, which was yanked and pulled until I made the move they wanted, to the feet of the officer. The soldiers were yelling at me, but I was not able to understand one word. I figured out by their sign language and by knowing that they did not like any guerrilla, that obviously they were pleased at having found one. They did nothing to stop the bleeding from my leg or my face, and once I was up on my own two feet, standing next to the officer, they searched me for weapons. They removed everything from my pockets: a small Filipino knife, a few pesos, and my copy of the *Pocket Book of Verse*. They placed these items in a small box, placed it on the front seat of a truck, shoved me into the bed of the truck, and with four or five soldiers standing guard over me, drove off.

Once in the truck and lying down, I tore my shirt in strips and used these strips of cloth to bandage my leg. This stopped the flow of blood, which made me feel a little stronger. Then I applied pressure to the cut on my cheek, trying to stop the bleeding. I had no idea where the guards were taking me or what they were going to do to me once we arrived. But as we drove, I thought, I'm still alive; stay that way. What they don't know won't hurt.

Now I had to plan my response to the interrogation that I knew would take place. I realized that time was at a premium. My mind started to think back to some of the experiences I had had during these past four months. Then remembering what I had been told at the guerrilla camp in the mountains, an idea came to me. I remembered that fateful day in December when we lost Lieutenant Morin's tank in the rice paddies. Four men got out of the tank and made it on foot to the hills. Two of the men were captured a few days later. I felt that I could make the Japanese believe, first, that I was one of the four in that tank and, second, that I was one of the two who had not been captured. Then I had to convince them that I had been hiding all this time in various barrios. If I could make them believe this, then maybe my punishment would not be too severe. I began putting together as many of the facts of that day as possible. I also had to remember not to respond to any question with "hai"; that would have been a giveaway.

We traveled for what seemed like two hours over roads that were severely damaged by heavy rains. The roads were filled with potholes and rocks. At one point we even had to stop while the driver removed a large tree branch that had no doubt fallen during a recent downpour. The truck traveled at about fifteen miles per hour during most of the trip. Then at about ten in the morning, we stopped at a large rural schoolhouse. I realized this building was the headquarters for the detachment that had captured me. I had finally arrived at my interrogation station.

And what an interrogation I got. When the truck stopped, I was herded into the main building and down a long hall to what was obviously the unit commander's office. Once inside, I was made to stand at attention while an officer gave me a chewing out and a lecture on being a "good boy." I did not really understand him; I just figured out what I would say under like circumstances.

Then in walked a young Japanese officer. His uniform was sparkling clean; his shoes, polished. His ornate samurai sword was not of the "issue" brand. Obviously, the officer was very proud of it. I could tell just by the way he held the handle while strutting over to where I was standing. He stood directly in front of me and then said, in as perfect English as any well-educated American, "I am here to interpret what the commander has to say to you. I caution you to be honest and to tell the commander everything he wants to know, for if not, you will be severely punished." After what I had seen of the Japanese treatment of prisoners, I had no doubt that he meant what he said.

At last in walked the commanding officer. He was as pompous as I expected, all five feet ten inches of him. He weighed at least 250 pounds and had a black, well-trimmed pencil mustache. He looked at me, smiled, and in almost a whisper spoke to the interpreter. The English-speaking officer then told me that the commander had said, "Tell me where the rest of the poor unfortunate soldiers you have been working with are hiding." The question was asked in a matter-of-fact way, without screaming or hands waving through the air. "Why didn't you use the surrender ticket we dropped from airplanes for your freedom?" I was asked by the interpreter. I rested a few seconds before I said anything. I thought to myself, You mean the one I chewed and swallowed when we arrived at Camp O'Donnell. Then I said that I had never seen one and that if I had, surely I would have given the option a lot of consideration.

Actually, five or six different freedom tickets were dropped from low-flying Japanese airplanes. The first one said, "MacArthur has left you . . . he will not return. Surrender now and we will treat you kindly." Another said, "Don't wait to die. Come forward now and you will live to see tomorrow." An illustration of the difference in our cultures and our approach to sexual expression was found in the surrender ticket that said, "Before the bombs fall, let me take your hand and kiss your gentle cheeks and murmur . . . before the terror comes, let me walk beside you in garden deep in a petaled sleep . . . let me, while there is still a time and place, feel soft against me and rest . . . rest your warm hand on my breast . . . come home to me, and dream with me." This flier, not using very good English, had a picture of a sexy Japanese lady surrounding the written message. And then I remembered one that was intended for the Filipino troops. It just said, "You are our Pals . . . *Our* Enemy is the Americans. This is your ticket to freedom."

The questioning continued, and the Japanese concern for the damage guerrillas were doing to them became evident. They demanded to know where the guerrillas were hiding. In the first place, I really did not know where the rest of the guerrillas were, because they moved to different locations quite often. Second, I was new to this and therefore did not know the exact locations where the guerrillas had taken me. Third, even if I did know, I was not planning on telling the enemy or even letting on that I knew. I had to answer, so I said, "If I knew, I would tell you, but I really don't know. You see, I was just passing through, trying to find a place to sleep and a little food." Obviously, they did not believe me. I could tell from their reaction that they had made up their minds that I was not going to tell them a thing.

For what seemed like an eternity, I just stood and waited for them to say something. At last the commander gave the interpreter instructions. A few minutes later, a guard came into the room, raised his rifle, flipped it around so that the stock of the gun was facing me, and with one swift movement hit me with the butt squarely in the face. With one fell swoop, I started to bleed from each and every part of my face. I knew that my nose was broken, that a few teeth were missing, and that it hurt like hell. Blood was gushing down my shirt to my pants. Everything was getting wet from the flowing blood. All the while the Japanese were having themselves a good laugh. I guess I was truly the butt of the joke.

While I was trying to straighten up, one of the guards hit me across the back with a piece of bamboo filled with dirt or gravel, and once again I fell to my knees. I got up as fast as I was able and stood at attention in front of the guards. I was left standing there for about an hour, then three guards came in and dragged me out to the parade ground, which had been the playground of the school.

Once outside, I saw they had another American spread-eagled on a large board. His head was about ten inches lower than his feet, and his arms and feet were outstretched and tied to the board. A Japanese soldier was holding the American's nose closed while another soldier poured what I later found out was salt water from a tea kettle into the prisoner's mouth. In a minute or two, the American started coughing and throwing up water. The Japanese were simulating a drowning situation while the victim was on land. Every few seconds an officer would lean over and ask the prisoner a question. If he did not receive an immediate answer he would order that more water be forced into the prisoner's mouth.

I could not believe my eyes. Torture of this nature was something I had read about in history books. It was used during the medieval times, certainly not in the twentieth century. My God, I wondered, what is in store for me? My entire body became clammy, and I felt a sort of internal shaking, where my insides seemed to be moving all around. My face grew hot and my eyes opened wide as I said to myself, "What now?"

It did not take long for me to find out. The guards forced me to the ground, in a sitting position, and then began asking a series of questions, shot at me quickly from two or three soldiers all at once. The interpreter came over, knelt down next to my ear, and repeated the questions in English. "Are you the officer in charge? Where are the other Americans hiding? Who gave you the guns and ammunition? Who has been feeding you? Tell us," he said. "Tell us, and you will live."

I was frightened. I did not know the answers to their questions, and I did not know the punishment that was being planned for me. After what I had seen on the march, my imagination just ran rampant. I thought of every one of the atrocities I had seen. Were they going to cut off my head? How will I act when they tell me to kneel down? Maybe they were going to shoot me; that would be easier, I thought. But what if they were going to make me a dummy for bayonet practice? Without realizing what I was doing, I replied, "The Geneva Convention said all I have to give is my name, rank, and serial number, sir."

The interpreter burst out laughing. Then he informed the officer in charge what I had just said. The officer also belched out a loud laugh. I was then informed that the Japanese did not sign the Geneva Convention; therefore, they did not have to abide by those rules governing prisoners of war.

I did not realize it at the time, but my response must have saved my life. The Japanese officer had been present at Camp O'Donnell when the camp commander had hollered and raved the same thing about the Geneva Convention. As I looked back on this experience, the Japanese must have felt that I had never arrived at O'Donnell or I would have known this little fact. After a few more minutes of laughing at me and my serious state- ment, the officer in charge stood up and went to where they were tortur- ing the other American prisoner. I heard the American yell out, "I'll tell, I'll tell! Please stop, please!" The interpreter kneeled down in front of the man and wrote down what he said. Then, without a moment's hesitation, the Japanese officer pulled out his revolver and shot the man in the head.

Oh my God, I thought, the chances of being killed were no better if you told or not. Death was still the price you paid. What a horrible thing to have to watch—and what a way to die—torture, then death. I thought about what I had just witnessed and decided right then and there I was going to stick to my guns. "I don't know anything about anything. I'm just a dumb American soldier taking orders, like any good soldier would do"— that was what I was going to say.

I was questioned for about two more hours, and after each question I told them the same thing: "I don't know anything. I am only a poor private and followed orders." At first I thought they accepted my denial of any valuable knowledge, but then I saw a few Japanese soldiers erecting a hanging bar out on the field. I was told to stand, and before I knew what was happening, I was again hit across the face with the butt of a rifle. Then they shouted more questions, and before I could answer, the officer in charge took off his large military belt, swung it while holding onto the leather end, and hit me in the face with the buckle with the impact of what seemed like a kicking horse.

I was so scared, I wet my pants. I did not know what to do or what to expect next. Was I going to die right then and there, or was this just some kind of game they wanted to play with me? No, my life did not pass in front of me; I had neither the time nor the energy to think about anything. I just wanted to know what I had to do to stay alive. As I had decided while on the march, my goal was to get home to my family and my wife. I had told myself that I had to make up my mind about what I wanted, and then I had to do everything necessary to accomplish that goal. My final decision was always based on what would enable me to accomplish my goal without forfeiting my honor, my integrity, or my dignity. This basic philosophy is what pulled me through that day and many more days during the next three years.

Finally, the soldiers who were working in the field hollered something to the officer in charge, and I was dragged to the makeshift hanging bar. (I did not know what else to call it at the time.) The soldiers made me stand up and interlace the fingers of my two hands. The officer in charge then tied my thumbs together with pieces of stripped bamboo that looked like wide shoelaces. Then they ran the upper portion of the bar, the crosspiece, under my tied hands and raised the bamboo pole up to the top of the two supporting pieces. They raised the bar just high enough so that my toes would barely touch the ground. I later learned that the Japanese called this device a stretching rack.

What the Japanese did not realize was that I was so totally out of it by then that I could not have told them any secrets even if I wanted to. In fact, I was unable to hear, see, or talk to them, or even know what was going on around me. Their unrelenting torture was so severe that the victim was incapable of comprehending anything after the first ten minutes of any of their favorite torture schemes. The man I had heard say "I'll tell" most probably had been in the spread-eagle position for only a short time, and his level of pain tolerance must have been very low.

I hung on the stretching rack for a day and a half, and when they let me down, it was only to start another inhumane act. They tore my clothes off and tied a piece of wet bamboo splice, like a string, around my testicles. Then they hanged me again for the balance of the day. As the sun became stronger the drying bamboo contracted, becoming tighter around my testicles, until they were squeezed up into my abdomen. At the time I felt as if I was being castrated without the use of any anesthetic.

Next, in frustration and anger, they shoved small pieces of dried bamboo up into my fingernails and then set fire to them. The pain was excruciating, and my blood flowed from my fingers as if they had been cut off. When the fire reached my fingers and I smelled my flesh burning, the soldiers, with one quick movement, forced my hands into a bucket of cold water. My pain was relieved instantly, but within minutes, the pain returned to my fingers to join the nauseating pain in my testicles and my abdomen. During this torture, they sometimes bombarded me with questions, but I always answered, "I don't know anything. If I did I would tell you."

As this treatment continued, I felt that I was slowly going out of my mind. I really did not know yes from no, left from right, or up from down. I cannot even say I was expecting to die. Dying or living was not on my mind. Getting away from all the pain was all I thought about.

After what seemed like an eternity but was only a few days, the guards finally took me down from the poles and dumped me on the ground, where I was allowed to stay until I was able to move under my own power. The guards gave me a small bowl of rice and a cup of hot tea. While I was squatting and eating my meager ration of rice, the interpreter came over and informed me that I was going to be taken away.

I was placed in the back of a truck, and my few possessions were thrown in beside me. At last the motor started, and relief surged over me. I do not know why; after all, they could have been taking me out to kill me. Even so, I was leaving the source of my pain, and at that time, that was all that counted. It was during this "questioning" session that I became aware that my threshold for pain was greater than that of many others.

As the truck rumbled along the highway, it seemed to go out of its way to hit every hole in the road. Three Japanese soldiers guarded me during the entire trip. I never was able to figure out just what they thought I could do on my own. My hands were still numb, my fingers were swollen to twice their normal size, the pain in my stomach felt like a cat was tearing my insides out, and my back and face had deep gashes from the beatings I took from the Japanese soldiers. My arms still ached from having been hanged by my thumbs with my toes just barely touching the ground. My legs were like a bowl of Jell-O, with little or no feeling in them. And the ride continued, with me bumping up and down with every rotation of the wheels.

I started to wonder why they did not just kill me. After all, I was a U.S. soldier captured in a Filipino barrio, befriended by natives. The only thing

I could think of was that they bought my story of being in a tank battle and of escaping into the jungle after the tank was damaged. In addition, maybe they were accustomed to prisoners, after being tortured, being willing to confess to just about anything the guards wanted them to. But I was so knocked out by the torture that I could not say or do anything besides forcing myself to mumble, "I don't know, I don't know."

It was just starting to get dark when I saw the faint outline of barbed wire around a large open field. Then I noticed nipa huts scattered around the compound, and suddenly I realized I was back at O'Donnell. I made the full circle, in, out, around, and in again. At least I was alive—not alive and well, but alive.

It was dusk when the truck rumbled through the gate into the compound of Camp O'Donnell. The driver spoke to the guard at the gate and continued into the compound for about another fifty feet. Then I was dumped, literally, on the ground inside the camp on the area normally used for roll call. I just lay there, not moving a muscle, hoping that no one else saw my being thrown out of the truck. After a few seconds, the truck took off in a cloud of dust, and I began the painful process of trying to get up on my feet. My legs were still numb; my back and neck felt like someone was hitting me with a two-by-four. My arms felt like a ton of lead, and my fingers and thumbs remained grotesquely swollen.

I stood up and slowly stumbled toward one of the barracks, passing hundreds of men laying on the ground in front of slit trenches. The stench just added to my total misery. As I passed one of the men, he called out, "Hey, Ten-Spot, haven't seen you around for a while. Thought you went to Boot Hill. How ya been?" As I looked down, I saw my platoon sergeant and friend, Bob Peterson. We had fought many a battle together. For one confrontation with the enemy while on Bataan, Bob later won the Silver Star for bravery. We had shared many experiences on the withdrawal back into Bataan.

It was good hearing Bob's voice, and when he said "Ten-Spot," it brought back happy memories of how I got that nickname. I was one of a dozen men who got together to play poker at least once a week in our barracks at Fort Knox. Out of the twelve of us, there would always be six or seven who were able to play when needed. One night as the evening wore on and the betting got hot and heavy, I pulled the fourth ten to beat Bob's full house. As I was taking in the pot, Bob said, "You did it to me, Ten-Spot." And that nickname stuck ever since.

I looked at him and said, "I only visit Boot Hill on limited occasions, and I don't intend to make that my permanent residence any more than you do. Come on, Bob. Let's take a walk and I'll tell you a story." With that, Bob got up, pulled up his trousers, and started to walk next to me. I knew then that Bob was going to make it, and he did.

I found my place to sleep that night in the same hut I had used when I first arrived at Camp O'Donnell. It was funny; no one even realized I had been gone. In fact, I found myself a little hurt that no one even missed me. I guess every man was too concerned with himself and his own survival to miss someone who could have been taken to Boot Hill, to Z ward, or out on a work detail. We were all so sick that just trying to stay alive was consuming all of our energy.

Nothing different was happening at Camp O'Donnell, just the same old stuff: men waiting for hours to fill a canteen of water, 150 Americans being buried each day, the stench of dysentery filling the air, and not a smile or happy man among us. We were still living like zombies; our body movements were made by instinct, not by choice. So here I was once again at least alive, but unsure of what was going to happen or when it would happen. It made me sad to think that only a few short weeks ago we were calling ourselves the "Battling Bastards of Bataan" and now here we were, no more than beggars, asking for permission to get some drinking water or pleading for a small portion of rice.

Our high-ranking officers tried to establish some kind of organization and discipline in the camp, but some of them believed they were entitled to special treatment and larger rations than the enlisted men. Considering the conditions we were living under, we enlisted men laughed at these self-righteous, better-than-thou attitudes. At the beginning of the march, the officers had suggested that all the men throw away their dog tags to prevent undue torture or mistreatment of the officers by the Japanese, who would try to obtain military information. Most of the men complied with the request. But once we got to the camp, the officers wanted to be identified again so they would not have to go out on work details. They wanted all of the benefits of their position without being willing to pay the price. This was not true of all of the officers, but it did apply to many in camps in both the Philippines and Japan. This self-centered attitude caused many arguments and disagreements.

By my third day back at O'Donnell I began to feel better, but I knew I had to leave again if I was going to survive. I could smell the death in the camp. There still was not enough food and water. Only the drip, drip, drip of the spigot at the corner of the camp gave water, a little at a time. The lines for water were still long and tedious. Death sometimes came faster than the water out of the pipe.

By this time, what little medicine our medics had when they arrived at Camp O'Donnell was gone. The myriad illnesses and necessary surgical procedures for the captives went unattended. Our doctors lacked both the medical supplies and the surgical tools necessary to keep the men alive and healthy. In addition, the guards were becoming more aggressive as the prisoners grew weaker. It appeared that the guards were "coming in for the kill" as their prey lost the ability to defend themselves.

When I went to the camp medics seeking medical attention for the damage done to my thumbs during the hanging torture and some relief or medication for my injured testicles, the doctors told me they could provide absolutely no help. They did not have any medication not only for my wounds, but for any problem. Dr. Thomas Hewlett said, "If something doesn't happen real soon, and medicine is not made available to ease the dysentery, malaria, and pneumonia cases, we will all be dead by Easter."

Doctor Hewlett weighed about 135 pounds and stood only five feet seven inches, but he was more of a man than most of us put together. Doc Hewlett's hair was cut crew-style, and he had a Kentucky drawl that complemented the well-educated and refined southern gentleman that he was. Thom was raised and lived on the Kentucky-Illinois border, but he had spent most of his time on the Kentucky side. I was very lucky to have had Doc Hewlett on the ship to Japan with me and then for the next three years in our prison camp in Japan. He came home and was honored by the U.S. government for his role in saving lives while a POW in Japan. A wonderful man, he died in 1991 and was honored at the annual reunion of the survivors of Camp 17. No man from our camp could ever forget Thom's sincere concern for us prisoners. Hundreds of us owed our lives to Doc's medical and mental genius. His negotiating powers with the guards of our camp, as well as the commander, were pure magic.

# CHAPTER 7

# BACK TO BATAAN— TO WORK

I left sick call more convinced than ever that I had to find a way out of this hellhole if I was going to survive. In spite of the pain in both my legs and my fingers, I made up my mind that I was going to do anything and go anyplace to get out of the camp again. As luck would have it, two days later a rumor circulated that the Japanese were looking for volunteers to go on a work detail and look for abandoned or destroyed equipment. Apparently, the Japanese were looking for truck drivers, welders, and loaders. I made myself available for all three of the positions. In fact, I was available for any job they had to offer; I just wanted to get out of O'Donnell. I decided that if I did not know how to do a certain task, I would learn.

About ninety men volunteered or were drafted for the work detail. We were herded into three trucks without any food or water or any idea of where we were going or what we were expected to do. In addition, we had no personal gear, such as blankets, shoes, socks, shirts or pants, canteens, or rain gear, of any kind. In spite of all these problems, I still welcomed the opportunity to leave the filth, stink, and depression of Camp O'Donnell.

We traveled on the same road we had marched just weeks before. It appeared to us that we were going back to Bataan; we would be working for the Japanese where just weeks ago we were fighting them. As we passed through San Fernando, dozens of Filipinos stood along the road, waving and throwing food to us in the back of the trucks. San Fernando was a pivot city among Manila, Bataan, and Clark Field-Fort Stotsenburg and was on the main route to the country's most prestigious and lovely resort, Baguio.

Because of San Fernando's important location and its large population, we noticed occasional Americans dressed as Filipinos, with all of the characteristics of true natives, among the locals. As we drove by, these "natives" not only waved and threw food to us, but also gave us the "thumbs-up" sign. This simple American custom was never copied by the Filipino people; instead, they gave us the "V for Victory" sign. We figured that these few Americans were members of a guerrilla band and were merely spending the day in this community. Oh, I thought, how lucky you are. I knew what it felt like since I had been one of them only days before.

The ride to the work detail in Bataan took only four hours. I could not forget that, starting on April 10, my walk along this same route took twelve days. The ride brought back distressful memories. As we passed the carabao watering hole near Balanga, where the most brutal killing of marchers took place, I searched for some small visual detail to remember so that some day I would be able to lead concerned people to this infamous site.

We arrived at an old schoolhouse in Limay, a barrio only about twenty miles from where we were captured. This site was to be our home for as long as the Japanese wanted. We planned on making the best of a bad deal. Each of us workers agreed to cause no problem that would encourage the Japanese to take drastic action against any of the rest of us. Except for a few of the men on the detail who knew each other prior to the capture, most of us were strangers.

It became important to attach myself to a small group of men from whom I could seek help and strength. I quickly found a group of seven men that I felt comfortable with. We had no rules, no agenda, and no verbal agreement. We just enjoyed the comfort of being together for a few hours every night after work to talk about home, freedom, women, food, and the crazy things that happened during the day. The talk was slow, deliberate, and quiet. We did not want the guards to think we were having fun or that we were talking about them, so we spoke softly in a monotone and carefully chose every word.

Whenever the talk turned to family or loved ones, I always seemed to talk about Laura. On more than one occasion, I spoke about how much fun we had together, what we liked to do, what we read, and how we felt about each other. After a few hours of reminiscing about home, we would lie down in our bunks, and each of us would dream of what the future held in store for us.

Our job on this detail was to dismantle all the abandoned U.S. tanks, trucks, and other heavy-duty vehicles or equipment. The Japanese would then ship the steel to Japan for use in their war effort. I was chosen and trained to be a blowtorch operator to cut and dissect all the steel found on

Bataan. We worked from sunup to sundown, with a five-minute break in the morning and another in the afternoon.

The work was strenuous. Our bodies were not able to take the physical strain of the day-to-day demands. Most of us still had signs of malaria, many were suffering the aftereffects of dysentery, and all of us were underweight, weak, and malnourished. On the fifth day of this work detail, we tried to convince the guards that if we could hunt for a few carabao that roamed the fields, their meat would make us stronger and enable us to do more work. This initiative seemed to please the Japanese officer in charge of our detail, and he finally gave us permission for the hunt.

I was one of three chosen to go on the carabao hunt. We were instructed to kill and bring back two carabao. Cooked beef was to be our reward for working hard. What a treat this was going to be! Two guards came with us on the hunt. They gave each of us a rifle, and we were told we could have the ammunition after we found some animals to shoot. We left our camp at about 2:00 P.M. We climbed into the back of a truck and set out looking for our prey.

We had each been assigned a number when our work detail arrived at our camp area, and we were told if one man escaped, ten men would be chosen to die. As we had heard in rumors at Camp O'Donnell, the ten men would be taken from the five numbers below and above that of the man who escaped. So escaping was not on our minds as we drove through the small towns and villages of Bataan looking for "meat on the hoof."

About five miles from our work camp, we spotted three or four carabao. We all got out of the truck, and the guards handed us bullets to use in our rifles. The guards told us in pidgin English and sign language to bring back two carabao, but large ones, as they would feed more men. We walked about one hundred yards into the open field where we had seen the animals, and sure enough, there they were, proud as proud could be, standing still with their heads up high. I loaded the ammunition into my rifle and took careful aim at the water buffalo. I fired three times in rapid succession, and within moments, the animal fell. The other animal was dropped by the other Americans. We walked cautiously toward the animals, not knowing if they were dead. We knew the potential power of an injured animal of this size, and we were not going to take any unnecessary risks. While approaching the animals we looked around, and standing not more than fifty feet from us was a very large carabao, just looking us over. Then, without a moment's warning, it ran toward us like an enormous charging bull, ready for the kill.

The guards started hollering in Japanese at the same time the other two Americans started yelling, "Kill 'im, kill 'im, kill 'im!" The Japanese guards picked up on the Americans' chant and started hollering, "Kill, kill, kill!"

So without waiting for another command, I put my rifle to my shoulder, took aim, and shot two, three, or four times, bringing the beast down with the last shot no more than twenty feet from our position.

I never thought twice about killing the third carabao. After all, it was charging and threatening us, and the Japanese guards were telling us to shoot. So with this worry out of our way, we started to skin the animals and cut them up so they could be lifted onto the truck. While butchering the animals, Frank, a tall lanky guy from Kentucky, said, "Let's get the brains out and cut out the tongue. Where I come from these are delicacies." If Frank knew how and wanted to go about this procedure, it was OK with us. (When I saw just how the dissecting was done, I was not able to eat any of the brains or tongue then or today.) After several hours of skinning, cutting, and, in general, feeling pretty good about ourselves, we started to load the meat onto the truck. In spite of our poor physical condition, the mere thought of eating meat once again seemed to spur us on and gave us the strength to load the animals.

We decided to take all three of the animals we shot. After all, there was no sense in leaving a dead animal out on the open field, especially with so many men going hungry. Once all the meat from the three carabao was loaded, we took off for camp. Upon arrival, we got a hero's welcome from the rest of the prisoners. We had not eaten meat since we slaughtered one of the 26th Cavalry's horses at least three months ago, and horse meat, we fantasized, was much tougher than carabao meat. This was going to be more like beef than anything we could think of.

We unloaded the carcasses and handed them over to the Japanese guards for final distribution. We knew that the Japanese soldiers would take the best cuts and most of the meat, but at least we would get a share and that seemed real important at the time. The three of us "hunters" were resting inside the schoolhouse at about 5 P.M., when a runner came in and told me I was wanted at Japanese headquarters immediately.

I entered the commander's office and stood at attention. There were five soldiers in the room; one, of course, was the commander, the other four just looked like guards. No one was laughing or even talking as I came in. All at once the commander started to holler at me in Japanese and all I could say, or was supposed to say, was hai. I stood at attention, feet firmly planted in front of me, my back as straight as an arrow, and said in as loud a voice as I could, "*Hai.*"

Within minutes, the commander made four or five more statements, and each seemed louder. At the same time, he started to swing his arms wildly from top to bottom and from side to side. I started to sweat from fear, fear of the unknown. What is he saying? Why pick on me? What did I do wrong? That was all I could think of until I was shocked by a hard blow to the back of my neck. The blow shook my teeth and caused my eyes to roll sideways. Then the commander screamed some more and continued to wave his hands while the four guards bashed my head and neck. Each time something was said, they would stop and wait, as if waiting for my answer. But I did not understand anything the Japanese were saying, so all I could do was what I was told to do—stand at attention and say, "*Hai*."

By this time I was in great pain from the beating, so I used a coping technique I had learned years before. I knew if I was in a fight and unable to defend myself, just to "roll" with the punches and to minimize the harshness of the blows. After I had said hai four or five times, I noticed one of the guards starting to take off his uniform trouser belt. The belt was about thirty-five inches long, and its large metal buckle was four inches long, two inches wide, and at least an eighth of an inch thick. Soon I started to feel this striking my face, neck, or nose each time I said hai. The pain was beyond description, and there was no doubt in my mind that I was going to be killed that day. I did everything I could to control my need to defecate. Put bluntly, I feared they would literally scare the shit out of me. My senses were still intact, and I was well enough aware that urinating on the floor of the commander's office would not be tolerated, either, so I psyched myself to control my bladder as well.

My mind raced trying to figure out what I had done to deserve this punishment, but I came up empty-handed. I had done nothing different than any of the other men. So why me?

After the second blow to my face, my nose was broken, and blood flowed from my nose as well as my cheekbones. The beating continued for what seemed like an hour or more, and then it stopped. I tried to put my mind in some order, but I was bewildered and totally confused. What were they saying? What was I supposed to do? How was I expected to answer? Would someone tell me what was going on?

Then, in a flash, it dawned on me: what if they were saying, "So you think you are better than us?" And I was answering, "Yes sir." Maybe they were saying, "You think we are stupid people?" and I was still saying, "Yes sir." I started to realize that if this treatment was going to continue, I would not be able to survive. When the beating started again, I had to make a decision about what I was going to do at once. I was not too sure which option to take—keep saying *hai*, or just stop answering altogether. Either way, I figured, I would be a dead soldier if something did not stop this beating. I decided to keep quiet, say nothing, and not even try to answer them. Maybe then the guards would stop the beatings for good. So, for the next ten or fifteen minutes, I just stood at attention the best I could under these circumstances and took the repeated blows to my back, neck, and face.

Finally, they stopped hitting me and yelling at me. Things were quiet in the commander's office. I started to breathe a little easier, and I was still able to stand. Falling down, I feared, could be fatal. I remembered those days on the Bataan Death March all too well. If a man stayed on his feet, he had a chance; if he fell down, he was beaten, kicked, or killed. With this on my mind, I did everything humanly possible to stay upright.

Just when I thought the worst was over, more guards came into the office and pushed me outside. They made me kneel down on a piece of bamboo and then placed another piece of bamboo behind my kneecaps between my legs. This position, I quickly found out, cut off the circulation of blood to my legs. Then a guard put a wheel taken from a U.S. Army 6 x 6 truck into my hands and ordered me to hold it over my head. After a few minutes, I found myself slowly lowering the wheel as my hands and arms became very tired, but when the Japanese saw this, the beatings began anew. Finally one of the guards broke down and whispered in English, "You must keep hands up five minutes, then you will be allowed to go to your bed."

I lasted the five minutes by counting them off in a simple jingle that went something like this: "One, two, three, four, who are you for; five, six, seven, eight, don't you think I appreciate; nine, ten, eleven, twelve, you can find it on a shelf; . . ." I counted the full three hundred seconds, and in doing so, I was able to block out the pain. I was looking forward to lying down and resting. My thoughts then focused on living, not on dying. I was ready for anything the Japanese wanted to dish out, because I knew I was going to get home someday. While keeping that wheel over my head, my mind raced a mile a minute about what I would do when I arrived back in the United States, back in Chicago.

When the three hundred seconds were over, or thereabouts, a guard kicked me over on my side, and I let the wheel drop from my grasp. At the same time, I pushed the two pieces of bamboo away from my legs, and I just lay there on the ground, waiting for the next surprise. None came. I was left alone in the darkness of the jungle.

Within minutes, three of my friends came over and carried me to my bunk in the schoolhouse. One of them moved my legs back and forth, try-ing to restore the circulation to my limbs. Another friend started wiping the blood from my face and cleaning my nose, mouth, and eyes with cool water. A third later washed my back and neck and put bandages on the cuts made by the rifle butts and belt buckle. My friends, not the Japanese, took good care of me.

I fell fast asleep almost as soon as my head hit the bunk. I awoke early the following morning and made a vow that the Japanese would never beat me again just because I did not understand their language. I gingerly got up for roll call and answered, "*Hai*," when my number was called, then I crawled back into my bunk for a few minutes of rest and prayer.

When I started to feel better, my friends told me what had caused the beatings. It seems the commander had only wanted two carabao killed. When he asked who killed the third animal, he was told number 64. That was my number and I did shoot the third animal, but I felt betrayed by the Japanese guards who failed to tell their commander the whole story. As my knowledge of Japanese tradition grew, however, I realized that the Japanese soldier never, ever added anything to a conversation. They were expected only to answer the question put to them. The commander did not ask "Why were three animals killed?" He merely asked, "Who killed the third animal?" No further comment was elicited, so none was given.

A few days later, I saw the guard who had whispered in my ear, "Only five minutes." I bowed to him and said in English, "Thank you for making those last five minutes easy." When he did not answer me, I asked, "Please, will you help me learn Japanese? I want to understand and speak your language." To my surprise, he was delighted; he smiled and said, "I will help." This was the beginning of a new learning experience for me.

I took a pick from the tool shed, held it up to the guard, and said, "English for this is 'pick.' What is the name for this in Japanese?" He slowly pronounced the word *truabosh*. I knew then that I could count on this guard for help in order to learn his language. Within a few days, I had learned the names of ten pieces of equipment that we were using. When I was told to get a common tool, such as a shovel, pick, or hammer, I could respond without the guards' hollering and hand waving that usually accompanied a simple request for a piece of equipment.

When I was able to respond to a Japanese request, my friends would ask, "How did you learn the language so quickly?" "Very easy," I would reply. "Anyone can learn Japanese in ten easy beatings." The beating I took in the commander's office for not understanding Japanese resulted in my learning the language. Knowing the language helped me, and many other prisoners who worked with me, avoid some of the serious beatings that other men incurred for not responding immediately to the guards' commands. Although I was still physically abused many times during the next three years, never again was it because I did not understand what the guards were saying.

Thus, I made the decision that I was going to learn Japanese, and I did. I made the decision I was going to survive this experience, and I did. I believed (and still do believe) that I could accomplish almost anything I really wanted if I would only give it everything I had. My positive attitude got me this far, and I was going to depend on it for the rest of my journey.

The work on our detail was simple, yet demanding. Most of us knew how to drive a truck, but few knew anything about welding or cutting. Those few Americans on the detail who knew how to use a blowtorch and could weld and cut metal trained those who wanted to learn; those who did not want to become cutters became truck drivers or loaders. We were lucky because none of the Japanese guards knew anything about blowtorches and could not tell that we were working slowly and less accurately than they would otherwise have wanted.

When we first saw some of the trucks and tanks that we had disabled before our capture, it made our hearts heavy. "Just think," I said, "they never intended to use the equipment as vehicles. We did all that damage for nothing." All they wanted was the scrap metal to use in manufacturing their bombs.

Except for working slower, we could not do much for the U.S. war effort, although on a few occasions, when loading the scrap metal from the trucks to the docks via wheelbarrows, a wheelbarrow would tip and fall into the bay. Of course, the guards would holler and maybe slap or punch us, but every so often one of the Americans would just "let go." We always knew when a load was going to be dropped, because the man pushing the wheelbarrow would start to whistle the "Stars and Stripes Forever." Of course, only we Americans knew that tune, and whenever we heard it we would all join in. This whistling was sort of our way of paying the Japanese back, for everything we salvaged was not going to the enemy; some of it was destined for the sea.

The guards on this work detail had been fighting men just a few months ago, but now they were sick or injured. The Japanese had never planned on the malaria bug devastating their fighting force. In addition, many of our guards had been wounded during various battles on Bataan and held deep grudges against the Americans. Their actions toward us prisoners made this resentment quite evident. A few of the guards, however, respected us because we were frontline soldiers and they knew what it was like at the front. They admired our fighting spirit.

During the three months that we worked this detail, many unusual events occurred. First, most of us became experts within our own job responsibility after working every day, seven days a week, for ten hours or more. Second, one of our American sergeants, Mike Sullivan (not his real name), had become so friendly with the Japanese guards from our work detail that they allowed him to dish out our punishments. Prior to the war, Sullivan was a professional boxer from St. Louis. He was very strong and built like a young bull, with wide shoulders, a slim waist, and large biceps. When he first arrived on the work detail, he looked like most of us—thin, weak, and happy just to be alive—but that changed after the first few weeks. Sullivan started to hang around with the guards, and then he maneuvered himself as senior man on our detail, informing the Japanese officers that he would ensure our work was done right and fast. The U.S. officers and higher-ranking noncommissioned officers, not wanting to make waves, just kept quiet and let Sullivan take over. We did not know that once in authority he was going to punch us out physically for any infraction of the work rules.

Mike Sullivan seemed to beam with delight whenever he was able to show his superiority over the rest of us. Once when I was filling in as a truck driver and had to back up to a pile of metal that was going to be loaded onto the truck, I backed up too far and hit the metal pile. Nothing was damaged or lost, and the rear bumper of the truck merely grazed the pile of metal. Within seconds, Sullivan pulled me by my shirt from the driver's seat and threw me to the ground in one swift movement. With his left hand on the collar of my shirt, he lifted me up, made a fist with his right hand, and hit me in the face while calling me a "dumb jerk," "careless and uncaring," and "not sympathetic or understanding the Japanese cause." I started to strike back but was stopped by a few of my friends who saw the laughing Japanese guards pat Sullivan on the back and say, "Yeroshi" (very good). I quickly realized that the guards would not tolerate anyone hitting "their" man.

To set the record straight regarding Mike Sullivan, a few of the other prisoners believed that he actually saved some of our lives or, in some situations, actually saved some of us from a very severe beating. At the time, such punishment would have been very hard to take and, along with our serious health problems, could well have proved fatal. Those who take this position claim that had Sullivan not intervened and taken the initiative to punish us for our errors, the Japanese guards would have done a more thorough job of beating us. In other words, his fist to the face a few times was not as bad as a rifle butt to the face, followed by a belt buckle to the face, and then a few whacks on the back and head with sand-filled lengths of bamboo. Undoubtedly, this argument would stand up in some situations but certainly not in all of the cases.

The third unusual event while on this detail in Bataan was our discovery among the destroyed trucks, tanks, and equipment of dozens of machine guns, hundreds of handguns, and many vehicles still in operating condition. A few of the American prisoners hid some of the weapons and carried them into our camp as a precaution against the possibility that the Japanese might decide to kill us after our job was done. So we collected a small arsenal and hid it in and around the camp.

Word spread that some of the men wanted to use the equipment to annihilate the Japanese on our work detail and take to the hills as free men and join the guerrillas. So an escape plan was considered that included killing the Japanese and any man not willing to cooperate. We broke up into little groups and talked about the probability of success. My concern was twofold. First, where would we go? Second, what would happen to those who did not want to join in this plan? Could we justify killing our own soldiers? But if we took no action against those who chose not to participate, could we expect the Japanese not to punish them severely? The questions we raised had to be addressed before we could take any action, and as time went on and our plans became better organized, we had to face the problem of Mike Sullivan. Who would, or could, deal with him on this crucial issue? No decision on our part, however, became necessary. Mike got word we were seriously thinking about escape and tipped off the Japanese, who systematically searched the area and questioned every prisoner regarding their part in the escape.

For the next two weeks, there was never a happy face around the work area or at our camp. Each man was suspicious of the other; no one trusted anyone. No one was sure what had happened, but we all had our ideas. Finally, a few weeks later, a Japanese guard let it be known that Mike had discussed the potential escape with the camp commander. Once again we had to ask ourselves, did Mike save us from being annihilated, or did he turn us in for his own glory? We will never know, for Mike never did make it home. At the end of the war, he boarded the ship for San Francisco but never got off. Some say he was pushed overboard, others say he fell; but either way, we will never really know the reason behind his punishment of fellow POWs. Were his actions for the good of the men, or were they caused by conceit and the desire for a better life for himself?

With all the hours we spent working, we did not have much time for other activities. When we drove the trucks into Manila to unload the metal, we always passed little barrios housing large numbers of pro-American people. These folks would give us the V sign as we passed. The Japanese thought the people were honoring them, and so the guards were very happy and constantly smiling. The people along the truck route would throw us food of all kinds, from simple sugar cakes to the Philippine party cakes, or babinkas.

On one of the trips, the guards wanted to stop at one of the food stands along the way, where we had another extraordinary experience. We pulled up to a small store, and as we got out of the truck, the storekeeper lined up five of the freshest-looking, largest, and reddest apples I had ever seen. The Japanese guard bought one of the apples for two pesos, but he never realized the significance of the fruit on the storekeeper's shelf. We knew these were Washington State's Red Delicious apples, which do not grow in the Philippines or Japan, and that they had to come from the United States via

submarine. The American guerrillas arranged such displays to show the
Filipinos that the Americans were still thinking of them and keeping an
eye on everything. It was a great morale booster, for us as well as the
Filipino people.

Upon our return to camp and, I must admit, feeling better about our circumstances, knowing that we had not been forgotten by our countrymen,
we were given the rest of the day off. This rest period was the first since we
were put on this detail. We took the opportunity to wash clothes, to get
some much needed sack time, and to just buzz around meeting with
friends we had not seen in quite some time.

By early evening I started to think about Laura again. I wondered about
what she was doing and whether she was going to be there, with her love
for me still blazing, when I returned to Chicago. These thoughts and many
more raced through my mind. I wished I could tell her that I was all right,
that at least I was still among the living. As I slowly realized that I was just
dreaming and wishing wishes that could not come true, I started to cry
tears of sorrow, sorrow for Laura. As the evening wore on, I felt light-head-
ed and warm. I was tired and needed some rest, so I lay back in my bunk,
closed my eyes, and slept.

By late evening I was awakened by a horrible headache and the need to
urinate. So I went upstairs to the latrine, and when I finished, I noticed my
body becoming very hot. While on my way back, I fell down almost the
entire flight of stairs. I picked myself up from the floor and climbed into
my sack. My buddy in the bunk next to me, Woody (I never did get his full
name, but no one ever cared too much for formalities of that kind), felt my
head and remarked, "You're burning up, Ten-Spot. Let me put some cool
water on your head." I do not remember much after that except sometime
during the night I asked Woody for a Bible. I really did not think I would
make it till morning. Malaria was a killer, and I was burning up in what was
by far the worst attack I ever had.

I remembered another bad malaria attack I had had on the march, when
my friends Cigoi and Bronge just would not let me stop. They had carried
me till the changing of the guards, and we had stopped on the side of the
road near a fairly large, quick-flowing stream. I had talked about things
that had happened years ago, and Bronge and Cigoi thought I was going
out of my mind. Without a moment's hesitation, they had picked me up
and threw me into the stream. The shock of the cool water rushing over
my body had brought me to my senses, and within minutes I had gotten up
on my own two feet and walked back to the stream's edge. My life has
been like that of a cat: throw me down, or let me fall, and I will always end
up on my feet.

Later, in yet another remarkable experience, Woody came over to my sleeping area, pulled the mosquito net back over my head, handed me a small book, and then slowly walked away. I looked at the three-by-five-inch cover of the book and started to smile as I read the title, *Prayer Book for Jews in the Armed Forces of the United States*. Where in the world did Woody get it? As I held the book, it fell open to page seventy-six. I felt my energy slipping, and seeing the image of my mother and father looking down at me, I thought of Laura and what she meant to me. Then I found just enough strength to hold the little book open. I read the following passage:

> Lord what is man, that Thou regardest him, or the son of man, that Thou takest account of him? Man is like to vanity; his days are as a shadow that passes away. In the morning he flourishes, and grows up; in the evening he is cut down, and withers. So teach us to number our days, that we may get us a heart of wisdom. Mark the man of integrity, and behold the upright; for there is a future for the man of peace. . . . My flesh and my heart fails; but God is the strength of my heart and my portion forever. And the dust returns to the earth as it was, but the spirit returns unto God who gave it. I shall behold Thy face in righteousness; I shall be satisfied, when I awake, with Thy likeness.

I understand that I slept for twenty-four hours, and when I woke I simply got out of bed as I had always done that past month without a fever or a flushed face. I was hungry and ready to go to work. That was the last time during the war that I had such a serious attack of malaria. (By the way, that little prayer book is still in my possession today and is one of my treasures I will not part with.)

We worked in Bataan for another two weeks, cutting all the steel we could find, stripping away all of the electronic gear that we had torn apart only a few weeks before, and then loading everything onto trucks for the trip to Manila and eventually to Japan. We were sure that the Geneva Convention forbade such forced labor, particularly being forced to help the enemy in furthering its war efforts. It seemed that suddenly most of us prisoners became military lawyers. Every time we were forced to do some kind of work, we always talked about the rules and regulations of the Geneva Convention and found ways to illustrate that the Japanese were in violation of most of the rules of war, to say nothing of the code of common decency.

Finally our work was finished. We had accomplished what the Japanese wanted, and then we were divided into groups, each designated for a different assignment. We had spent three months on this special work detail, all working together while making new friends. These new friends I had made had some of the same positive attitudes I had, and this shared outlook had made my job a little easier. Working with these men did more for me than working with those who always complained about something and spoke about everything in a negative way. During these three months, I had found myself staying away from those men with poor attitudes. I could not afford to spend my valuable time with men who only thought negatively.

Once more we were separated from newfound friendships and were off someplace else to start making new friends all over again. Some of the men were sent to a work detail on the docks in Manila; this was known as the Port Detail. Some others were going south to another island to strip that area of all trucks, half-tracks, and other machinery once used in the U.S. forces' defense of the Philippines.

The group to which I was assigned was going to a new prison camp called Cabanatuan. All of us had come from the original camp, Camp O'Donnell. As soon as we heard about our destination, we remembered vividly that stinking, rat-infested hellhole, where Americans died at the rate of 150 or more each day. We had been away from O'Donnell for about three months, and when we heard about Cabanatuan, we expected a military camp in which all of the problems of the past would be straightened out. Food and water, we thought, would surely be more accessible as well as adequate medical supplies and treatment for the sick. We started to look forward to a clean and orderly camp environment. What we found when we entered Cabanatuan, however, was just what we had left at O'Donnell, only bigger.

# CHAPTER 8

# CABANATUAN

Before World War II, Camp Cabanatuan was a Philippine Army training facility located about four miles east of the city of Cabanatuan and about sixty miles north of Manila. This newer and larger camp was roughly fifty marching miles east of Camp O'Donnell, the first camp we entered after the Bataan Death March.

Around June 1, 1942, the prisoners from O'Donnell were sent to Cabanatuan. This transfer was completed within four days, with the men who could walk marching the distance. Those too sick to walk were sent by truck.

The few books written about prison camps in the Philippines all discuss Cabanatuan. After all, it was the biggest and by far the most important POW camp the Japanese had. Its size was hard to judge, but it was estimated at one hundred acres, with the prison farm adding another three hundred acres. The Japanese quarters were in the center of the camp, on the southerly edge; the hospital area was on the west side; and the barracks for the POWs covered the entire east side of the camp. Guard towers were everywhere, and the camp was laced with old and rusty barbed wire. In fact, when I first entered the camp I thought the barbed wire was in the process of being taken down. On the southeast side of the camp was the infamous farm.

The medics, knowing the potential health problems caused by those with dysentery, set up an isolated ward for the infected on the northwest side of the camp. Close to the dysentery ward, the medics also set up a Zero ward for those considered unable to survive.

When our truck stopped at the gate to this new camp, we were turned over to a group of Japanese guards who laughed and joked about our arrival. They looked like a welcoming party, they were so glad to see us.

Within minutes we were forced to stand at attention as one of the guards began his tirade about what was expected of us. As he did not speak English and we had no interpreter, we merely assumed what was meant.

We were then pushed and shoved out onto the parade ground, where we underwent first a search of our belongings and then a hand search of the clothes we had on and our bodies' orifices. Some of us were forced to strip and then were fully examined. Those who did not have to undergo the body search had to drop everything from their pockets onto the ground in front of them. Then the guards put their hands into every pocket to make sure we followed orders and were not concealing anything. By this time, we knew the consequences of not following orders, so none of our group was punished for disobeying.

Each of us was assigned to a barracks, and as we walked to our new homes, we were shocked to see the same conditions as had existed at O'Donnell. The men we saw walking around camp were living zombies, with their eyes sunken, heads bowed down, and their backs curved in defeat. Most were skin and bones, after losing between fifty and sixty pounds from their normal weight. Those men not able to get up on their feet were obviously dying of malaria and dysentery. Men were also lying next to a slit trench, ready to defecate at a moment's notice.

Once inside the barracks, we each were assigned a number and told the rule regarding escape. Five men bearing the numbers on each side of the man who escaped would be taken out and shot, bayoneted, or beheaded, depending on the whim of the officer in charge.

When I saw the conditions in this camp, I realized that I was one of the lucky ones. The Bataan work detail had afforded me the opportunity to get out for a brief time and a chance to breathe fresh air, to see and hear people laugh, to take a walk without seeing a burial detail carrying those poor souls to their shallow, unmarked graves. Already my thoughts were once again centered on how to get out of this living cemetery.

When we arrived at our new barracks, we found much the same living accommodations as in O'Donnell, except these buildings were bigger and held more men. The camp was much larger than the old one, and more men seemed to mill around. After the first shock of seeing so many sick men wore off, I realized that the healthy-looking men walking around were captives from Corregidor. These men had not made a forced march; they had come by rail in the same small, cramped cars that carried thousands of men on the death march from San Fernando to Capas. The men from Corregidor were not malnourished prior to their surrender, for they had had adequate supplies until the end of their war on May 6, 1942.

So this new camp had two distinct types of prisoners. The first were the tired, starved, and beaten transferees from O'Donnell who had malaria,

The author in front of his barracks at Fort Knox, Kentucky, in September 1941. *Author's collection*

Tanks and men of the 192d Tank Battalion on maneuvers in Louisiana in September 1941. The unit performed so well that it was selected to go overseas immediately. *Author's collection*

The author (second from left) and fellow crew members in the
Philippines in mid-December 1941. *Author's collection*

A Japanese attempt
at psychological
warfare during the
battle for Bataan.
*National Archives*

On April 10, 1942, Japanese soldiers entered the author's bivouac area, captured an American soldier, and walked him to the main road. Thus began the Bataan Death March. *National Archives*

Prisoners rest on the first day of the march. *National Archives*

Some had to march for days with their hands tied behind their backs.
*National Archives*

Prisoners were made to raise their hands for this Japanese propaganda photograph
*National Archives*

The Japanese forced Filipino civilians to view murdered troops.
*National Archives*

Burial detail at Camp O'Donnell.
*National Archives*

A Japanese soldier enjoys a
drink from a GI's canteen.
*National Archives*

The POW barracks at Camp 17, located near the town of Omuta on the island of Kyushu and about thirty-five miles east of Nagasaki.

Japanese workers building a retaining wall in Camp 17's dangerous coal mine. Each eight-man team of Allied prisoners was headed by two Japanese civilian supervisors, many of whom were as brutal as the Japanese soldiers. *Author's collection*

A Camp 17 coal mine tunnel about to collapse. *National Archives*

Crematorium used to
dispose of prisoners'
bodies at Camp 17.
*National Archives*

A misleading but prudent postcard sent by the author from Camp 17 to his father.

福岡俘虜収容所俘虜郵便　　IMPERIAL JAPANESE ARMY

Received letters.   Glad to hear all are well
and in good spirts.  Send pictures.  I am
in good health don't worry about me.  Our
quarters are comfortable, we have many
recreations.  Working each day which we
receive pay.   Regards to family.
Remember me to friends and relatives.

The author (center) back in the Philippines in September 1945 with fellow members of Company B, 192d Tank Battalion. The hilt of a souvenir samurai sword is just visible on author's left side. *Author's collection*

The author (left) and his friend Lew Brittan, two of the sixteen survivors of Company B, in a Chicago nightclub after the war. *Author's collection*

Forty-three years after the battle for the Philippines, Senator Barry Goldwater presents the author with the Bronze Star for gallantry in action. *Ahwatukee (Ariz.) News*

dysentery, beriberi, scurvy, pellagra, and pneumonia. The death that hovered over O'Donnell seemed to follow us to Cabanatuan. The second group, mostly all taken prisoner at the fall of Corregidor, was different. Relatively healthy, these men had come into camp as a group with little or no malaria, and only a handful of the men had dysentery when they arrived. In addition, except for those who were wounded during the last few days of battle, the men were mostly able-bodied and capable of caring for themselves. The men from Corregidor had fought just as fearlessly as the men on Bataan, but they did not make the death march, undernourished and diseased, and they did not have to bury their buddies alive or take the consequence of being killed.

The first group of prisoners at the original Camp Cabanatuan came in around May 26, 1942. By May 30, six thousand men had arrived in camp, all Corregidor defenders. This camp was referred to as Camp Number 3. The men from O'Donnell were sent to Camp Number 1, about five miles away. The subsequent death rates for each camp illustrate the drastic differences between the two camps. From the opening of Camp Number 3 to October 29, when both camps merged, sixty-nine men died in that camp. During the same period, twenty-one hundred men died in Camp Number 1. The morale at Camp Number 1 plummeted. Seeing death all around us made us tremble with constant anxiety regarding our own mortality. The small rice supply coupled with the alarmingly high death rate played havoc with the men's desire to live.

Given the men's overall condition, the officers who arrived from Corregidor were healthier and appeared more capable of taking charge of the camp. Obviously, a healthy officer would command much more respect from both the American prisoners and the Japanese soldiers than would an officer who was sick and disabled, regardless of his rank. Thus, when our small group from the Bataan work detail arrived in this new camp, we found the healthy ones assuming control. While we could expect this, we still found it hard having someone who had never been beaten telling us how to handle ourselves if we were ever put into the unfortunate position of being punished by the Japanese.

At the time of the surrender the medics from Corregidor took large quantities of medical supplies with them. We prisoners still wonder whether all of these medicines and supplies were turned over to the doctors at the camp hospital when the Corregidor contingent entered Camp Cabanatuan. Neither the men suffering from malaria nor those suffering from dysentery could obtain any medicine available to help them. We will never know whether men died because of selfishness or discrimination as to who would receive necessary medication. A few of the medics sold or bartered the medicine in their possession to the highest bidder, leaving those without resources no relief. At times word went out that if a prisoner had money he could buy certain types of medicine, such as sulfa or quinine. If those men who sold medicine lived to come home, they have had to live with the knowledge that they played the role of God for money. May God help them overcome their transgression.

As time wore on the lack of shoes and clothing also became a serious problem. Without a shirt or pair of pants, a man's body temperature would soar from the extreme heat. And without shoes or other foot protection, men commonly suffered from blisters, cuts, and infections. The Japanese never issued clothing to us POWs. Instead, we took clothes from those who died and buried them nude so that their clothes could be washed and then given to those men with the greatest need. In those cases where men no longer had shoes to protect their feet, they went barefoot until they found a pair of shoes their size among the remnants of the dead.

Before long we learned that the Japanese wanted men with technical experience for the better jobs in camp or for the better details out of camp. So many a truck driver turned engineer overnight. Those without special technical skills, or who were not smart enough to fake it, were made laborers and were given the dirtiest as well as the hardest jobs in and outside of camp. The one job that almost every man was assigned to at some time or other, however, was to labor on the camp farm.

At Cabanatuan, everyone had a chance to learn farming the hard way. We had to do everything by hand, for we did not have any machines to help in the digging or harvesting, and we put in long hours to accomplish the tasks required by the Japanese. Work started at 6:00 in the morning and lasted till about 11:00, when we were given a bowl of rice and a cup of colored water called soup for lunch. We could rest until 2:00 in the afternoon, and then we worked on the farm till dark. This routine went on day after day, without a break, and we were not allowed to talk while in the field, planting, picking, or digging. We thought that the food was for us, we were so foolish. The Japanese either ate the food or traded what we grew for favors in town from the local Filipinos. The farm produced large quantities of beans, squash, corn, sweet potatoes, okra, and eggplant. As a rule, we POWs got the tops, while the Japanese ate the vegetables. And of course if anyone were caught eating any of the vegetables while working on the farm, a beating was the price he paid.

The men doing farm detail had nicknames for many of the guards watching over them. American soldiers anywhere assigned nicknames based on facial expressions, verbal characteristics, actions, or just about anything else that could connote a guard's personality. "Big Speedo" was so named because no matter how hard the men worked on the farm, he would yell out, "Speedo, speedo," meaning of course, to work faster. Every time the guard named "Donald Duck" spoke or hollered at us, he would speak so fast in Japanese that he sounded just like the cartoon character. Almost without exception, the nicknames chosen were names that everyone understood and were able to relate to the correct individual.

My first day on the farm started at 6:00 in the morning. The temperature had already reached ninety-six degrees and was expected once again to reach the mid-hundreds by the afternoon. I no sooner walked onto the farm area, when *wham*, one of the guards hit me with a shovel right in the small of my back. I had stepped on a plant that was just starting to grow, and this was my first punishment of the day. Within two hours I received two more whacks on the head with bamboo sticks filled with sand. I just was not working fast enough. Later, when I got down on my knees to pull some weeds, two guards cornered me. One hit me on the neck with the stick end of a shovel, while the other pounded my head and shoulders with his heavy-duty walking stick. I learned another lesson that day: I could not kneel down, but only bend down from the waist. When the whistle finally blew, indicating the end of work for the day, I was bleeding from my back, head, and shoulders. Surviving this ordeal was not going to be easy.

I fell to the ground after the guards left the field, and a few of the other workers helped me up and to the barracks. I was planning on going to the medics for treatment and possibly a "no work" badge for the next day, but my friends told me that some of the Japanese guards who worked the farm hung around the medics' building just to see who went in. The next day, that person would really get a beating, within an inch of his life. Sometimes the guards did not even leave an inch, and prisoners died right there in the field. That way, their cause of death could be listed as heatstroke.

Strong evidence suggests that the guards in Cabanatuan were, for the most part, the poorest educated and least respected men in the Japanese army. It appeared that if they had not been guarding prisoners of war, many of these soldiers would have been shipped back to Japan and given jobs guarding bathhouses. Some of the guards did so many stupid things that their superiors often beat and humiliated them in front of us American and Filipino prisoners. These miserable guards would then take their pain out on us, beating us for any infraction of a regulation or minor rule. In fact, in many cases these guards would make up their own rules to justify torturing, beating, and denying food to the "big" Americans. The only difference among the guards was the degree of their sadistic treatment of the prisoners.

After taking all of this, I knew that getting out of this camp was the only way I was going to survive. Then one night at roll call, five men did not answer when their numbers were called. The guards became frantic, screaming for everyone to sit down in our places on the parade field. They did not make any effort to determine if any of these men were sick or had died; the Japanese just assumed that if they did not answer roll call, they had escaped. For a while we thought that ten of us would be put to death for every escapee; but after about two hours, the guards came back to our area and informed us that they had captured the five men.

The guards were pleased with themselves, laughing and slapping each other on the back. We were ordered to stand at attention; the commander wanted to talk to us. About ten minutes later, he strolled in with his interpreter. He explained that many of us were saved because the guards did such a good job of locating the escapees. Only the men who attempted to escape would be put to death the following morning.

Rumors and camp scuttlebutt indicated that four of the five men had, in fact, tried to escape. The guards had found the fifth man hiding under the floor of one of the barracks, so sick he just wanted to die in peace. He had defecated all over himself just hours before and had been burning up from a bad case of malaria.

As we walked off the field, we saw that their punishment had begun. The guards were beating each man with wooden clubs and kicking him, first in the stomach, then in the middle of his back, and finally in the kidneys—all of this after the man had fallen to the ground. The guards then led the prisoners, with their hands bound behind their backs, to the rear of the parade ground, where they were tied to a post usually reserved for whippings.

After falling in for roll call the following morning, we all looked toward the rear of the parade ground for the five men. They were tied to the fence just on the other side of the border of our camp so that the Filipinos who walked by could see how the Japanese punished anyone caught trying to escape.

The five men remained tied to the fence for the next two days. No food or water was brought to them. The only thing they got while standing in the broiling sun all day was more beatings from various guards. Some of the guards kicked them. Others swung their belts in a wide arc and hit the men repeatedly over their faces, arms, and heads with the heavy metal buckles on the end of their belts. Other guards jokingly played the part of executioner, feinting with their bayonets toward the hearts of the tortured men.

Two of the noncommissioned officers pulled their samurai swords from their scabbards and started to swing them as if practicing to decapitate the men. In fact, with the prisoners unable to stand erect and with their heads bowed because of the intense heat, some of the sword movements came so close to their heads or necks that from a distance it looked as if their heads were in fact separated from their bodies.

On the third day, ten armed guards marched the five men to the cemetery. The prisoners—weak from starvation these past days, sick with malaria and dysentery, broken in body and spirit—were forced to dig their own graves. When they finished, these brave and proud men spontaneously stood at rigid attention, ready for whatever the Japanese had in store for them.

After their hands were tied behind their backs, the Japanese commander placed a lit cigarette in each prisoner's mouth and turned to face the guards, each one with his rifle aimed at one of the five Americans. The commander raised his sword above his head and quickly brought the sword down in a gesture that indicated "Fire." Four of the five men fell instantly. Within seconds, the guards fired another round, and the last man fell to the ground. The commander walked over to the fallen men, their prostrate bodies still quivering. After removing his revolver from its holster, he put one more bullet into each man's head. They were now dead, having paid the price of trying to escape. To all of us watching the message was clear: try to escape and death will surely follow.

Once again, this psychological trauma was getting to be more than I could bear. I kept wondering, if there was a work detail I could volunteer for or whether I could go someplace else that would give me a better chance of surviving this holocaust. My mind raced a mile a minute, trying to figure out how I could avoid becoming a sad statistic of this war.

As luck would have it, I was called out of line the following morning and told to gather whatever belongings I had; I was being shipped out with 499 other men. All five hundred of us were herded together on the parade ground for a roll call and inspection. We asked ourselves, "What was going to happen? Where were we going? Why the inspection? Why the hurry?" Within minutes, the rumor mill started pumping: the Red Cross was nego-tiating the release of American prisoners of war. For an exciting few hours, just the thought of being free made us forget our troubles. Soon after the inspection, we were herded onto trucks headed toward Manila. We could feel it in our bones. We were going to board a ship for freedom.

# CHAPTER 9

# THE NIGHTMARE SHIP

After working on Bataan for three months and then on the Cabanatuan farm for a few weeks, I was ready for any change of guards and environment. Although the rumor mill predicted we were being returned to our forces, we found out soon enough it was indeed just a rumor.

We did board a Japanese freighter, the *Toro Maru*, but our destination was not the United States; it was Japan. From the looks of it, the ship was at least thirty years old and aging fast. It needed a paint job just to keep the steel from rusting out, and as far as freighters go, it was small compared to a few of the others docked alongside. The Manila docks were bustling with activity, with dozens of men doing a variety of jobs. Some were loading scrap metal on board our ship; others were loading thousands of sacks of rice.

The men in our group slowly disembarked from the trucks, and the guards, in sign language, ordered us to form a line, two abreast. Then we had to have a formal count to satisfy the dozen officers on the dock. The leader of the Japanese soldiers, Lt. Tanaka San ("San" stands for the English word *mister* and is always used after the name), asked who in our group knew how to cook, or was a cook in the U.S. Army. I raised my hand and was chosen, along with three other men, to be a cook aboard the ship. We were told the officers on the dock were there to bid farewell to the first ship leaving for Japan with prisoners aboard. We realized that we were going to be relieving some of the Japanese citizens from certain menial jobs, against the principles of the Geneva Convention, thus freeing them for military service to fight for the emperor.

It was a very hot day, and the sweat poured off my head and face. My tattered shirt was soaking wet. As we started to board the ship, we saw a contingent of American POWs sitting on the dock and eating their meager rice ration. They watched us while we marched aboard and gave us the V sign, along with a farewell wave. In spite of the fact that I wanted to leave Cabanatuan, I really was not excited about going to Japan in this so-called oceangoing ship. Rusty and obviously old, it did not look seaworthy, even to a landlubber like me.

We walked up the plank onto the ship's deck, where I was pulled out of line along with the other cooks and led to where the cooking was to be done. To the rear of the main deck we found the "galley"; we could not laugh out loud for fear of insulting the Japanese. What we saw were four very large kettles, which could hold about forty gallons of water each. The one on the left, we were told, was for soup, the two in the middle were for cooking rice, and the one on the right was for tea.

We were to serve two meals a day: one at 8:00 in the morning, the second at 4:00 in the afternoon. We were to remain down in the hold with the rest of the men from 6:00 in the evening till 6:00 in the morning and then from 11:00 in the morning until 2:00 in the afternoon. In other words, we were able to stay topside five hours in the morning and four hours in the  afternoon. Working out in the fresh air was an advantage, and I was sure that any one of the men would have loved trading places with any one of us cooks.

The *Toro Maru* set sail from Manila about September 5, 1942, with its human cargo of slave labor. I was not a good sailor. I was seasick within hours of our ship leaving Manila, but I was able to assist with the cooking that first night out. By morning I was really sick. I made frequent trips to the side of the ship, always with an excuse of throwing something overboard. I did not want any of the guards to see me heaving my guts over the side, or my role as a cook would come to an immediate halt. I must admit I liked the freedom the job carried.

On the third day out as I was starting to feel a little better, one of the other cooks, an old navy hand, asked me, "Do you know how we can tell a real sailor from a bad one?" I fell for his question, hook, line, and sinker, and answered, "No, tell me." With that he said, "Well, you tie some salt pork on the end of a piece of string, then you swallow it, and when you p-u-l-l it up, if you don't throw up, you're a real Navy man." He did not have to say another word. Over to the side of the ship I went and heaved everything inside me. To my chagrin, the Japanese officer in charge of our group was standing just a few feet from the railing over which I discharged the entire contents of my stomach. That was my last day as cook. He put me down in the hold with the other 496 men for the balance of the trip. My seasickness got worse without any fresh air or wide open spaces to look at and, worst of all, with a limit on how much rice and soup I was able to eat.

Later I often kidded that former sailor about the not-so-welcome joke he pulled on me. A tall, slender man, Ard had flaming curly red hair that hung down to his neck. For the next two and a half years, he was the number one cook in our camp and the best fed.

So I was back in the hold for twenty-four hours a day. The hold measured fifty feet by fifty feet, for an allocation of about five square feet per man, which was not much space for five hundred men to spend twenty-four hours a day for a twenty-eight-day trip. Of course, the trip could be made in ten days if traveling at full speed, but this ship was so old that traveling at anything above ten knots per hour was unthinkable.

The hold was about twenty feet high. It had no electricity, and our only light came when the hatches were opened. A ladder was in the middle, going up to the hatch cover. We found out that we were going to dispose of our body waste by hauling buckets of it up through the hatch and then heaving them overboard.

The insides of the hold were bare metal walls with wooden planks over a metal floor. The hold was intended to carry cargo, not humans, and had been recently used to transport horses to the Philippines. We slept on the wood planks, which had soaked up all of the odor of horse urine and still had marks where the horses had relieved themselves. We had to live with this smell all the way to Japan. Our clothes and our bodies took on the smell of horses. We would have given everything we owned for hot baths and for anything that would get rid of the stench that permeated the air down in that hold.

We designated two corners of the hold as latrines. Each day we were allowed to send four men topside who would work with four men in the hold to dump out our waste buckets. It was not a very sanitary way of living, but then again, who said we were living? After a few days of emptying the waste material during the day, we decided to get permission to empty the buckets at night, just before we retired. Then we would not have to sleep with the continuous stink and worry of the bucket either overflowing or tipping over at night.

One of our officers suggested that we exercise while in the hold to keep ourselves physically fit. We did not respond to his idea with much enthusiasm. In fact, being fed two skimpy rations of rice a day along with a cup of watery soup did not give us enough energy to keep our bunks neat, let alone exercise. The lieutenant commander's recommendation made all of us feel that he was going to be a man to contend with once we arrived in our more permanent Japanese camp. This man, who became known as "The Henchman," was later responsible for the deaths of at least three Americans in our camp and the severe torture and beating of four others. In Camp 17, he was in charge of food and the entire mess hall operations, which included the cooks, the cooks' helpers, and all those who assisted in any way with the kitchen detail. In a situation where food was so critically important, his job gave him more power and authority than any other man in camp. He decided what we had to eat, how much we would get, and when we would get it.

By the fourth day at sea, many of the men in the hold experienced sickness again. By the time we boarded this ship, most of us had lost between 30 and 40 percent of our normal prewar weight. Most of the men still had bad cases of dysentery, and half of the men had malaria. At least once a night someone would have a malaria attack, crying for blankets because he was cold and shivering and a few minutes later screaming that his body was burning up. These diseases, along with a variety of other ills afflicting us, made sleeping and living in close quarters very difficult. When there was nothing to do and it was totally dark, the hours became a burden to most of us. The sounds of some of the men tore through me like fingernails scratching a blackboard. Men cried because they could not take it any longer; some moaned because of the severe pain caused by either wet or dry beriberi.

Wet beriberi causes the legs, abdomen, genitalia, and finally the face to swell. This is due to the increase of water within the body. To alleviate the pain associated with this type of beriberi, a doctor will usually tap the patient's body in order to draw out the excess fluid. Dry beriberi, on the other hand, is the elimination of fluid, and the end result is severe pain, which is caused by what seems like electric shocks, usually attacking the feet and legs. The only relief we were ever able to get from dry beriberi was to place our feet in a bucket of cold water and then just sit there and wait for the pain to subside. We later found out that one of the long-term effects of beriberi was a severe heart problem.

On more than one occasion during this trip, in the unquiet night, my mind would race. Oh, how I wanted this to be a bad dream, a nightmare that I could just wake up from and find gone; but the truth of the situation overruled my dreams of happiness. I often wondered what Laura was doing and how she was taking my being a loser and my surrendering. I worried whether she was embarrassed to admit she was my wife and my lover. Most important, was she waiting for me? Night after fearful night these dark thoughts circled my mind. The daytime allowed us to talk, to tell stories, and to be active within our limited confines, but nighttime was different. To survive I had to have something to do, something different to think about, something to make the time pass faster and take my mind off this horrible dream that was all too real.

Wherever there are American servicemen gathered, a man will always be able to find a deck of cards or a pair of dice. I soon found one of the

men sleeping near me had a pair of dice, and after negotiating a fair partnership, we started a craps game. This newfound friend was from the coast
artillery. His name was Silva, and he hailed from El Paso, New Mexico. He
had been mobilized into the service from a National Guard outfit just like I
was. Silva, I discovered, was the one who had led the singing and whistling
of American marching songs during the loading of the ship in Manila. He
loved to create funny scenes involving Japanese actions. He would scream
in pidgin Japanese and then he would holler at the man nearest him,
always imitating what one of the guards would have said. A funny guy,
Silva was bright, honest, and proud of being an American. We were going
to get along fine.

Once we teamed up, I drew a craps table layout on my blanket, and we
became the "house" in a craps game. We agreed to split all profits fifty-fifty,
although what little money the men had was not worth much. All the
Filipino or U.S. money in the world was useless down here in this bloody
hole. With all this in mind, we announced the game was to begin the following day.

Within minutes, twenty men congregated in one corner of the hold
around our blanket. For the next eight or nine days, things were going
fine, with money changing hands ten times a day. Men pushed and shoved
to get near the craps blanket, just to have some fun and a diversion from
our horrible trip.

If anyone ran out of money, we evaluated whatever he had to trade.
Silva and I made the decision of what an item was worth. The variety of
items offered at this late date of capture was surprising. If we named it,
someone in the hold would have it. We had to assess values on watches,
rings, precious stones, and wallets. As the game progressed, even shoes
and shirts would get values placed on them. The one item we would not
deal in was food. A man's ration of food belonged to him, and Silva and I
agreed that no one would trade or gamble it away with us.

The long boring days thus became more exciting. Now we had something to look forward to. The evenings, which seemed to last a lifetime
and were filled with loneliness, took on a new dimension. Now the time
was used to inventory and value the many items we had won the day
before. Our pangs of loneliness slowly vanished and sleep came a little easier when it became too dark to see.

We made a great deal of money those first ten days. Then it happened.
Either this fellow got a hot hand, or he understood how to throw dice so
that he could come up with his point on a regular basis. After many hours
of continuous play, he broke the bank, taking not only all our money and
valuables, but the dice to boot! My partner and I had fun, and from what
everyone said, all the men did too. At least we were able to take our minds

off the trip, and in many cases, some of the men who had been feeling sorry for themselves all of a sudden had a new outlook on survival.

We learned that the Japanese had chosen for this trip men who at one time or another had exercised some of their rights or protested in some way the treatment we were given. All five hundred of us men were classified as "bad ones." I guess my not being able to take orders and shooting an extra carabao put me in that category. Maybe I was written up in a report that followed me to Camp Cabanatuan. As I looked back on this experience, I could only say how lucky I was.

The next ship that left the Philippines right after we did never got into the open waters of the South China Sea. Torpedoes from U.S. submarines found their mark. With a great explosion and a burst of flame, the ship was hit broadside with such force that the cargo hatch was blown off its hinges and some of the prisoners below were catapulted topside.

As the war intensified and the Americans began their offensive in earnest, the Japanese moved greater numbers of prisoners to Japan. The war records show that by August 1944 the ships carrying American POWs were subjected to torpedo destruction and to attack by U.S. aircraft. U.S. submarines and aircraft were inadvertently responsible for sinking twenty-five Japanese freighters, many carrying American prisoners of war. Thousands of Americans died this way because the Japanese, for whatever reason, refused to identify those ships carrying POWs with Red Cross markings.

Our ship arrived at Formosa fourteen days after leaving Manila. We docked alongside six other Japanese freighters, none of which carried POWs. The first day in port we were allowed out of the hold for two hours. Then on the second day, we were told that for our "health and welfare" we would be allowed to work on a farm, picking bananas. We picked bananas for five days, but we were told not to eat any part of a banana or we would be punished severely. Each day after work we were herded back to the ship and put in the hold for the night.

Because I had learned enough of the Japanese language to survive, I spoke to some of the guards about various daily activities. During one of these conversations, I found out that the reason for the delay was our ship needed some repairs. The Japanese officers figured that as long as we were in Formosa, we might as well pick fruit, load it aboard the ship, and take it with us to Japan. We had hoped that the fruit would be distributed to us during the final leg of our journey, but this was wishful thinking. The fruit was for the Japanese people in Japan, not for us Americans.

When the repairs were completed, plans were made for our departure. While we were on the dock watching the ship being loaded with various items for Japan, a guard came through our ranks distributing sheets of paper with the heading, "Regulations for Prisoners." In essence, the regulations concerned our restrictions aboard the ship—what we could and could not do. These were in two parts. The first dealt with general guidelines that if not followed would result in punishment. The second set of regulations stated that if these were disobeyed in any manner, the result would be immediate death.

To the best of my recollection, the first set of guidelines included such items as:

> Prisoners should eliminate both their bowels and bladder before boarding the ship.

> Prisoners should not complain about the small amount of food or the condition of the ship.

> Prisoners will get only one portion of rice, twice a day.

> When the toilet buckets and cans are full, they will be brought to the center of the room, and a guard will be notified that a pulley is needed. Buckets will be pulled up and the contents thrown away by prisoners, who will work with the guards to accomplish this order.

The second set of prohibitions are recalled below. If a prisoner did any of the following, he would be executed:

> Climbing ladders without orders

> Touching or fooling with any of the boat's materials, wires, lights, and so forth

> Taking more food than his share

> Disobeying any orders or instructions given by any Japanese soldier or officer

> Talking in a loud or mean fashion to the guards

> Walking around or moving anyplace except the hold of the ship without Japanese orders

No one wanted to challenge or test these rules; instead, we tried our best to comply. We found out that any punishment doled out to one of the men had a negative effect on the rest of us.

On the third day out from Formosa, a prisoner suffering severely from malaria and dysentery started to scream that he wanted to go out on the deck to get some fresh air. We all knew that the poor guy was out of his mind, but we could not stop his yelling. A guard opened the hatch and invited the man who was screaming to come up on deck. As this sick man stuck his head out of the hold, the guard pushed his bayonet into the poor man's neck with one mighty thrust. The man toppled backward down the ladder. As he fell to the deck of the hold, the blood poured from his neck wound. Our medics ran to him and tried to stop the bleeding. Two men took turns holding pressure on the wound until after what seemed like hours the bleeding stopped enough for the medics to sew up the hole. Our friend lived to see another day, and we all learned a lesson: the Japanese meant what they said. The following day, the officer in charge informed us that we would get only one ration of food that day because we did not control our friend and stop him from breaking one of the rules. So, we all suffered because of the actions of one.

For what felt like a lifetime, we sat in the stinking hold telling each other lies. First, we were going to be traded for Japanese prisoners. Then, we were going to be taken to a neutral port and wait out the war there. We heard countless rumors of what was going to happen to us, but not one of the rumors ever mentioned our being executed or killed. That possibility was never discussed, although most of us thought about it many times.

The days just dragged on, with nothing to do but sit and talk about nothing in particular. By this stage in our journey, everything was starting to irritate us. The men started fighting among themselves for the slightest reasons. We simply got on each others' nerves. Actually, by this time we had heard each others' stories a dozen times and were so bored that we could not bear to hear the same tales over again.

In addition to the boredom and despair, we found it necessary for many hours of the day to hold our breath systematically. The odor of urine and feces from the men aboard, as well as the horses that had previously traveled in our accommodations, made us all nauseous. As the days wore on, we longed for an end to this boat ride. Anything, we thought, would be better than what we were enduring.

Then, as if in answer to our pleas, we heard the ship's horn blaring with two short and then one long blast and loud voices giving what seemed to be commands. We also heard other motors and horns from other ships. We felt sure that something important was happening. When our ship was bumped by what we perceived as a pilot boat, we knew the end of this hellish voyage was in sight.

# CHAPTER 10

# THE COAL MINE

When we landed in Japan, each of us had lost an average of fifteen pounds since leaving the Philippines. If I had been able to weigh myself that day, I probably would have weighed 105 pounds, for a loss of 43 percent from my prewar weight. In spite of being in Japan—enemy territory—we were happy to be off the *Toro Maru*. Many of us were unable to walk without holding on to someone else, our legs were so cramped from lack of exercise and from sitting in one position for long periods of time.

After we disembarked, the Japanese herded us into a large warehouse right on the docks. They told us to take off all of our clothes and to throw them into the trash bins spaced along the wall of the building. Standing there in our birthday suits made us even more painfully aware of our poor physical condition. Soon a half dozen Japanese entered, dressed in uniforms covered with what appeared to be canvas coveralls and wearing long gloves and face masks. Each had strapped to his back (Or hers? we wondered, as we stood shivering) a large tank, like a scuba diver's oxygen tank, and from the tank ran a long rubber hose with a spray attachment and an on-off lever. These six people walked up and down the rows of naked men and sprayed our bodies and hair with a chemical. Had we known about the German concentration camps, where people were gassed to death in a similar fashion, we would have thought that was what was happening to us. In fact, we were only being deloused. The Japanese wanted to eliminate any chance of our bringing parasites into Japan. This whole procedure took roughly two hours, but it seemed like an eternity.

We were then issued Japanese-style clothing and typical Japanese rubber and canvas working shoes that buttoned on the side and had a split section just for the big toe. The shirts and pants were all one size, but their legs and sleeves were much too small for most of us Americans. The waist and chest sizes were just right; after all, we were down to skin and bones. Our last piece of clothing was a strip of white cloth, about thirty inches long and twelve inches wide, with a string going around one end. We tied the string around our waists and pulled the other end of the cloth up, through, and over it like a loincloth.

Ready at last with our new clothes, we could move on to the next leg of our journey. We stood another hour waiting for instructions. Everyone wanted to know what we were going to be doing, where we were going, and how we would survive this new experience.

A young naval officer stepped onto a platform at the far end of the building. When we saw him, we all stood at attention and stopped talking. The Japanese officer spoke perfect English. In fact, when I turned my head away, I could have sworn I was listening to one of my own officers speaking. As he started to speak, he announced, "I was born in Long Beach, California, went to school at Stanford University, but I am Japanese and will always remember my heritage. We will win the war against the American threat of boycotting our country and depriving us of our very existence to live.

"You are prisoners, and don't forget it. You are here to work, and to work hard for the emperor," he shouted. Then he explained that we would be taken by train to our new "home," where we would be indoctrinated into the work habits of the Japanese.

We were then marched to a nearby railroad station, where waiting for us was a very old steam engine with seven very antiquated passenger cars in tow. The engine bellowed dark smoke from its smokestack, and the hissing sounds and the belching of steam from the release valves made us wonder if this engine would ever be able to get started while pulling a load behind it.

The guards ordered us to start boarding the train, but instead of allowing us to board on our own, they pushed and shoved us so that we would hurry up our boarding procedure. I did not move as fast as the guards wanted, so the one closest to me hit me on the head with the butt of his rifle and hollered, "*Hayaku, hayaku*" (faster, faster). I turned to look at this guard who had just struck me, and as I did so, another guard who had been watching the whole episode stepped in front of me. With his rifle turned so that the butt was directly in front of my nose, he swung his gun in a wide arc, hit me squarely in the face, and hollered, "*Domi, domi*" (no good, no good).

Blood gushed from my nose, and from the pain, I believed he had broken my nose once again. The bleeding also seemed to come from my forehead, so I put my hand up to my head to put pressure on the spot where I thought the bleeding was coming from. I did all of this while boarding the train. I had no intention of stopping to look back; I knew the second guard attacked me after he caught me looking back with disgust at the first guard.

At last we were all aboard the train, still without having the faintest idea of where we were or where we were going. We no longer fantasized that we were going to be traded for Japanese prisoners, for we felt certain that our time as prisoners of war was going to continue until the war ended. This unhappy bunch of Americans felt that we had lost whatever chance we had of being released now that we were in Japan. The thought of U.S. forces coming into the Philippines to release us had at least kept us dreaming. We had had hopes, plans, and dreams—all of which were now shattered.

I wondered how we could make it now that we were so far from friendly forces. I kept thinking of all the Filipino people who had waved at us, showed the V sign, and had been our friends. What was it going to be like here in enemy territory? How long would this go on? If only I had some idea I could count the days and have something to look forward to, but this uncertainty could drive me crazy.

I could not figure out the answers to my questions. I did arrive at some important conclusions, however, while on that train ride through Japan: I would make it, I would go home, and I would get even with those bastards, the ones who beat and tortured me, the ones who deprived me of my dignity, the ones who killed my friends.

This little speech that I made to myself helped me figure out how I was going to deal with each day's activities and problems. First, I decided that I would have to keep busy. Even if I was tired, I would have to do something each day to stimulate my mind and to make me want to face tomorrow. Second, I would not just sit back and let the Japanese do whatever they wanted to me. Instead, I vowed to have a voice, even if only a small voice, in any decision that affected me personally. Third, I would use my knowledge of the language to communicate on a regular basis with the Japanese I encountered. And last, I would never forget my main objective: to survive and return home. Therefore, everything I did from that day on was weighed against "the probability of my going home, if I do such and such." Like the days on the Bataan march when I looked down the road to fix my eyes on a goal, a place to aim for, I would search for anything that would help me reach my objective.

After six hours, the train blew its whistle and the bell rang, announcing its arrival. The train continued slowly for another ten minutes and finally came to an abrupt stop. At the command of the officer in charge, we began disembarking. When I stepped off the train, I saw for the first time what a Japanese city looked like, and I was not impressed. As I looked around, I could have sworn that I had seen this town before in a magazine or newspaper. It was so typical of what I expected that I was not shocked, as some of my friends were. The homes were made out of bamboo, with thatched roofs. I saw only one building constructed of brick, and that looked like a government facility. Few automobiles were on the street, and they seemed quite old, just barely chugging along.

Some of the townspeople had gathered at the train station to see what we Americans looked like. They just stood there, in their typical Japanese attire, waiting for something to happen. As we marched off the train, we took a look around, just to get our bearings, and saw civilians gawking and pointing at us as if we were animals in a cage. With muffled laughs and derogatory gestures, they made us feel as if we were cowards. Without a single word, they stripped us of our dignity. We felt they were thinking that we had been afraid to fight, that we had just given up. We even looked like beaten men. We had been taken like animals in a trap, beaten and tortured, and made to feel worthless. Now once again, we were being humiliated.

Once we were all off the train, the guards counted us to ensure that all of us who had survived the voyage were present. We then began another march, but not as bad as before. We walked for about four miles before we saw in the distance a large compound with a wooden fence six feet tall that was topped with two feet of barbed wire. As we approached the area, one-story wooden barracks came into view. Then as we got closer, we could tell that this was going to be our camp.

Once inside we saw row after row of barracks, all on the right side of the camp. Apparently the Japanese were expecting at least another thousand men. Our original contingent of 500 prisoners was augmented early in 1944 by another 800 American, 200 Australian, and about 150 Javanese soldiers captured in the battle for Sumatra. Then in February 1945, the last group of Americans arrived: ninety-five men who had survived the bombing and torpedoing of the Japanese freighter that was ferrying them from the Philippines to Japan. This brought the total number of POWs in our camp to seventeen hundred men.

Each of the thirty-five barracks was identical: about sixty-five feet long, fifteen feet wide, and divided into seven rooms. The  front room was reserved for the barracks leader and his assistant, and the other six rooms each housed eight men. Running the length of the barracks was one three-foot-wide interior corridor on the side of the building. From this aisle, we entered our sleeping room by stepping up onto a small, foot-high platform, which also served as our sitting area, in front of the room and then sliding the wood-framed door covered with rice paper either to the left or the right. The wooden floor was covered with typical straw mats. Each room had a large window that could be opened, but in winter, the cold breeze seeped through the many cracks caused by poor construction. Each prisoner had one thin mattress, stuffed with straw, and one heavy, coarse blanket. When it was cold, all eight of us in the room would move as close together as possible to allow our body heat to generate more warmth. Extending the full width at the very front of the barracks was our latrine. It consisted of four cubicles with nothing more than holes in the floor where our body waste was collected. Little did I know then that I would be spending the next three years in this environment.

Up to this point we still did not know what we were supposed to do. What was our work going to be? That was the question of the day. We were counted off in groups of fifty and assigned to one of the barracks. I was assigned to barracks number 4. In the middle of the compound we found the POWs' showers and our mess hall, and on the left side of the camp were the Japanese headquarters, their barracks, and their eating area.

That evening we were each given our own *bento* box. About seven inches long, four inches wide, and two inches deep, it had a cover with a one-inch lip that just fit over the bottom section. It was made of wood, and the outside was lacquered a shiny deep brown.

The following morning, the Japanese told us that we would be working in the coal mines. They also told us that we were expected to salute or to bow to any Japanese guard or officer we saw or thought we saw. Whenever we left our barracks and came out into the open street, we had to stop, face the location where the guard would normally be stationed, and bow. We had to do this, we were told, even if we could not see the guard. Any failure to bow would result in severe punishment.

The Japanese then instructed us that once we went into the mine we would be divided into three groups for exploration, construction, and extraction. Those doing exploration would look for new veins of coal and would work in hard rock. The construction team would shore up the ceilings of the laterals, whereas the extraction team would blast and dig out the coal. The first few days, according to the guards, we would all go down into the mine and do a little of each job, just to get a feel for what had to be done.

Next, the Japanese guards marched us to the mine, a distance of about three miles, and then turned us over to civilians for the actual work in the mines. The shaft mine was underground. We had to either walk or ride down. Most of the time Japanese workers filled the rail cars, so we had to walk, carrying jackhammers with five-foot-long bits, shovels, axes, saws, hammers, our bento boxes, our cloth caps with their light in the front, and battery packs on belts strapped to our waists. We would start down fully clothed, but as we progressed into the coal area, we would start taking our clothes off until we had on nothing but our loincloths. Inside the tunnels it got hot and stuffy. Very little air got into the lateral areas, which were far away from the main tunnel.

The shaft went down at a 15 percent grade. That meant that for every one hundred feet we walked, we went down fifteen feet. (The steepest grade allowed on most roads in the United States is 6 percent.) The deepest part of the mine was about half a mile down. Although we walked down most of the time, walking back up really got to us, especially after working for twelve hours shoveling coal, moving coal troughs, and bracing the ceilings so that we would not be injured in a cave-in.

I will never forget that first day down in the mine. We were allowed to ride down the shaft in one of the cars, and it took about five minutes to reach our tunnel. Our first job was building ceiling supports. When I asked why this was needed, one of the civilian workers told me that the mine had been shut down years before because all the coal that was safe to extract had already been removed. Now we were really going after the proverbial needle in the haystack; that was how difficult it was to find more coal that could be safely extracted.

I then found out that in mining coal a supporting lateral sixteen feet wide was saved for every sixteen feet of coal extracted. What we were doing was extracting that lateral support. This meant that we had to enter the area from which the coal had already been taken, put up supports to help prevent the ceiling from coming down, and then extract the coal from the side that had been used as the original ceiling support. In other words, we were stripping the mine of all the remaining coal.

We paid the price for doing this. We experienced serious accidents that cost many of our men their lives, an arm or leg, and in a few cases, broken backs. Many injuries, often fatal, were caused when the ceiling collapsed in what was known as sidewall cave-ins. It made no difference how many accidents we had, however; the work had to go on.

On that first day in the mine, we were divided into groups of eight. Each group had two Japanese civilian miners working with it. The group to which I was assigned was being trained to build rock walls in the tunnel that had already had all of its coal removed. We started to build a wall sixteen feet wide and sixteen feet long up to the ceiling. The tunnel we were working in that day was sixteen feet wide by about eighty feet long. Thus, we had to construct three retaining walls, each separated by sixteen feet of space. Therefore, for every sixteen feet of space we had a sixteen-foot wall.

The Japanese supervisor of our group told us that we had to start the base of the wall with the largest boulders we could find. Then we would build on top and to the side of these first boulders with smaller rocks to form a well-structured wall. As the wall grew to three feet in height, the supervisor instructed us to shovel whatever debris was on the ground nearby to the other side of the wall. Then we threw smaller rocks into the wall for packing. We continued building the wall until it got to be about five feet high. Then we followed the same procedure as before, filling the inside of the wall with whatever we could find. We repeated this process until the wall hit the ceiling, about seven feet. To top off the wall, we made wooden wedges and then crammed the top boulders firmly against the ceiling.

Here I was, a Chicago boy who had never seen the outside of a mine let alone been inside one, working below ground in the most unsafe and archaic conditions imaginable. By then, I was about sixty pounds under my prewar weight and was still fighting the malaria bug and amoebic dysentery. And I was no exception. Most of the men working in the mine had the same problems.

As we were building the wall, we found out how weak we had become. Trying to lift some of the large, heavy boulders into place, it would take two or sometimes three of us just to get the boulder from the ground up onto the wall. At about this time, the Japanese working with us would start laughing and say, in sign language, in pidgin English, and in Japanese, "Americans are big but weak; Japanese small, but strong." When we tried to get one of the big boulders to the wall, we would roll it, end over end or any way we could, just to get it there. Once again the Japanese would laugh at us and then say, "Two Americans to move that boulder, but it would take only one Japanese." They were really riling us, but how could we respond to this constant harassment? I spoke enough Japanese to be understood, and the men in my group wanted me to say something that would get them off our backs. After thinking for a few minutes, I realized that if one Japanese could do the work of two Americans, we could finish our work faster and have time to rest.

I waited for the next time that the Japanese were going to say something nasty about our not being able to do something. Sure enough, as soon as we tried to lift another heavy boulder onto the wall, one of the Japanese laughed and said, "Two Americans for what one Japanese can do." This was my chance. I motioned to the one in charge and said, "Why don't you show us how you would do it?" Within seconds he got up, spit on his hands, grabbed the boulder around the center, and lifted it into place on the wall. I started to applaud, then the rest of the men caught on and also applauded.

Not to be outdone, the other Japanese man went over to a boulder much larger than the first man's, and with a loud grunt, he lifted it up onto the wall and shifted it around until it fit into place alongside the others.

Once again we all applauded. The two Japanese men took a bow and started to help us build the wall. They were so proud to have Americans applauding them that they wanted more, and we gave it to them. We thanked them, bowed to them, shook their hands, patted their backs, and applauded some more. They loved it all. We knew what we were doing—just using some very simple psychology on them—and it worked.

When we finished this ten-hour work shift, we were allowed to ride the cars topside. Then we were herded into a huge "bath" room, literally, a room with three tubs of hot water that were heated by a large gas water heater. Each tub was about twenty feet long, ten feet wide, and three feet at its deepest part. A seat went around the entire inside of the tub. We also had soap, small wooden dunking buckets, and an assortment of small rags. I discovered in short order that I should not use the soap in the water. Instead, I got in the tub and soaked, letting my body relax. Then I got out of the tub, soaped down, and poured buckets of hot water from the tub all over me. When I finished that routine, then I returned to the tub to soak for a little while longer.

As we found out later, the shift that finished work first enjoyed clean hot water, the second shift got dirty hot water, and by the time the third shift finished work, these men got murky, very dirty, hot water. Most of the men who worked the third shift never bothered to bathe at the mine, preferring to walk back to the camp and take a shower there before turning in for the night.

Our wall-building project continued for another week. We were working to make the area safe before the first coal-extracting team of prisoners came in to begin their work. Working under these conditions was a constant strain on our minds as well as our body. That first week toughened us up, though. At least we knew what was expected of us, and if we performed the way we were supposed to, the Japanese did not beat us. If we goofed off, however, then we could expect the consequences. Of course, this basic premise did not follow any type of pattern. We were beaten for any reason the Japanese civilians wanted. If their food was in short supply, if the Americans bombed a Japanese city, or if the supervisors that day wanted more coal than was produced, they beat us. We quickly found out that there was no need for an excuse; we were punished any time the Japanese wanted to vent their anger and frustration.

We slowly learned to accept our fate that, while in Japan, we were going to work in the coal mine. As day followed dreary day, we carefully watched everything that went on down in the mine. We noticed that the large motor that ran the main conveyor belt from the bottom to the top of the mine was connected to all of the tunnels and laterals and transported the coal out of the mine and onto ships for destinations unknown. We quickly realized if that one main motor could be stopped, all of the work in the mine would grind to a halt. So while in camp that week, our work group of ten men made plans to sabotage the motor the next time we had to walk down the mine's main tunnel to our work station.

A few days after planning our strategy, we arrived at the mine and picked up all of our equipment only to be told that we would be walking down the tunnel that day because the rail car was broken. We marched down single file. About halfway down, we saw the motor. It looked like a fifty-horsepower motor, huge by anyone's standard. The first man to pass the motor, as planned, loosened the wing nut to the oil reservoir. The second man removed its cover, and the next six men dropped into the open oil reservoir rocks, hard coal, and anything else available in the mine that could cause damage to the motor. The last two men in our group were responsible for replacing the oil cover. We continued to our work area, knowing that sooner or later the motor would stop. Then we would have accomplished two things: first, we would be able to stop working for a while, and second, we would have contributed, in some small manner, to the U.S. war effort.

An hour later, all hell broke loose. The belt in the main tunnel, the one taking the coal topside, stopped. We found out about the stoppage when the coal in our side lateral trough started to bunch up; it would not move out onto the belt. This backup of coal signaled that something was wrong with the main coal-carrying belt, and our work group had to stop shoveling coal because we had no place to put it. Our plan had worked! We just sat down and rested for about three hours, until the motor was replaced or repaired and things got back to normal.

Each day, once we reached our workplace in the mine and got ready for work, we always had to wait for a supervisor to come into our tunnel and tell us how many cars of coal he expected our group to produce. At the beginning of one shift, about ten minutes went by before in strode a Japanese man, standing about six feet tall, with a husky build and a wide smile covering his face. He was dressed all in black in a high-necked tunic and tight-fitting trousers. His uniform had four white stripes on the tunic's sleeves; I later found out they indicated he was a high official of the mine. We referred to him as the "Four Striper."

The Four Striper began tapping the walls of our area with a stick he was carrying that looked like a cane. After a few minutes, he looked at me and said in Japanese, "Twelve cars of coal today." I was amazed. Did he really know how to calculate the number of cars of coal just by tapping the walls? He must have noticed my surprised look, for he said, "Yatte miru" (try it). I then realized he knew no more about coal mining than we did. Because I was the one who understood and could communicate with the Japanese, I decided to test him right there and then. I borrowed his cane and tapped the walls all around us. When I finished, I looked him in the eye and said, "*Dai-hachi, yatte mimasho*" (eight I will try for; that's the best we can do). He looked me in the eye and stared me down for what seemed like one full minute. He then smiled and said in English with a Japanese accent, "OK."

At the end of our shift, we did in fact produce eight cars of coal. When we got topside, the Four Striper looked for me and with a big smile said, "*Yeroshi*" (good). Then he proudly handed each man in our crew a big red apple. We tried to imagine how coal miners back in the United States would respond to a reward of an apple. What the Four Striper did not know, however, was that we completed our work in just five hours. We then sat down in our lateral, took off our headlamps, buried them light first in the loose coal, and slept. That was the beginning of an almost daily routine for the next few months.

We negotiated the number of cars of coal each day, and I might add, the Japanese always settled for the number we bargained for. Then after we made our quota, we would find a place to rest where we would not be discovered. This scheme usually meant at least four or five hours of rest each day. Unfortunately, we hungry men did not get an apple each day.

When the work day was over and we walked up the mine shaft to reach topside, we had a choice of bathing there or going back to our barracks. The men on our shift always voted to return to camp unless we were the first ones finished. Only if we were on the first shift did we vote to take a hot bath in crystal-clear water. When we were ready to march back to the barracks, we would line up four abreast in front of the mine entrance and start our three-mile march back to camp.

Our daily routine of marching to the mine, working in the mine for ten hours, being forced to walk up the mine shaft to topside while carrying all of the coal-digging equipment, and then walking the three miles back to camp became almost impossible. Those first few weeks in the mine were devastating, by far the most trying of my three years in Japan. Each day became worse than the day before, as we started to hate the very thought of working in the mine. We knew that each day brought additional challenges and dangers. Our continued forced labor exhausted us and exacted a heavy toll on our emotions and our survival attitude.

By the end of the first month, we were accustomed to the routine. We then needed something to take our minds off the continued harassment and beatings by both the Japanese soldiers and the civilians in the mine. As our group marched back to camp, I kept searching the streets, the people, and the terrain for telltale marks that would give me some relief from the tensions of the workday. Surprisingly enough, some of the people lining the road from the mine to our camp seemed to have a very sad and questioning air about them. If only I could talk to them, to ask them how the war was going and what the future held for us, maybe then I could carry on in a more positive spirit.

When we arrived at camp, the guards searched our bodies as well as all of our clothes. What were they looking for? The guards did not communicate with us or give us any indication that anything was wrong. We did not know what was happening. Finally one of the officers explained that on selected days they would conduct searches for specific items. This day the guards were looking for contraband. They wanted to see if any of us had picked up items that belonged to the Japanese civilians in the mine. They did not find anything, so we were ordered back into camp, then dismissed. We were allowed to go to our barracks, to the showers, to the mess hall for our evening meal, or just to wander throughout the camp.

That evening as Doc Hewlett and I were talking about the day's events, Doc explained that he could not keep records of the men's health conditions and wished that he had some way to write down each man's sick call diagnosis and the treatment given. This information would be quite valuable to the men in the future, Doc felt, for a record of a man's condition, his treatment, and his prognosis during the time he was a prisoner would help immensely in treating an illness, sickness, or injury once back home. Then Doc said once we were released the proper authorities would have a better chance of improving our overall physical condition if we had medical records available detailing what happened to us and the treatment we received while prisoners. I promised Doc that I would try to obtain some writing paper for our medics' use. I did not know how, but I felt that I could find a way.

My chance came only a few days later while shoveling coal in the mine. One of the Japanese civilian overseers, knowing that I spoke a little Japanese, approached me and asked whether I knew where he could buy a tube of American toothpaste. I told him that I would try to locate one when I got back into camp. He instructed me not to say anything to anyone else, to keep quiet. I smiled a knowing smile and said I understood. Then I asked what he would pay or trade for a valuable tube of American toothpaste. He said in Japanese, "Anything. How about tobacco?"

Tobacco really meant cigarettes, and cigarettes were our medium of exchange in camp. So I agreed. "How many?"

He replied, "Ten, twenty, maybe thirty." I told him I would try to find some toothpaste, but whether I could get any was going to depend on how many packs of cigarettes he would trade for the toothpaste.

I started to think. Would he be able to get me some writing paper, in any form—a booklet or loose sheets—that our medics could use for record keeping? I felt that I had found someone with whom I could begin a good trading relationship. He and I both knew that this bartering or trading was against Japanese policy and that we would be punished if caught. But, what the hell, I was already living on borrowed time. I figured I might just as well have a little excitement in my life and at the same time help the medics keep health records of the prisoners for their future use. Little did I know then how important a copy of my wartime medical records would be when seeking assistance from the Veterans Administration once I got back to the United States.

I introduced myself to the overseer as Tenney San (Mr. Tenney). He said his name was Moto San; he came from Kyoto and was here just to work in the mine and train the prisoners on how to produce coal. He asked where I came from and in what city in the United States was I born. When I replied Chicago, he laughed, pointed his finger at me, and said, "Caponeee— Gango." I understood what he meant at once. First, I was from Chicago, Al Capone's town, and at that time, everyone knew that Capone was a gangster. Second, I was about to do the same things a gangster would do, things that were against the law.

Moto San was a small man, about five feet four inches tall and not more than 120 pounds. He had jet-black hair, which he kept short because of all the coal dust, and he looked much younger than his forty-five years. The one thing that set him apart from the rest of the prison guards were his eyes. Bright, shining, and the happiest eyes I had ever seen, they looked mischievous, but loaded with fun. Although Moto San spoke a little English, he was very patient with my speaking what I later learned was "gutter" Japanese. He explained that I had learned the language from the soldiers on Bataan, who undoubtedly were from the poorer areas of Japan and did not receive as good an education as their compatriots.

Back in camp I had to find someone with toothpaste. We Americans had never received any Red Cross packages, so when seeking something that would normally be found in a Red Cross box, we contacted some of the POWs in our camp from as far away as Australia, China, England, and Java. The Javanese soldiers arrived in excellent health, not having endured the Bataan march, and the Japanese did not hate them as much as the guards hated us Americans. Of course, the English and Australians were Caucasians, which led the Japanese to dislike them almost as much as they despised us Americans. Generally, the Javanese prisoners were treated much better than the Filipinos or Americans.

In my search around camp the next few days, I found that the Javanese prisoners had hoarded dozens of items, from toothbrushes to cans of coffee. Apparently, when a Javanese prisoner received a Red Cross box while a prisoner in Java, he kept the contents for future use. When I questioned them about this practice, they said they had saved the goods for a "rainy day."

The fact was that I could find almost anything simply by passing on the word that I wanted an item. Cigarettes would buy just about anything in the camp, from rice to having an experienced bone breaker fracture a bone or two, just to keep a man out of work and the mine for a week, a month, or maybe forever. I could also purchase it with U.S. currency or IOUs that were properly signed and witnessed by our camp commander and made payable after the war ended. These IOUs were supposed to be paid in U.S. dollars once we received our back pay from the government. Maj. John Mamerow, our American camp commander, told me privately that the notes would not stand up in any court and were not even worth the paper they were written on; but, if they were what the Javanese men wanted, it was agreeable with him. One of the reasons Major Mamerow felt the notes could never be collected was that the prices asked were outlandishly high and undue pressure was applied to influence the exchange. For example, an aspirin tablet would require a promissory note for one hundred dollars, or for a ration of rice, an IOU for one hundred dollars. None of the note signers ever intended to renege on their debts, but hunger and pain can cause anyone to promise anything to get relief.

Before long, I found someone in the Javanese barracks with a nice new tube of Colgate toothpaste, still in its original box. He wanted ten packs of cigarettes for it. At this time in camp, a bowl of rice cost three cigarettes, so the Javanese prisoner asked a mighty handsome price just for a tube of toothpaste.

The price of rice fluctuated daily, depending on the probability of cigarettes being issued that day or the length of time since they were last issued. Our experience showed that we could expect one pack of ten cigarettes every four to seven weeks, give or take a few weeks in either direction. In other words, it was anybody's guess as to when cigarettes would be issued. This measure of uncertainty kept the value of rice and soup constantly fluctuating. In addition, of course, the value of everything else varied along with the inventory or availability of cigarettes. One thing was certain: the number of cigarettes available for trading diminished daily. While the non-traders smoked them, the traders kept their supply safe and well hidden—safe not only from theft but from the possibility of the tobacco drying and falling out, which would make the investment (the cigarette) lose some of its trading value.

At my next meeting with my newfound Japanese friend, Moto San, I told him I had located a tube of toothpaste, but the owner wanted twenty packs of cigarettes for it. Moto San did not blink an eye. He said, "OK, tomorrow I bring tobacco." I then said that I would like to have some paper to draw or write on and asked if he could bring me a little paper notebook as my gift for getting him the toothpaste. He was excited and seemed very happy to accommodate my request. He said, "Tomorrow, tomorrow I bring you gift." Thus, the stage was set for a new enterprise; a new business was going to operate right here in Japan with a partnership between Moto San and Tenney San. What experiences lay ahead?

The difference between what my Javanese friend asked for the toothpaste and what I told Moto San was my commission, or profit, for the risk I was taking, the risk of being caught and put to death. Why was I willing to do this? Was it for the excitement or just the chance to eat a little better? I really did not take the time to think this through; I just decided to start trading. It seemed like an easy way for me to get more food and, at the same time, to provide some good benefits to my fellow prisoners in the camp. Of course, I liked the thrill of doing something daring, something different, and I would enjoy the attention from the medics after I was able to supply them with the paper necessary for recording our medical histories.

I knew I had to be careful. First, I had to figure out how to avoid handing over the toothpaste before getting paid. If I did not receive my payment, I would still be obligated to pay the Javanese for his toothpaste. My second concern was to come up with a way to carry twenty packages of cigarettes in my clothes without being detected by the guards. A Japanese pack consisted of only ten cigarettes, making them smaller and easier to carry back to camp and to hide than the larger American packs of twenty cigarettes. And last, I had to face the fact that on the day I was carrying in the contraband the guards might search me upon my entry to camp.

Finally the day came for the trade. The arrangements were all made. Moto San knew I was bringing the toothpaste down into the mine that day and that he had to have twenty packs of cigarettes ready for me in just a plain wrapper. No one was supposed to know anything about our transaction. For my part, I carried the toothpaste out of the camp in one of my pockets. I knew the guards never searched us on leaving camp, only on coming back in. So I left camp, anxious for my first trading experience.

We walked our normal route to the mine. Once there, the Japanese guards turned us over to the civilian workers. We arranged for the tools we would need that day: a jackhammer, four five-foot long bits, a can of lubricating oil, three picks, four coal shovels, our headlamps, batteries and belts, and of course, five sticks of dynamite, blaster caps, and dynamite cord. Once we gathered all of the equipment, we entered the room where our Japanese civilian supervisor was waiting. I spotted Moto San at once, and he acknowledged me. That day, our group started down the mine shaft in a rail car, which was a real treat.

Once in our lateral, we assembled the jackhammer and inserted a starter bit into the head. At about that time Moto San spoke up, "Today we get only seven cars of coal, no problem." With that he sat down on the outside of the lateral and called me over. He asked me if I had the toothpaste, and when I responded, "Yes," he opened his tunic and displayed twenty packs of cigarettes, just as he had promised. I explained as best I could that I did not want the cigarettes then; I would get them right before we started to go topside. He agreed to this and instructed me to go back and work with the group to get seven cars of coal.

All during that workday, I was as nervous as a cat. All I could think of was what I would do and say if I got caught. How was I going to get these cigarettes back to the camp? Then I had an idea: I could tie them around the inside of my thighs with some of the dynamite cord. That way, even if I was searched, the guards would not find them. They rarely did a complete body search, especially on the 4:00 A.M. shift I was working. The Japanese had instituted three twelve-hour shifts, and every ten days we rotated shifts. We used to joke wryly that the Japanese invented the thirty-six-hour day with the ten-day work week.

Anyway, the day shift got searched most often and the other shifts just occasionally, so I waited to trade until I was on a shift that was met by only a few guards at the camp's entrance. If the Japanese wanted to do a complete search, they would have to search about six hundred men.

When we filled our required seven cars of coal, we were told to rest for a while. Each of us knew that meant to bury our lights in the loose coal and stay quiet, for even the Japanese civilians wanted a little rest now and then. I approached Moto San and showed him the piece of dynamite cord I had saved for tying the cigarettes to my thighs. When he saw and heard what I was going to do, he said, "Very good, very good." He opened the top buttons of his tunic and slowly brought out the cigarettes, which were wrapped in two packages of ten packs of cigarettes. He placed these two packages next to my bento box. At the same time, I picked up my jacket and pulled out from one of the pockets the tube of toothpaste in its original carton. When I handed Moto San the tube of toothpaste, his eyes flashed a warm, happy acknowledgment. I then attached the cigarette packages to the inside of my thighs with the dynamite cord. When I finished, Moto San handed me two notebooks of plain lined paper. The notebooks were small, about three inches by five inches, and without thinking I slipped them into my jacket pocket.

After walking up the mine tunnel and then walking the three miles back to camp with twenty packs of cigarettes tied to my thighs, I realized that I had earned my ten-pack commission. As I had expected, when we arrived at the entrance to the camp, the guards simply opened the gates and herded us in. Once inside, the guards started to give us a cursory search, just patting our bodies for contraband.

Oh my God, I thought, I forgot about the notebooks of paper. What would happen if they found them? When the guard got to me, he patted my jacket, and when he reached the pocket, he stopped. He inserted his hand and brought out the two books of paper. He opened the books and flashed through them. He looked at me, laughed, and said, "*Iie o-kane*" (no money). He was only looking for Japanese money coming into camp illegally, not for paper notebooks. It seemed that if the guards were given orders to search for one particular thing, that was all they looked for that day. Any other type of contraband could come in unchallenged. When the guard finished flashing through the two notebooks and found nothing in them, not even any writing, he put them back into my pocket and waved me through to the barracks.

I had sweated profusely during the search. I was scared not knowing what was going to happen and knowing I was breaking the rules. As I walked toward my barracks that morning, I said to myself, "Yep, I made it! I made it, and tomorrow I will eat good. I'll buy an extra ration of rice."

I felt good that night, and as I got ready to sleep, I wondered what would be next on my list of wants. I wanted to go home, but this was not possible now. I wanted to hold my wife in my arms and to caress her and tell her how much I missed her, but this also was impossible. It seemed that the few things I really wanted, I could not have, so I resorted to the desires that I could fulfill. I was not alone in dreaming about my home, my family, my wife. Whenever a small group of us got together to talk about the past, we would always come around to our loved ones and our home life. What else was there to dream about, live for, and want to come home to?

# CHAPTER 11

# CAMP 17

As time went on and our work became more routine, many of us were virtually able to fall asleep while shoveling coal. Our bodies were so totally exhausted and our energy so sapped that we were able to do the shoveling as an action of our subconscious, sort of from rote memory. Like Pavlov's dog, we were conditioned to respond a certain way under a certain set of rules or circumstances.

When the work or conditions became unbearable, when a man felt that another day down in the hole might be his last, either he paid to have someone break a bone in his body, or he broke his own hand, arm, or foot. We had some experienced bone breakers, who, for five rations of rice, would break a hand or foot. It would cost ten or twelve rations to have an arm or leg broken; after all, they needed greater expertise to ensure a clean break with no repercussions once it was healed.

Different methods to get out of work had a long-term negative impact in a few cases. We found out that after smoking iodine-soaked tobacco, one's lungs would show up on X-ray film with dark spots similar to those found in tuberculosis (TB) cases. A few enterprising men smoked cigarettes that had been soaked in iodine. Then they started imitating a bad cough. After a few weeks, they went on sick call and continued the annoying cough in front of the Japanese and American doctors. The Japanese were deathly afraid of TB, and when they heard the man coughing, they would order him into town for a chest X ray. Then the news would come back that the man had signs of spots on his lung and that he should be isolated from the rest of the men and the Japanese guards. A special room had been set up far from any other camp activities, and the men with signs of TB were placed here for the duration. They were allowed outside for exercise only thirty minutes a day; the rest of the time they were confined. Unfortunately, the TB room housed some men who really were infected with tuber-culosis. As a result, the ones who were faking it ended up catching TB from the ones who were truly afflicted.

Although Doctor Hewlett was very capable, competent, and extremely innovative in treating us, we were still well aware that all of his treatment and operations were performed without the necessary surgical instruments, medical supplies, or sterile conditions one could expect in a more normal hospital. To put it mildly, Doc operated wherever and whenever he could and under whatever conditions that prevailed at the time. He would not help us get out of work, but he always made those of us who took matters into our own hands more comfortable. Once one of us would get out of work due to an illness or accident, Doc would do everything in his power to keep us out for as long as possible, bearing in mind that the Japanese placed pressure on him to send at least 95 percent of the men from each barracks to work.

While working in the mine one night, I felt that if I had to go down in the mine the next day it would be my last. So I picked up a steel cable-car locking pin, about ten inches long and two inches in circumference, and placed it close to my *bento* box. I waited for the time when the Japanese miner working close by would leave and check on what was happening at one of the other laterals. Then I picked up the pin with my right hand, placed my left hand on the end of a skinned tree trunk used to support the ceilings, and with one mighty blow, hit my hand as hard as I could with the steel pin. The pain was excruciating. I did not yell but tears came to my eyes. I saw a huge red bump on my hand, and where the pin had pierced the skin, my hand started to bleed, just a little at first. I was sure I would not have to go back into the mine for a few weeks. A two-week vacation—with full rations because the injury occurred while in the line of duty, working for the emperor—was due me.

When the Japanese worker returned, I was pretending to shovel coal from a wall that we had just blasted down. After a few minutes and with the precision of an engineer, I placed my shovel far enough under the wall of coal to cause a slight break. Coal fell from the top and crashed down on the floor. As soon as this happened, I let out a yell and held out my hand so the supervising Japanese worker could see my damaged and, I hoped, broken hand. All went well so far. All the workers felt sorry for me and within minutes brought me a clean piece of cloth to wrap around my bleeding hand.

That night when our group entered camp, I was taken at once to the medics' office. Doctor Hewlett took a look at my hand and said, "Looks pretty bad, but you're lucky. It's not broken. You'll be able to go back to work tomorrow." I thought, Did the Doc know what I went through to try to get this darn hand broken? Did he know the pain I endured, the chance I took? Next time, I determined, I will get an experienced bone breaker to do the job, and get it done right.

When I went back to the mine the following day, I was sort of a hero in the eyes of the Japanese, who thought I was coming back in spite of a painful broken hand. I felt what they did not know would not hurt them, and I did not tell them any different.

Although I failed at my first attempt to break my hand, I succeeded the next time, and despite my earlier resolve, I did it myself. I did not want to run the risk of someone else doing it wrong and then having to suffer the consequences. I broke my hand about a month after the earlier botched-up job. It hurt so much more the second time. As I was right-handed, of course, it was my left hand that I damaged; after all, I did not want to take a chance of permanently injuring my good right hand.

One of the more ingenious inventions to get out of work was the home-made ulcer. Making an ulcer was really quite simple. One time when I wanted to get out of work in the mine, I first took a sharp instrument, like a pointed knife or pin, and pricked my foot, just above the ankle, about twenty times to make it bleed a little. Then I made a paste out of a little piece of our lye soap and some of the powdered lye we used in our latrine to sprinkle over our excrement. I then formed this paste into a small ball, about the size of a nickel, and placed it over the bleeding area and secured it with a bandage. The following morning when I removed the bandage, I found a nice burn scab. With a little work and a little pain, I removed the scab and in its place was a beautiful, fresh-looking ulcer the size of a nick-el. The medics confirmed that I had an ulcer forming and issued me a no-work order for a few days so the ulcer could start to heal. I was deter-mined, however, that my ulcer would not heal until I wanted it to.

To get out of work a little longer, I waited a few days and then did the same thing except I made the ball of soap and lye the size of a quarter. I placed it on the open sore and bandaged it overnight. The next morn-ing—voilà!—the new ulcer had grown to the size of a quarter. I did this for about a week, until the ulcer was half-dollar size, then I started to let it heal so there would not be any undue questions asked of either the medics or me. That one more week out of work was a great vacation.

The reason for always putting the ulcer on the lower leg was to prevent me from walking to the mine, and certainly it kept me from working in that dirty environment. The homemade ulcers were so real that no one could distinguish them from the genuine thing, not even the medics, though I am sure that somewhere along the line they had a pretty good idea of what was going on. At least two hundred other men used this ulcer ruse, and we put a crimp in the Japanese war effort. Although it was a minor crimp, it sure made us feel good at the time.

Getting out of work in the coal mine was a real challenge. Not only did a man have to break a bone, get caught in a mine cave-in, or develop ulcers on his legs, but he wanted to be sure that, whatever happened, it happened in the mine. That way, if he stayed in camp on sick call, he would still get full rations. If he had an accident while in camp that prevented him from working in the mine, he would only get half rations. And if he got sick, he only got two meals a day.

On a few occasions, a man in our group would start screaming, literally going berserk. The confinement within the mine, the working conditions, or the constant fear of dying caused many men to go off their rockers—some for just a few days, others for the duration. If the Japanese thought a man's dementia was incurable, they placed him in an isolation room adjacent to the TB room. If they thought he was faking it, however, they took him out to the parade ground, and three or four guards would hit him with wooden planks, rocks, sticks, their wooden slippers, and anything else they could get their hands on. This beating could last for upwards of an hour or two, depending on how the guards felt at the time.

In the meantime, I guess the word got out about my trade with Moto San, for I was approached by another Japanese worker in the mine who said he would pay fifty packs of cigarettes for a pair of size eight shoes. Another civilian worker in the mine wanted an American watch. I was in great demand as a trader of items found in our camp; I even traded with a few of our camp's guards. I got a kick out of it, and I always insisted that each trade include some kind of writing paper as part of my payment. I realized that this much-needed paper was crucial for keeping the medical records of those men, myself included, who would survive this ordeal. But for now, my job was to find a pair of size eight shoes.

I let the Javanese prisoners know that I was looking for a pair of size eight shoes, in good condition. I also announced that the price was no object. As I expected, it did not take long before one of the Javanese men contacted me, saying he had a pair of size eight shoes. He even brought them over to show me that they were just as good as new. He told me he wanted thirty packs of cigarettes and ten rations of rice and soup. I countered with twenty packs of cigarettes and ten rations of rice and soup. He accepted. All I had to do was arrange the trade, smuggle the shoes to the mine, and get the transfer of ten rations of rice and soup. None of these problems would be easy to solve.

Whatever my commission was on this transaction, I was really going to earn it. The only way I could get size eight shoes to the coal mine was by putting them on my size ten-and-a-half feet and walking them three miles to the mine. Getting the rations to the Javanese prisoner was another story. This part was going to be more difficult because he was in a different barracks, did not work on my shift, and had a different job. I was a shoveler, and he was an explorer, so we did not see each other in the mine. I did have an alternative, however. During the past six months, I had had occasion to negotiate with a friend of mine who had broken both legs in a mine cave-in and was since assigned to the kitchen staff as a "nail pusher."

Let me explain the role of a nail pusher. At mealtime, all the men from the same barracks went into the mess hall at the same time. When we first arrived in camp, the Japanese assigned to each man in a barracks a number that was his alone and was printed on his shirt or jacket. When the barracks leader was ready for the men to come through the chow line, the nail pusher would set up that barracks' board with all of the men's numbers on it. At each man's number there were two holes, one above the other, and when a prisoner came through the chow line, the nail pusher moved the nail from the top hole to the bottom hole to show that the prisoner had received his ration for that meal.

Because I traded for cigarettes and the men pulling kitchen duty within the camp had no such opportunity, I supplied some of the kitchen crew with cigarettes in exchange for extra rations. The first time I went through the chow line the nail pusher would only pretend to move my nail from the top position to the bottom. He would move it only after I went back in line for my second ration, the one owed me for the cigarettes I had traded. This worked out so well that I had planned on using it to pay the Javanese prisoner for his shoes. Unfortunately, when I explained what I had in mind to the nail pusher, he refused, fearing it could lead to a shakedown by others in the Javanese man's barracks if someone saw him returning for a second ration. I had to agree.

I renegotiated my deal for the shoes, and the Javanese prisoner settled for thirty packs of cigarettes and no meals. A pack of cigarettes increased in value as more time elapsed after the last cigarette issue, but at no time did a ration cost more than one pack of cigarettes. So, with the extra ten packs, the Javanese could at least get the extra ten meals he wanted.

All went well on the day I walked gingerly to the mine in the pair of size eight shoes. The cigarettes and writing paper were there waiting for me, and I was able to get them into camp with no trouble, just large blisters on the heels of my feet and my skin on the inside of my thighs rubbed raw.

My friend in the kitchen had been right about the shakedown. On one occasion, while I was collecting my payment of cigarettes and the nail pusher did not move my nail to show I had already been through the chow line, I heard the man behind me say to the nail pusher, "The guy in front of me has gone through twice. How about me? You don't want me to tell, do you?" After we went through the line and had finished eating, I waited for this fellow at the door to the mess hall. When he finally came out, I grabbed him by the collar, turned him around, and told him, "Don't horn in on someone else's deal. Go find your own. If I'm told about this kind of pressure again, I'll see you floating in the fire-water pool, and if I can't do it, I'll find someone else who will."

He did not say a word for what seemed like one full minute. Then he said, "You're right, I was trying to horn in. I was thinking of blackmailing the nail pusher, but that's not right. Don't worry. It'll never happen again, and I'll keep my mouth shut."

In spite of my trading, there still were many days that I went hungry. I was fed, but the small bowl of rice I got for each meal just did not satisfy my hunger. I knew others were hungry, too, so I got together a plan with three friends of mine in our barracks. We designed and cut a solid block of wood just a fraction smaller than a bento box. Then when we carried our ration of rice with us into the mine, one of us would also bring the small piece of wood. Once inside the mine, the one whose turn it was that day would eat all but a few spoonfuls of his rice. Putting the rice aside, he would place the carved block of wood into his empty bento box and then spread the leftover rice over the false bottom. It would appear that his box was full of rice. Then he would store his bento box in a very hot part of the mine so that the rice would sour. That night in the chow line, the man with the sour rice would show his bento box to the cook. After looking and sniffing at it to make sure it indeed was a full box of sour rice, the cook would say, "Throw it in the waste barrel. You have an extra ration due you today." Then the man two places behind the one who had just received the extra ration would dig down in the barrel for the piece of wood, and the next day he would get the extra ration.

This scheme went on for six or eight months but not every day. Sometimes, we would wait three or four days before the next person would use the carved block of wood for his free ration. We hungry men thought up more ways of getting more food. After a while we would sell the block of wood to someone in another barracks, and the "better eating system," as we called it, would continue for another few months.

It is important to understand that we did not take food out of the mouths of other prisoners. Maybe the cooks did not eat all they could hold that day, or the Japanese issued the kitchen crew more rice for feeding the men. We knew that the cooks gave rations away anytime they received something of value in exchange, so we figured that made what we did an acceptable practice. And not only that, we had fun doing something to help ourselves. In spite of the trading I did in the mine to earn cigarettes for extra rations, fully 90 percent of the 840 days I spent in that camp I did not get enough to eat.

Back in the mine, work went on as usual. We had a fairly good gauge of what was happening with regard to the war: if the Americans bombed a city in Japan, we would be beaten but for no apparent reason. If the Japanese lost a ship during a naval battle, we would be beaten once again.

The guards and the civilians would also get mad as hell when we would not believe their stories about how the war was going. At one point, one of the Japanese civilian workers brought into the mine a copy of that day's newspaper. On the front page as big as life was a picture of Hollywood, California, showing the intersection of Hollywood and Vine. Standing next to a street sign were four Japanese soldiers with their arms around two of America's famous movie stars, Rita Hayworth and Ginger Rogers. The headline I was told, said, "Hollywood beauties meet Imperial Japanese soldiers in United States' most famous city, Los Angeles." When I started to laugh, a Japanese overseer hit me across the face with the scoop portion of a coal shovel, breaking my nose, cutting a two-inch gash under my lower lip, and knocking a couple of my teeth loose. He simply wanted to remind me that the Japanese paper told its citizens the truth, and we should not laugh at or doubt the stories.

Most of the crews working in the mine had at least two Japanese civilians as overseers or guards. This arrangement made trying to get even for beatings an almost impossible task. Also, we could not do anything or escape afterward much less muster the energy or stamina to retaliate. We found out early that each of us had to play the game openly the Japanese way, but secretly, we had plenty of ways of evening the score with our enemy.

On one such occasion, we found ourselves working just a few hundred feet from a Japanese crew. Both of our crews were shoveling coal. First we drilled, then we blasted, and finally we started to shovel coal into the trough that carried the coal out to the waiting cars. We noticed that although they started at different points, the Japanese crew's loaded cars ended with our cars on the same single track leading to the unloading bin topside. As each car was loaded, we placed a metal disk bearing our group's number on a hook on the front of the car. These disks were used to monitor the number of loaded cars that each group produced, for an attendant would remove the numbered disk from each car that arrived at the unloading bin and would record it as a credit toward each group's assigned quota.

This particular day I was leader of our group, and we developed a plan to get credit for the Japanese group's cars. First, we had to take up some of our track leading to the main tunnel and move it so that we could push the Japanese workers' cars from their location onto the new track and into our location. Once we had accumulated six cars of coal produced by the Japanese, we moved the track to its original position and then placed our tags on the newly acquired coal-filled cars.

Our quota was ten cars of coal that day, and when the day was over, we produced ten cars: six from the Japanese crew and four of our own. When we arrived topside and waited for roll call, we were greeted with a gift of appreciation—a pack of cigarettes and an apple. We silently laughed and accepted our reward with grace and dignity while the Japanese group that had been working near us was chastised for only producing four cars of coal. Not one in the Japanese group would speak out and explain that something was wrong. Instead, they just stood at attention and responded with a loud, "Hai." That day we worked twice as hard stealing the coal as we would have if we had shoveled it, but we had the satisfaction of outwitting the enemy as well as making our small contribution to the war effort.

It was the beginning of winter, a light snow was falling, and our barracks were as cold as an icebox. Working in the mine at least kept us warm, so one day the Japanese told us, "For your health and welfare we will allow you to work in the mine an extra hour each day." Of course, no clock recorded our comings and goings; when we stopped working was all up to the civilian workers. Obviously, if we were still shoveling coal from a recent blast, we had to stay until it was all done. This one extra hour usually stretched to two.

One of my most interesting recollections of the years I spent working in the mine occurred around Christmastime. One of the Japanese civilians who was then working with us told me that he loved flowers and plants and asked me if I knew anything about flowers. I realized at once that if I said yes I might very well get out of doing some hard work. So I said, "Yes, I also love flowers. What would you like to know?" He explained that he wanted to be a horticulturist and wanted to know the English names for many of the plants and flowers. "Of course, I will help," I said. "Bring some pictures down into the mine, and I will give you the English names." This pleased him very much.

Although we had nicknamed him "Happy San" after the character in Snow White and the Seven Dwarfs, his real name was Sato Kibi San (Mr. Sugar Cane), and he asked me to call him "Sato San." His nickname came about because he was always happy-go-lucky; nothing seemed to bother him. He was only about five feet six inches tall, weighed about 140 pounds, and was all muscle. Sato San said he was thirty-five years old and that he had been married since he was twenty. Unlike most of the Japanese men I had come into contact with, he was polite to everyone—to his own countrymen as well as to American prisoners of war. In his own way, he seemed to apologize for his countrymen's cruel treatment of us POWs.

The following day, Sato San came down into the mine with a magazine filled with pictures of flowers, trees, and shrubbery. He was so excited he could hardly wait for our lunch break. Then, as we all sat down to eat, he came over and asked me to sit with him over in a corner of the tunnel. I knew right away what he wanted, only I did not know one flower from another. What in the hell was I going to tell him? Just the day before I had told him I knew all about flowers, but I sure did not expect a "test" on flowers the very next day. I flipped through the pages of the magazine quickly, spotting those few flowers that I did know. A rose is a rose is a rose, so that was the first one I recognized. Then I spent a long time telling him the colors of the various roses, four different shades of red, white, pink, and any other color I could think of. After about an hour, we all went back to work, and Sato San told me he would bring the magazine back the next day. What was I going to do? Then it hit me. He would not know the English name of one flower from another. So I developed a plan.

After returning to camp, I asked my friends who were from the southern part of the United States just to name a few flowers for me. I did not want their descriptions, just their names. I thought people from the South saw and understood more about flowers than city boys like me, who only rec-ognized flowers when they were in vases on a table.

After getting a dozen or so names of flowers, I went to sleep that night feeling that the next few weeks could be more relaxing than normal, in other words, with less work and more talk. I felt really good, not just for myself, but for our whole group, as we were all in the same boat together. If one sat out, we all sat out; that was the way our group voted when we started out. We had all assumed that a supervisor or civilian worker would someday take time out to converse with me, because I understood the Japanese requests better than most of the men in our group.

The following day, just as we had expected, our Japanese worker wanted to talk about flowers during our lunch break. All of the men sat down in a corner of the tunnel, took off their headlamps and buried them in the coal, laid back, closed their eyes, and did not make a sound. While the men rested, I took Sato San to a far corner of our work area, sat down with him, and went over some of the flowers in the magazine. Even though I did not know a tulip from a violet, here I was ready to bullshit this Japanese into believing I was a horticultural hotshot. I convinced myself all I had to do was remember names of flowers; after all, he would not know which flower was which.

On one occasion, when I reported for sick call and was allowed to stay in camp because of my "ulcers," Sato San asked a friend of mine whether he would take a gift to me. My friend certainly agreed. The next day Sato San brought a can of sweetened condensed milk into the mine and passed it to my friend to give me. The only way the man could bring a can of this type and size into camp was the same way I was smuggling in cigarettes, tied between his legs with dynamite cord.

That night, after our evening meal, my friend came to my barracks and presented me with Sato San's magnificent gift. I invited a few of my barracks mates to partake in a spoonful of this gold-plated treat. We all gathered around my sleeping mattress and, with happy smiles on our faces, started to savor the can's contents. We saved enough to put on our rice the following morning. I paused to think about what a friend I had in the mine and about my friend in the camp and the risk he took in bringing the gift to me.

After a few days out of work, I finally went back to the mine. On that first day back, Sato San was there to greet me. With a big smile on his face and a gleam in his eyes, he asked me in English whether I received the milk and if it helped me get better. I told him how much I appreciated the gift, and I was sorry that I could not give him a gift in return. He was such a gentleman. He said he understood and that all he wanted was for me to stay healthy until I returned home. Then we sat down and started all over again with the flower magazine.

His education continued for about four weeks, and each day he would bring into the mine a little something for each of us. One day it would be candy; the next day, a can of fish for us to put on our rice to add a little flavor. A few of the days he would give each of us a pack of cigarettes. He just wanted to show his appreciation for the time I was willing to spend with him and his sorrow for what we had to go through. Each day he would point to a flower in the magazine and ask, "In America, what is name?" I would then recall one of the names I had memorized. I would slowly pronounce the flower's name, try to spell it, and then write it down for him to take home and study. Each day when we finished, I felt like a fool, not knowing any of the true names for the flowers he showed me. I also felt guilty giving him these god-awful names for all of those lovely flowers. It became harder and harder to face him each day and to accept the little things he was always trying to do for us. During one of our sessions, Sato San told me about his always wanting to move to the United States after the war and to become a horticulturist at the Golden Gate State Park in San Francisco. That was his big dream.

Eventually, the workday would end, and we would make the same march back to camp, face the same guards, and do the same things at the same times. To relieve the boredom in our lives, I asked the Japanese officer in charge of our work detail if we could have a little entertainment on the day set aside for changing the shifts in the mine, or our day off, so to speak. To my surprise, he was happy about the idea, but he wanted me to give

him more specifics before making a firm decision. In addition, he also suggested that I talk to Major Mamerow. The next few days I was filled with
excitement. Planning something to do out of the ordinary—something
that would require creativity, organization, and a different kind of hard
work—was music to my soul. No doubt it was the best therapeutic medicine I could have had at this time of my life and in these circumstances.

# CHAPTER 12

# FUN AND GAMES

We were all tired of our forced labor and felt that we could not go on much longer. It was not just the work that got to the men, but the fact that we had nothing to keep our minds busy. Everyone in camp was bored with the daily routine of twelve hours of working, a little eating, and then a lot of dreaming. We needed something to take our minds off of our miserable circumstances.

I listened to some of my friends singing, others telling stories, and a few just hamming it up. Four fellows in my barracks had the sweetest harmony I had ever heard, and they entertained us by singing a few songs. That is when I got the idea for putting on some type of formal entertainment in camp, something we could look forward to each day off.

Based on the Japanese officer's suggestion, I asked Maj. John Mamerow what he thought about our putting on some type of entertainment in the camp. Major Mamerow quickly agreed it was a good idea and something we needed for the men's morale. He then gave me permission to address the group during evening roll call. I wanted to tell them about my idea and get some feedback from them. I asked first if they were even interested in this idea. Second, I wanted to know if any of them played a musical instrument or had other talents that we could use in putting together a show. If anyone was interested and able to recite poetry, act, sing, tell jokes, or do anything else that could amuse or entertain us on our day off, I asked them to see me in the mess hall after roll call. Imagine my surprise when I got to the mess hall and found about twenty-five or thirty men waiting for me.

Our inventory of interested and talented men consisted of two piano players, six men who played a variety of musical instruments, a quartet that had been singing together for almost a year, a variety of actors and storytellers, and five men who simply loved the idea of being female dancers in a musical. As the evening wore on, I realized we had the makings for a good musical comedy show. Everyone agreed to practice whatever part they would get in the upcoming event. The volunteers gave me unofficial authority to come up with an idea for a show and assured me that they would be behind me 100 percent.

Major Mamerow was present at that first meeting; he was as excited about it as I was. He said, "Ten-Spot, we need to do something to break the monotony here. If we don't, the men will go berserk. You can count on my help. I'll do anything I can." He then got permission from the Japanese to proceed with our plans.

The major was quite a man who never asked the men to do anything that he was not prepared to do first. He stood at least six feet tall and was well built, even under these conditions. With his nose a little out of shape and a firm jaw, he looked just like a prizefighter who was willing to take on all comers. Major Mamerow was about thirty-seven years old, an old man for what we had to endure.

On the day our group met, we agreed it would be great if we could have some type of entertainment every "rest" day. Major Mamerow warned us that we would get no special consideration and that we would still have to work every day in the mine, just like the rest of the men. We all agreed to the terms set out, and now we were ready for some action. When I analyzed the group of the volunteers, I thought immediately of Ziegfeld—not the man, but the follies.

During the following week, I used whatever spare time I had to plan a show. While walking to and from the mine, while eating, and even while shoveling coal, my mind was on getting a show together. My mind kept coming back to the film *The Great Ziegfeld,* and the more I thought about it the more I liked the idea of a follies. I reasoned there would be music that all the men would enjoy, dancing "girls" who would get a roaring welcome, comedians to make fun of our situation, dramatic scenes and poetry readings that might bring a little seriousness to the occasion, solo singers, and of course, our prize quartet to sing songs that would stir up memories as well as allow all of us the opportunity to sing along whenever we knew the words.

With this as our nucleus, six of us—all extroverts interested in doing some creative thinking—got together to develop plans for the show. We agreed to call the show "The Ziegfeld Follies of 1944." We would use the following introduction: "Brought to you through the courtesy of our camp commander, Captain Yuri, and his Camp 17 guards, here in the heart of Omuta, across the bay from Nagasaki, and through the courtesy of the emperor."

Now we had to locate a few musical instruments that our men could play, keeping in mind that those who played a wind instrument might not have the energy, the lip, or the chops for it at this time. Our Japanese commander obtained the few instruments we did get. The two fellows who played piano said they thought they could play with just a little practice. The rhythm man, the one who played drums, said he would have no problem at all following the others. His drum set was a series of empty boxes, with cymbals made from pieces of scrap metal found around camp or in the mine. He fashioned drumsticks from pieces of hard wood we found in the mine.

So, it was all set. We would start rehearsal the next time we had a day off. These were the only truly happy days of all the three and a half years I spent in prison camp, and I found that the men involved with the show had the same feelings. We felt good doing something creative, and the show got our minds off of the horrible past, the dismal present, and the uncertain future. Although we toiled in the mine for our full shift, after work we still found the energy to plan for the show. The show was our therapy. We rehearsed every spare minute, many times in lieu of resting or of doing something with other friends. The practice paid off, the show started to take shape, and we liked what we saw.

Then we faced the problem of making the dancing "girls" look their part. We wanted them to be scantily dressed and to wear huge headpieces. Our camp tailor, a man named Timmons, was too old to work in the mines so he repaired the men's garments and shoes. He had a sewing machine that made the work easier. Timmons was a jolly guy, and despite his wartime weight loss, he still had a roly-poly look. When we asked him to sew the costumes—skimpy bottoms and halter tops—he agreed at once. In fact, Timmons told me that he would use his influence to obtain anything we needed.

Finally, I came up with an idea for the headpieces. We would use cardboard boxes that the Japanese usually threw away, cut them into various shapes and sizes, and then glue on some sparkling pieces of crushed glass. The Japanese let us have the cardboard boxes and reluctantly gave me a few dozen empty glass bottles of various colors and textures that we deliberately crushed into tiny particles. We then sprinkled them onto the headpieces to act as glitter. We then asked the cooks for a couple of cups of raw rice, rice that was never washed or hulled. They complied, with Major Mamerow's encouragement.

Then began the creative part of this endeavor. First, we cut the cardboard into shapes representing diamonds, hearts, circles, triangles, and so on. Each headpiece shape was about fifteen to eighteen inches high and eight to twelve inches wide. We then took the raw rice, placed it on a smooth surface, and rolled it with one of the large empty bottles. In no time at all the rice started to form a powder, or a rice flour. We mixed it with water to form a paste, which we smeared all over the headpieces. We then sprinkled the glittery crushed glass over the sticky cardboard headpieces. A headpiece was then secured to each dancer's head atop a turban-style headdress. Under the circumstances, the "girls" looked great, and they loved every minute of it.

The men who wanted to be the dancing girls were all homosexuals. In the years we men were incarcerated at Camp 17, we knew who the gay men were, all eight of them, but we who were not gay just ignored those who were. Many evenings we could see a few of the gay men caressing their lovers and stroking their hair, but it did not involve us, so we overlooked their sexual preference. I must admit I could not see this "lovemaking" without feeling a little sick to my stomach. I had never been exposed to this lifestyle, so it did offend me. As far as the show was concerned, however, I knew their lifestyle would not interfere with our putting on a good show. The men who took the part of the dancing girls became an integral part of the show, and by the time it was over, my feelings about them changed. I saw them and spoke to them as individuals. Once I understood what their lifestyle was all about and once I realized they were just like me in every way but one, I became more tolerant.

The night of the show, I was as nervous as a cat on a hot tin roof. I worried about how it would go over and what the men would think of it. I also hoped the Japanese would accept the jokes making fun of some of their commands and movements. This was one of the parts that I had volunteered to play, and before putting the sketch in the show, I had asked one of the Japanese officers if he thought it would be all right. After giving him a preview of what I was going to say and how I was going to act, he laughed and said, "Yeroshi" (very good).

The show opened with the song, "A Pretty Girl Is Like a Melody," and when the "girls" came dancing out, dressed like real Ziegfeld girls, it brought the house down. All of us who worked on the show were so thrilled when we got a standing ovation. To my surprise, our Japanese camp commander had invited a few of the higher-ranking Japanese officers from Tokyo to attend our performance. These officers brought with them Baron Mitsui, the owner of the coal mine in which we were working.

At the end of the night, we knew the show was a hit. Everyone loved it, and they showed it with their clapping, whistling, and yelling. To this day I am not sure if the show was that good or if the men were simply that starved for entertainment, but either way, we accepted the accolades with grace and dignity. Immediately after the show, I was introduced to the baron, who informed me that he had asked the Japanese high command to give me a special privilege: I would be allowed to send a message home to my family as my reward for producing and directing the show. The following morning, the Japanese gave me a piece of paper and a pencil and told me to write down whatever I wanted to say, with certain limitations.

They said they would broadcast my message over the radio, and most certainly it would be picked up by our government for relaying to my family within a few weeks.

I wrote the following message, which the provost marshal general of the United States received on June 17, 1945, almost a year after I was granted permission to write it. He, in turn, sent the telegram to my mother and father in Chicago. In addition, the message was also picked up by half a dozen shortwave radio enthusiasts in the United States and aboard some of the U.S. Navy ships at sea. My family received a few copies of my message that people forwarded, the most interesting of which was a phonograph record of the message as read by a Japanese announcer.

> Washington, D.C. June 17, 1945, 9:49 A.M. Following enemy propaganda broadcast from the Japanese Government has been intercepted, quote.

> Dear family: Hope this message finds everyone in the best of health. I am feeling fine. Glad to hear about Louis' new son. Tell Laura I still love her as much as ever and I hope she is waiting for me. Inform Mrs. M. Martin of Maywood that Bob is with me and is in good health. Also notify Mr. K.J. Bashleban of Parkridge, the same. I hope to hear from you soon. Write and send pictures. Closing now with all the love in my heart to all and give my regards to relatives and friends. Your loving son. Lester . . . Fukuoka, Japan.

Of course, I did not know what happened to this message until I returned home, but when I wrote it, I felt real good that I could let my parents, Laura, and my buddies' parents know their sons were OK. Bob Martin and Jim Bashleban were also from Company B, my outfit, and when I had the opportunity to write home, all I wanted to transmit was that at the time of the message we were all right.

With the Great Ziegfeld show out of the way, we began planning for the next show. We had hoped to put on a show of some kind every off day, or rotation day, which came every ten days. During the next fourteen months, we produced thirteen shows; at least nine were musicals, and all of the men were able to sing along with the performers. The continued planning, rehearsing, writing, directing, and creating new ideas allowed me, along with many others, to forget the day-to-day tribulations of being a prisoner of war. My work in the mine continued as before, and I continued trading not only with the Japanese in the mine but with the guards in our

camp as well. One thing had nothing to do with the other. Although I was
engrossed with the work of the entertainment program, survival was still
my top priority.

One necessary element for the human body's survival is salt. The Japanese never gave us any salt in all the time we were in Japan even though
we sweated profusely while working in the mine for them. Our camp
health committee—Doc Hewlett, Major Mamerow, Lt. John Little, and Lt.
Steve Jenkins—decided that we should build a salt-gathering contraption,
whereby we would bring in sea water and, through a series of operations,
would end up with sea salt.

Our camp was located on the edge of the bay, so saltwater was going to
be easy to obtain. We built a desalting plant that consisted of a trough to
bring the water into camp, a fifty-five gallon empty drum to boil water in, a
fire pit, and a series of wooden ladders down which the water would drib-
ble, leaving the granules of salt behind on the wooden steps. After the first
successful week of "making" our own salt, each man in camp was given a
spoonful to put on his rice or soup. Unfortunately, some of the fellows
traded for more salt and got heart palpitations from ingesting so much salt
at one time.

While trying to get enough food and at the same time build his financial
empire, a prisoner would trade cigarettes for rice that would be collected
at some future date. It could be for as soon as tomorrow or as far away as
two weeks. I played this supply-and-demand game. It worked like this:
when cigarettes were in great supply, the trading value for rice could be as
high as ten cigarettes for one ration of rice. As time wore on and the cigarette supply was literally going up in smoke, one cigarette would buy one
bowl of rice. Then when a pack of ten cigarettes was issued by the
Japanese, the value of a ration of rice went way up again. This fluctuation
showed supply and demand at work. When one ration of rice would trade
for ten cigarettes, that was the time to sell rice. Conversely, when cigarettes had not been issued for five or six weeks and one ration of rice could
be bought for only one cigarette, that was the time to buy rations of rice.

Next came the hard part. First, I figured out how I could save or store
rice for five, ten, or more days without it becoming sour and inedible. By
trading rice for one day or more in the future, I could keep my investment
intact and at the same time keep my rice hot and fresh. With maybe ten
rations of rice to trade it was necessary to offer "rice today for rice tomorrow." If that failed to get action, I would offer "rice today for rice next
week." If I also felt that it was necessary to get "interest" on my investment, I would offer "rice today for rice and soup next week."

Second, after I had accumulated sixty or seventy cigarettes, I had to find
a place to store them for safekeeping while I worked in the mine. We had to

hide our valuables because a few men in camp turned to stealing in order to get more to eat. I hid mine under my barracks, near my sleeping area. Even if the tobacco got stale, it still had a market value of one cigarette.

Of course, there were always some men who would trade their future meal of rice without any idea how they would pay back their debt. If they could not pay back the ration when due, they would end up being harassed, beaten, and deprived of food by those to whom they owed that meal. Often a man who ended up owing more than he could repay would seek what we established as "bankruptcy protection." To many of the men in camp, it seemed like the mafia at work, but food was more important than money could ever be. When a prisoner gave someone his ration of rice, he gave the recipient his very existence, his lifeline; and he had a right to expect the debt to be paid as promised.

Our bankruptcy laws were different than those back home. First of all, the bankrupt person had to pay back everything he owed. Nothing was forgiven. Second, while he would have to give up one meal a day until he had paid his debt, he was allowed to eat two meals a day without fear of being molested by those to whom he owed rations. Our informal bankruptcy court would put out a notice to all barracks announcing the name and number of the person who had just declared bankruptcy. Then anyone who had rations due him from this person would come to headquarters at a specified time and face the bankrupt person for proper identification and acknowledgment of his debt. Once the preliminary details were completed, the court prepared a list specifying the day and the meal (breakfast, noon, or evening) that would be paid to the person(s) owed the ration(s). Because some of the men to whom bankrupt men owed rations would still try to strong-arm their way into collecting their debts, we established a system whereby a guard, usually one of the bigger men, would walk through the chow line each meal with the bankrupt person. The guard prevented anyone who was not on the list for that day or that meal from getting the ration of rice. The guard got paid one ration from the bankrupt person's food rations every ten days for providing protection and for administrating the list of rations due.

Everyone in the camp knew who the bankrupt person was. Anyone trading with the bankrupt person from the date of bankruptcy was told that he would do so at his own risk. He would never be able to file a claim for food from the bankrupt person.

After doing so much trading during the year, I decided to do something different. Even after my twelve-hour stint in the mine, I had to keep active. I put together a raffle. As the prize, I wanted to offer the unusual: an entire Red Cross package. To locate all of the items would keep me challenged for a month or more.

I had enough cigarettes stored away to be able to trade for just about anything, so my first stop was the barracks of the Javanese prisoners. I told them that I was looking for one of everything normally found in a Red Cross package and that I would pay in advance with cigarettes. Within three days, I had located and negotiated for at least half of the items I sought.

Knowing that I was on my way to success, I started to sell tickets for the raffle, which would be held in thirty days. I obtained the numbered tickets from a Japanese civilian I was trading with. The writing on the ticket was in Japanese, but the numerals were Arabic. Because the tickets could not be duplicated, the probability of cheating was greatly reduced. Each ticket, or each chance for the Red Cross package, cost the buyer one package of cigarettes. I was gambling on the idea that every one of us wanted a full Red Cross box, and I encouraged the men who did not have a full package of cigarettes themselves to team up with other men who also did not have enough cigarettes for a wager.

During the next thirty days, I located every item normally found in a Red Cross box. My total purchase price for the entire contents of this box was 420 packages of cigarettes.

In the thirty days that I sold raffle tickets, I collected 675 packages of cigarettes. I hid cigarettes all over my barracks, and I gave more than one hundred packs to Doc Hewlett for the men in the hospital ward. My close friends in camp shared the remaining profit from this unusual adventure.

We held the raffle on one of our days off. At our noon meal in the mess hall, the number was pulled, and the winner jumped up on one of the tables. He shouted, "I'll live now, my dream's come true! This is the second thing I ever won in my entire life—the first was being drafted!"

I also shared the cigarettes with about ten kitchen helpers and cooks. At the evening meal, I traded for all the rice and soup I could eat. I felt real good about the whole episode. As I was enjoying my soup and rice, all of a sudden I felt an excruciating pain in my jaw. I pushed my food aside and made my way to the medics' barracks.

Doc Hewlett was still there. He took one look at my mouth and told me I would have to go into town and see one of the local dentists. Doc did not have any provisions for any type of dental work. That night I just sat up and bit down real hard on a piece of cloth. I could not sleep the whole night.

The following morning, upon my arrival at the medics' building, I was told to wait outside and that one of the Japanese guards would drive me to town to see a dentist. The truck and driver arrived about an hour later and drove me into town. The ride only took fifteen minutes, and when we arrived the dentist was waiting for me. His office was old and filthy, and the dental chair looked like something out of an old western movie. The dentist motioned me into the chair. After I had opened my mouth, he said, "Tooth out, OK?" I did not believe he was actually asking me a question; he was just telling me what he was going to do.

As he gathered his instruments on the tray in front of me, I saw that he was not going to give me a shot of Novocain. He was just going to pull the tooth. He grabbed his forceps, and without any warning, he proceeded to pry the tooth loose. With one mighty jerk, he pulled the tooth out of the socket. The pain was awful. I clutched the arms of the chair until my knuckles turned white. I must have moaned and groaned, even yelled a little, but I do not remember what I did when he pulled my tooth. I was so happy when the dentist showed me the tooth and said, with a big grin on his face, "Finished. You can go now." I climbed out of the chair, bowed slightly from the waist, and said "*Arigato goraimasu*" (thank you). Then the guard pulled me out the door and down the steps to the waiting truck.

Upon arriving back in camp, I was immediately put into the next group of workers going to the mine. The Japanese were not going to allow me a day off work and wait for my regular group just because of a toothache.

# CHAPTER 13

# "WE HONOR YOU
# WITH HEAD CUT OFF"

I had returned from my twelve-hour shift in the mine, eaten on the good side of my mouth, and retired to my bunk for a little rest, when all of a sudden an American runner from Japanese headquarters dashed into my barracks. He hollered, "Tenney, you're wanted at headquarters on the double. Let's go!" I grabbed my shoes and started to put them on while walking, as the runner hollered, "Make it snappy. This is no laughing matter. Mamerow told me to inform you to tell them everything; they know it all." What in the hell was he talking about? I started to run as fast as I could, thinking, what can they want me for? What have I done? Then right before I got to Japanese headquarters it dawned on me that someone may have told them about my trading with the workers in the mine.

We entered the headquarters building, and the runner escorted me to a large room with only a small desk, a chair, and a lamp. Sitting behind the desk was our Japanese camp commander. Standing alongside it was the camp interpreter. At the door stood two Japanese soldiers, with their rifles cocked and aimed at me, as if they were needed to protect the commander from the likes of me. I walked into the room, stood at attention, and waited for instructions.

Within a few seconds, the commander spoke to me in a soft, pleasant voice. The interpreter said, "The commander wants to know your name." As the question sank in, I realized that no one had ever asked me that before. The only time anyone had asked for my name was when I met Riley, the guerrilla leader, and then he only said, "What's your moniker?" Tenney was all I told him, and that was all he wanted to know. (Only the men from my own outfit knew my name. During the march, no one had cared who anyone was. In Camps O'Donnell and Cabanatuan, we were all so tired and sick that no one bothered to ask a man his name, not even the doctors. When Moto San had asked my name, I had simply told him Tenney San.)

Here I was in the Japanese commander's office, and he wanted to know who he was talking to. I replied, "Lester Tenenberg, sir." He then asked me a series of innocuous questions, such as how old I was, if I was married, and where my home was in the United States.

Then, out of the blue, he asked, "Do you know anyone in this camp trading American goods for Japanese goods?" Without blinking an eye, I said, "*Hai.*" The commander said to the interpreter in Japanese, "*Donata desu ka.*" The interpreter looked at me and demanded, "Who?" I quickly replied, "Me, sir."

I could see that both the commander and the interpreter were taken by surprise. They blinked their eyes, moved closer to each other, and looked at me as if I was crazy. With wide open eyes, they asked, "Did you not know it was against Japanese law?" I answered, "No sir, I didn't know it was not permitted." Then they asked who I traded with and what I traded. I said that when a Japanese man asked me if I could get him a tube of tooth-paste, I just said I could. I did not even know who the Japanese man was; I was just trying to do what he asked.

"When did you do this trading?" they asked. Remembering the runner's instructions from Major Mamerow—whom I trusted—to tell them everything, I made up my mind to do just what he recommended. I answered, "I have been trading for about five months." Next they said, "Tell us everything."

I began by telling them that I traded because I was hungry and the work in the mine took more of my energy than I could get from my ration of rice. I told them I did not know any of the Japanese guards or civilians by name and that I could not even identify them because it was dark in the mine. I did say that I traded with more than one or two Japanese, but I stopped there.

At first the commander was furious. He jumped up and grabbed his sword. I thought he was going to cut my head off right then and there. Then just as quickly, he sat down and became calm, almost as if a load was removed from his mind. He dismissed me, telling me to go to my barracks, which I did gratefully.

The following day I was made aware of the serious consequences of the trading incident. At our noon meal, I was in the mess hall just finishing my rice and soup when in came two Japanese guards with fixed bayonets. They had no sooner entered than they started to holler, "*Ni-hyaku roku-ju-yon*" (number 264). They were looking for me. I raised my hand and hollered, "*Hai!*" The guards ran to me, grabbed me, and pushed me toward the door. Once outside, they took each of my arms, twisted them behind my back, and led me to the guardhouse in the center of the compound. I was shoved inside the building, and to my surprise, there were seven other men in there. All of them, I learned later, had been trading with workers in the mine.

They pushed me into a cell with such force that I was thrown about two feet inside, and when I fell, my head struck the floor hard enough to open a two-inch gash in my forehead. I had the cell—a space about five feet long, four feet wide, and five feet high—all to myself. It was not big enough to stand up in or long enough to lie down in. It had solid walls on three sides and bars in the front; I could not see the other men once I was inside. About two hours later, the interpreter came in and informed me that I would get no food and only one small glass of water per day. And, I was told, tomorrow we traders would learn what our punishment would be. I was scared stiff, wondering what was going to happen.

At the morning's roll call, we were all marched out of the guardhouse and onto the field in front of the entire prisoner population. After the roll call, the Japanese commander marched over to us. He seemed very nervous and paced back and forth in front of us. He informed us that we had to be put to death for trading with the Japanese in the mine. Trading was against Japanese law, we broke the law, and we had to be punished for it. With a wave of his hand, we were surrounded by about ten soldiers, all with rifles and fixed bayonets. Two of the officers were swinging their samurai swords from right to left, in a full arc. One of the officers abruptly assumed the warrior's position, squatting down with his feet planted firmly on the ground and the sword held poised over his head with both hands. Then *swish-sh-sh!* He swung his sword down, catching the wind as he imitated a blow to the neck of a victim.

The guards lined us up, and the commander told each of us how we were going to die. "You, bayonet. You, shoot death. You, number 264, you do good show; we honor you with head cut off." At that moment I lost control over my bowels. I defecated in my pants.

The Japanese commander paraded in front of us like a pompous ass, but he was an ass with the power of life and death. First he said, "Like in America, who wants last cigarette?" Not one of us wanted a cigarette. Then he said, "Like America, who wants blindfold?" Again no takers. Finally, the commander said, "Like America, anyone have last words to say?"

At last he gave me an opening. Obviously, the next move was going to be my last, so I said I would like to say something. He told me to take one step forward and say whatever I wanted. The speech I gave that day was truly extemporaneous, but I believe it saved my life and the lives of the other men waiting to be executed. I stepped forward with my hands tied behind my back and with tears in my eyes. My voice cracked as I said, "Men, don't try to fool the Japanese; they are very smart. Do what they say and you will live to see your families again. Do what I did, and you will die here in Japan." The Japanese camp commander began waving his hands and hollering, "*Yeroshi, yeroshi*." His face glowed with excitement, he stood more erect than ever before, and his chest was puffed out to its fullest. He impressed us all as being one very happy man.

I rejoined my fellow prisoners, who were waiting for their executions to begin. Then the commander shouted, "No more heads cut off! No more shoots to death! All men go to *esso* [guardhouse]. One glass of water and one meal each day for ten days, then free." I could not believe my ears. The tears in my eyes, first caused by fear, were now from happiness. The six other men condemned to death gave muffled sighs of relief.

The guards led us back to the guardhouse and put us in our cells. I was alive, that was all I could think of. I had just met one more goal in my quest for returning home. On the second day in the guardhouse, our one meal was brought in by my best friend, Bob Martin, who had been injured in the coal mine and was unable to walk without a very bad limp. He was assigned kitchen duty, and one of his responsibilities was to feed anyone in the guardhouse. When he got to my cell, he filled my bento box to the very top and packed it down real tight to get as much rice as possible in the box. Eating one ration a day was not going to be easy, but I would have to contend with it if I wanted to go home someday.

The following evening one of the guards came in, and as he looked at me, he banged the metal bars of my cell with a club he was carrying. He screamed at me, using a Japanese expression that we Americans knew well: "*Dami, dami*" (no good, no good). He looked at me and put his fingers to his lips, indicating that he wanted me to keep quiet. He then whispered, "Number 264, what are you doing in here?" I told him I was caught trading with the Japanese in the mine. I quickly added, "I didn't tell I was trading with you, only those Japanese in the mine." At that moment his face broke into a wide smile. He laughed a little and said, "*Tomodachi, yeroshi*" (my friend, very good). As he left, he waved to me, mumbling something under his breath.

Around midnight I heard a hissing noise. As I opened my eyes, I saw the same Japanese guard outside my cell, trying to get my attention. When I became fully awake, through the bars he handed me two large rice balls, with the rice firmly packed around a little something extra in the center. One had pieces of chicken and the other had small pieces of fried fish. I quickly and quietly devoured the food; actually, it was the best meal I had had in months.

Between Bob and the grateful Japanese guard, when I was released from the guardhouse at the end of the ten days, I weighed several pounds more than when I went in. Still, I did not recommend this weight-gaining program for anyone else.

# CHAPTER 14

# BOMBS AND BEATINGS

The winter of 1944 in Japan would be hard to forget. Food was in short supply, and the U.S. fighting forces were getting closer and closer. As the war moved directly into Japanese cities, the people became more and more resentful of our very existence. The guards and the civilians in the mine found all kinds of excuses to beat us. Instead of merely hitting us with their hands or fists, the Japanese used shovels, picks, and sections of steel chain, which was used to move coal from one place to another. They swung the chains around overhead until they reached a high speed. Then, using the chain's momentum, they inflicted brutal blows upon our bodies.

I was hit with the swinging chain three times, all within a month or two and always for the same reason: the Americans had bombed one of the Japanese cities and killed some of the residents. I had expected some form of retaliation. When I was hit with the chain the first time, it fell across my lower back. I felt as if my back had been broken in two. Down I went with a THUMP, flat on the mine floor. When I was finally able to get up, I was bent over like a question mark. Someone took me to the spot where the train picked up riders who wanted to go topside. Once I arrived at the top, I asked if I could get into one of the tubs. Apparently, the officer in charge noticed my bent position and the bleeding marks on my back, so he allowed me in the tub at once. The hot water felt real good on my back muscles, and I soaked in the water at least thirty minutes.

After I hobbled back to camp, Doc Hewlett put me onto a stretching bed he had made out of thin slats of wood. The bed formed a slightly convex curve from the head to the toe. With my head at one end about six inches lower than the center and my feet also six inches lower than the center, I felt my body being stretched out. I stayed in this position on and off for three days; then when I felt better, I went back into the mine.

The second and third times I was hit with the swinging chain happened within a few minutes of each other. During this attack, when one Japanese worker finished with me, he handed me over to another one. The first man had caught me squarely in the chest with the swinging chain and knocked me about twenty feet from where I had been standing. The second man hit me right in the middle of my face. The pain was so severe that I forgot about the pain in my chest. My cheekbones were gashed; the skin above my eyebrow was broken; my nose, once again, was smashed; and my entire chin was gushing with blood. When the second Japanese worker saw what he had done, he became very nervous. He realized that if he had hurt me too severely I would not be able to come back to work the following day, and that was not acceptable to the mine operators.

When I got back to the camp that day, Doc Hewlett just looked at me in disbelief and asked, "Did you want to get out of work that badly?" While the effects of this beating appeared only on my face, Doc noticed a grating sound as well as a bone movement in my left shoulder and right leg. He found my left scapula was broken near the shoulder. He put my left arm into a sling that was pulled tight across my chest to prevent any movement of my arm or shoulder. Then Doc said, "You can still shovel coal with one hand." He could not find anything wrong with my leg except a severe contusion.

The medics watched my progress for weeks. After a consultation between the doctors and the medics, they decided that I had a disease of the bone and that they should amputate my left arm at the shoulder. At my insistence, they agreed to wait till the last possible moment before operating. Until the operation, however, I still had to work in the mine because by this time so many men in the camp were too sick to even walk to the mine, let alone work in it.

I tried to comprehend why the Japanese were beating us so often and so severely. I even accepted the fact that the grief and frustration of finding out that a relative or good friend was among the dead or injured in that day's bombing could cause our captors to go temporarily insane. In the mine one day, a Japanese civilian went berserk when he saw me picking at the coal in a very relaxed manner. Without warning, he rushed at me and screamed in Japanese that I had killed his father. He brandished a pick in wide circles over my head and then crashed it down onto my skull. I was lucky; it hit me broadside instead of with the point. I was knocked unconscious for what I was told was a good five minutes.

We did not have newspapers to tell us how the war was going, but we used the way we were treated as a barometer. We would often infuriate the guards or Japanese workers by laughing while being beaten. Of course, the reason for our odd reaction was that we were in effect getting our news on the war's progress.

It was near Christmastime when I received some mail from home. The cards did not say much—after all, they had been censored by both the Japanese and the Americans—but just getting some mail made me feel that I was missed. One piece was postmarked August 2, 1943, from Detroit, Michigan, and I got it sometime in November 1944, fifteen months later. It still was nice to hear from my family. Better late than never.

During this period of our captivity, the Japanese commander called me into his office for questioning. The interpreter handed me a Christmas card that was addressed to me but had been opened by someone else. The card had the normal holiday salutation and then personal signatures all over it. The front, the inside, and the back of the card were covered with names. Under each name, I saw was a code number, and the Japanese wanted to know the secret of the code. Nothing short of telling the commander the actual code would do, but I did not know what the code was. In fact, I did not even recognize any of the names on the card. I saw names like The Shelbys, and then right below the name was a number, say 1204. It was this number they wanted to know about. I told them I could not help them because I did not know anything about a code.

My answer did not satisfy the commander, and he told the interpreter to bring in the guards standing right outside his door. When the guards came in, I heard the commander give them a series of instructions. One phrase I caught was, "*Bassuru, bashhinai*" (punish, or punish him). The guards hollered for me to stand at attention and then began beating me with their rifles. Only a few minutes later, they started hitting me with a wooden baseball bat. They continued to ask me questions about the Christmas card and the numbering code. I kept insisting that I did not know.

After a good thirty minutes of continued beating, it all of a sudden dawned on me that the numbers under the names were apartment numbers. My folks lived in a building of about forty-eight apartments. At last I had figured out the code, but I did not know how to explain it to the Japanese. I began by saying, "*Watasewa hanashi*" (I will talk). They stopped beating me and pushed me to the commander's desk. There I asked for a piece of paper and a pencil, and I drew a picture of a large eight-story building, with six apartments on each floor. I then numbered each apartment and placed a name alongside each. I looked at the commander, whose face flushed with anger. It then changed to a slow smile as he said, "*Ah so*," meaning he understood. He laughed and tried to brush aside his embarrassment. He then handed me a few more pieces of mail and allowed me to return to my barracks. With blood oozing from my face, head, and back, I fell on the floor next to my bedding, read the brief messages on the cards, and then passed out.

In the spirit of the holiday season of 1944, Major Mamerow informed all of us Jewish men that he wanted to help us celebrate Chanukah. He offered to post a series of American guards at the entrance to an air-raid shelter so that those of us who wanted to attend religious services inside could do so without the Japanese disturbing us. We had discovered long ago that the Japanese were very anti-Semitic. In our conversations, a few of them insisted that Adolf Hitler was doing the right thing in imprisoning the Jews, that the Jews caused the war, and that President Roosevelt was Jewish. They even went so far as to accuse John D. Rockefeller of being a Jew. According to the Japanese, if a man in the West had power or money or owned a newspaper or radio station, he had to be Jewish.

In our camp of about fifteen hundred men, only ten were Jewish; that is, only ten who would admit to being Jewish. On more than one occasion, while working in the mine, a Japanese civilian worker would ask a prisoner, "Is number 313 Jewish? Is number 264 Jewish?" A positive answer always resulted in a severe beating for the Jewish prisoner. So, a strong possibility was that the camp housed men of Jewish ancestry who refused to be identified for fear of Japanese reprisal. Major Mamerow did what he had promised for Chanukah, and we Jewish prisoners enjoyed services without any interruptions. When the services were over and we walked out of the bomb shelter, the Americans standing guard greeted us with a hearty, "Happy Chanukah . . . and a Merry Christmas."

Although Mamerow lived to come home and kept his vow to see us as often as possible by attending almost every reunion of the Camp 17 survivors, he never really seemed to be a happy man. As the officer in charge of the prisoners at Camp 17, he saw so many of his men die at the hands of the Japanese that it was just too much for him to cope with. He carried the burden of every beating, of every torture, and of every needless death by disease and starvation with him to the end. At times while still in camp I thought I could sense an impending breakdown just under the surface of Mamerow's steadfast exterior.

When Mamerow died in 1991, we survivors paid him our respects and honored him as one of the few real yet unsung heroes of the war. He practiced what he preached, he gave of himself to all who needed him, and he was a true leader of men. What he could not accept, however, was that although he did everything he could in Camp 17, the Japanese still killed dozens of his men. The Japanese high command had made its message clear: even a lowly private in the Japanese army had authority over any American officer of any rank.

We saw an example of this mind-set when Doc Hewlett refused to send the required number of prisoners to work in the mine. Out of a barracks of fifty, the Japanese expected no less than forty-seven to report for work each day. On this particular day, our barracks had only forty-five men who were well enough to go down into the mine. Of the other five, three were in the hospital ward, and the other two were so sick that Doc Hewlett had put them on bed rest. The Japanese guards responsible for taking us men to the mine would not accept Doc's explanations. Although we did not know it then the owners of the mine, the Mitsui Company, gave our camp's guards a monetary bonus for every prisoner who went to work each day. Thus, greed was the main incentive for the guards' insistence on a high labor turnout.

When Doc Hewlett refused to send the men on bed rest to work that day, the guards threatened him with time in the *esso*, or guardhouse. The Japanese and Doc went round and round on this request. Doc Hewlett declared, "The men in the hospital ward belong in the cemetery, and the men on bed rest belong in the hospital. I won't sent any man to work who I believe is too sick to work."

The guards brought the Japanese commander into this disagreement, and he sided with the guards. They gave Doc Hewlett a choice: put forty-seven men from barracks number 4 to work or go into the guardhouse. Doc Hewlett said, "My mind is made up. I can't send any of these sick men to work today. I would rather be put in the *esso*." As he was marched away, the commander called after him, "One more chance to obey, or you will stay in the esso for ten days, with one bowl of rice and one cup of water. You'll be sorry."

In stunned disbelief we watched as they marched Doc Hewlett to the esso, removed everything from his pockets, and pushed him into the main guardhouse. We were all horrified that a good man like Doctor Hewlett, a man to whom most of the Japanese guards came for medical advice, was being treated like a common criminal. It was heartbreaking, but through it all the Doc stood tall. He briskly marched and entered the cell without ever looking back. Everyone in the camp, all fifteen hundred of us, stood at the end of that night's roll call and shouted out in unison, "Give 'em hell, Doc!" Some of the men talked about striking to get him released, but we quickly dropped the idea when we realized the futility of such an endeavor. Where did we think we were, back in the United States?

The following morning, when the early shift was ready to leave for the mine, the guards accepted only forty-five men from barracks number 4. They never mentioned the men in the hospital or on bed rest. In addition, the guards did not say one word about Doc Hewlett. We continued to go to the mine, as usual, and when needed, we would go to the medics and be treated by one of the medical corpsmen.

We all counted the days while Doc was in the guardhouse. During roll call on the sixth day, to our surprise, out of the guardhouse strode Doc

Hewlett. He marched right into line where he belonged and answered "*Hai*" loud and clear. If we had not been afraid of retaliation by the guards, we would have all yelled, "Welcome back!" Doc needed a shave and looked a little thinner, but his spirit was not broken. In fact, if any spirit was broken it was that of the Japanese high command. Doc Hewlett had not given in to the brutality of the Japanese guards and officers of Camp 17; he had refused to compromise his medical ethics.

After Dr. Thomas Hewlett returned home, he received many awards and decorations for his bravery in the face of Japanese death threats and for refusing to obey their barbaric commands. Like Major Mamerow, Doc labored under the sorrow from the days he was powerless to save men's arms, legs, or lives, and he always felt a sense of responsibility for these losses. He grieved from the time he returned home until June 1990, when he carried that burden with him to his grave.

As the years wore on, we became more accustomed to our everyday situation and to the unyielding brutality. Our monotonous routine—get up, eat some rice, walk to and from the mine, shovel and load coal, suffer beatings by the Japanese for the slightest infractions, take a shower, go to bed—was a sorry and unpleasant one but one we had to follow. Thank God we had the occasional diversion of preparing for one of our shows. This gave me a little break from the otherwise meaningless days. We were always on the lookout for any diversion, and we even looked forward to the days the *benjo* (toilet) personnel came by to empty the contents of our latrines.

Each barracks had four toilet cubicles. About once a month, these outhouse type latrines required emptying. Surprisingly, we did not have to do this dirty work. Instead, the Japanese sent into camp three *benjo* girls, whom we would eye with excitement. After all, we rarely saw a girl up close, and we had not even talked to one for what seemed like a lifetime. The *benjo* girls pushed or pulled a cart that held a very large drum-shaped receptacle that had a hinged lid at the top. The girls also carried long poles with scoops at one end to ladle out the waste. After bringing the waste up from the depths of the toilet, the girls would dump it into the receptacle. Of course, to do this work, the girls had to enter our barracks, that is, our sleeping quarters. This was all that a few of the men needed, just a chance to get "friendly" with the girls.

During one of the *benjo* girls' work details, an aggressive man in our barracks propositioned one of the girls. He offered her an apple, which he had obtained in the mine for meeting his shoveling quota, for a few minutes of pleasure. With some giggling and a shy motion with her hands, she nodded her head yes. Within a few seconds the girl was herded into one of the sleeping rooms and disrobed, and our friend had an exciting three or four minutes. Afterward, the girl quickly got dressed, bowed politely, and went outside to join her friends. As the girls pushed the cart away, we could hear them giggling and whispering to each other.

We talked about this escapade for days. The word was out: "We screwed the Japanese!"

# CHAPTER 15

# OUR WAR IS OVER

In late June 1945, we listened to the Japanese civilians in the mine worry about the war coming to their homeland. Then in camp early one morning, we heard the sound of aircraft, loud and clear. Within seconds, we saw streaming down at us from the west six fighter planes bearing the emblem of the United States of America.

The planes roared in directly overhead, and the pilots dipped their wings at us as they flew low over our area of camp. Then, they made a tight turn and came back. This time they came down and across the side that housed the Japanese guards. As the planes neared the buildings, they opened fire with their machine guns. After strafing the entire Japanese side of the camp, they then turned, dipped their wings once again, and sped away. At that moment, the better part of valor caused us to control our obvious emotional rejoicing, and instead, we patted the backs of those standing closest to us, smiled, and said, "The time is getting closer."

As soon as our planes left, the guards rushed us into the bomb shelter. They hollered, they pushed, they poked at us to hurry. We got into the shelter as quickly as we could, but not without wondering whether we would ever get out.

About four hours later the guards told us to come out, that it was all clear and safe for us. They cut our food ration in half that day and hit more of us than ever before, and we knew why. We got the message: the Allies were winning the war, and time would soon tell the story of how the rising sun fell. When I was beaten that night for a minor infraction of the regulations, I stood tall and took it with pride. Their time was coming, I thought, maybe not today, but soon, real soon.

On August 6, 1945, we noticed a marked difference in the attitude of the Japanese civilian workers in the mine. In fact, the guards were also obviously uneasy. We figured it was just a lull in the storm, but the guards were suddenly so docile and not their usual sadistic selves. Something was going on that we knew nothing about. We discussed how we would be able to tell that the war was over. We all finally agreed that we would know that the war was over when (1) we did not have to go to work in the mine, (2) we received a Red Cross food parcel, (3) we got all the rice we wanted to eat, and (4) we did not have to salute the Japanese guards any longer. We had this all figured out. No one would have to tell us when the war was over. With these four signs, we would know.

That morning we marched to the mine and entered to go to work as usual. We took our assignment, picked up our tools, and started the long walk down to our working lateral. Just as we started down, a Four Striper stopped us and told us to take one of the cars down. We wondered why all of a sudden he was showing some concern for us. Down in the mine, the civilian workers were waiting for us. Sato San took me aside and said, "Many Japanese killed by big bomb." Their tragedy meant our ordeal was almost over, but I did not dare smile or show in any way my happiness. I knew something was in the air just by the way the Japanese civilians talked among themselves. We finished work that day and rode up on one of the cars. Then we walked back to the camp, as usual; but the people on the streets did not look at us, and the guards walked in front of us without saying anything to us, which was most unusual.

August 9, 1945, started out like any other day—up at dawn to eat a little rice, then walk to the mine to shovel some coal, and so on—but later, something very different happened. Looking toward Nagasaki, about thirty-five miles southeast of our camp, we saw what appeared to be a large floating cloud, with a large stemlike cloud at the bottom. The top of this cloud looked perfectly flat, sort of like a pancake. In fact, Doc Hewlett called it a mushroom cloud because of its stem and large upper body. Doc made a bet with me that the war would be over in ten days. I took the bet, saying that cloud we had just seen was a floating airfield and that the Japanese were going to have airplanes land on this cloud and float it over the United States. There, I continued, the Japanese planes would take off from this floating airfield and bomb their targets. We made the bet for dinner at the finest restaurant we could find whenever we met again after the war.

We later learned that we had witnessed the rising cloud of the second atomic bomb—the one dropped on Nagasaki—that the United States used against Japan. Not in a million years could we have dreamed of a weapon like the atomic bomb and the destruction it caused. As far as Camp 17 was concerned, there is no doubt that dropping this devastating bomb saved our lives, as well as the lives of millions of our Allies and our enemy, the

Japanese. Although about two hundred thousand civilians were killed in both Hiroshima and Nagasaki, the benefit to us prisoners was immediate.

Since July, our sick bay had more cases of malnutrition, beriberi, and downright depression than it could handle. We had lost all the weight, strength, and energy we could afford. There was nothing left to lose, except our lives. As our energy level dropped, so did our ability to work efficiently and with a safety-first attitude.

Freedom came at last on the morning of August 15, 1945. Our first shift left for the mines the same time we always did, but we never went down into the mine. When we asked what we were supposed to do, the Japanese told us, "*Yasumi kondo*" (rest time). While topside we saw the Japanese huddled together, talking, and no one was working. In all of our years in Japan, this was the first time we did not see some type of work being performed. Without explanation we were marched back into camp. Excitement in camp grew, for the first of our four indicators that the war was over had happened.

At noon when we went into the mess hall and gave our bento box to the cook, he filled it to the top and pushed more rice into the box until it could not hold any more. Our soup, which usually was nothing more than warm colored water, was full of vegetables. I looked at some of my friends and just grinned. The second of our four signs had taken place.

Excitement ruled the day. Most of us could not even talk about it; we did not want to wish ourselves something before it was real. For the first time in three and a half years, I really felt that we were going to be released. Then the Japanese ordered everyone into the mess hall, where we were handed a Red Cross food box—a *full* Red Cross box, one box per man. The war had to be over. What were we waiting for? At that moment, we felt as if God really was on our side.

Our excitement built up to a frenzy. Was this the end of the war? Were we going to be free men by the day's end? The only thing left on our list was not to have to salute the guards. Because I spoke Japanese a little better than most of the other fellows, I was prodded to go out onto the parade ground area and just say hello to one of the guards, without saluting or bowing. I took the challenge. Out of the barracks I went, and I walked on the parade ground until I saw a guard. With one mighty heave of my hand, I waved at him and said, "Hello." He smiled at me, bowed, and said in English, "Hello."

I knew then it was all over. The war was over! At twenty-five, I was going to live to see my family and Laura. I was going to be a free man any minute now.

# CHAPTER 16

# "AMERICA AND JAPAN NOW FRIENDS"

Before long we were all herded out to the parade ground. We lined up, waiting for roll call or for whatever was going to happen. Nothing the Japanese could do to us would surprise us after three and a half years of putting up with their idiosyncrasies. During our incarceration in Japan, we kept asking ourselves, "What will happen to us when the Americans win? How will we be treated when the war is over? Will the Japanese try to kill us because of how badly they have treated us?" Our concerns increased as time went on, for we were at the mercy of the Japanese and did not know our fate.

As our bodies stiffened to attention, we heard the roar of trucks coming onto the parade ground. We counted seven trucks, each with a manned machine gun mounted on the roof of the cab and dozens of soldiers standing on the running boards or in the bed of the truck. The camp commander strutted onto the field in his usual peacock fashion. He looked as if the Japanese had just won the war, and he was here to inform us of their victory. Once in position at the center of the group, he cleared his throat and said, "America and Japan now friends. War is over." Then he jumped onto the running board of the lead truck, and with the other six trucks following, he pounded his fist on the top of the truck and hollered, "*Yuka*" (go).

We were left standing on the parade ground. For a moment no one spoke a word. The silence was overwhelming. Then we realized we were free. We cheered. The war was over! We had won! My only thoughts at that time were, How do we get out of here? When can we leave? It's over. . . . By golly, it's over, over at last. I *will* see my family again! Thank God.

While we were still dazedly standing on the parade ground, Major Mamerow cautioned, "The war is over and we will be going home soon, but for now we have to keep our dignity and remember we are Americans."

His first order of business in camp was to put one of the navy officers who was in charge of the mess hall and kitchen into the guardhouse for safekeeping. Major Mamerow knew that this officer, if he was not protected, was fingered for murder by at least a dozen of the men. This lieutenant commander, who happened to be an Annapolis graduate, was directly responsible for the deaths of at least three, and possibly four, fellow Americans. He also turned over to the Japanese four Americans who were tortured unmercifully—whatever the enemy wanted to do was all right with him—because the hungry men had stolen food. Because of his inhumane treatment of fellow American POWs, we had nicknamed him "The Henchman." Without exception, no one in Camp 17 had the slightest regard for this officer. In fact, we all wanted him court-martialed, if and when we ever returned to the United States.

After attending to the protection of our mess officer, next we established a prophylactic station in our camp for those POWs who wanted to go into town and have some fun with the geisha girls or whatever other girls were willing and available. Some of us also went into town to look for a few of the civilians or the guards who had been beating us unmercifully these past three years. We certainly were not hoping to have a drink with them or to chat. What we wanted was to give them the same treatment they had given us, except we wanted it to end in a lynching or something close to it. Apparently, however, word got out to the civilian miners that we were looking for those who had punished or tortured us prisoners. Most of them seemed to have just melted away. We did manage to find a few of the workers, and we accomplished our goal: we got even. We beat the few guards we found with our fists—not with sticks or stones—until there was no life left in them. Maybe we went a little berserk, but we did what we had to do. Although we also sought out the guards from Camp 17, most of them were long gone by the time we went looking for them.

In the early afternoon of August 18, we heard the loud roar of aircraft approaching from the south. As I looked up, I was flooded with emotion, for flying low in the sky was the largest and the most tremendous airplane I had ever seen. As it came over our camp, its bomb bay doors opened and we saw a hole so large that we bet our tanks could have entered it, side by side, with plenty of room left over. The aircraft made a large loop around our area and then made a pass, coming in low over our parade ground. At just the right moment, as we were looking skyward, dozens of parachutes floated out of the bomb bay with precious cargo attached. As the packages left the airplane, their chutes opened, filling the sky with unbelievable color. Slowly the parachutes drifted to earth with their cargo of much-needed food, medical supplies, and clothing.

When the first parachute hit the ground, three cases of canned fruit salad broke open, and the fruit salad was strewn all over the ground. We ran to the spot and started to eat the food with our bare hands. We laughed, we cried, and we could not believe our eyes. Our air force had found us; we were not as isolated as we had thought.

When the second aircraft came over our camp, someone in the airplane threw out a black leather cylinder. Inside we found a map of Nagasaki, Kumamoto, and Omuta, where our camp was located. The note attached to this canister explained that an atomic bomb had been dropped on Hiroshima. The second fell on Nagasaki, but if it had been closed-in due to bad weather, our area was the alternative. Omuta, with all its mines and shipping capacity, would have been the target area. The note went on to explain the damage the bombs did to Hiroshima and Nagasaki. It was then we realized just how lucky we were.

The next couple of days were stored in my memory bank as filled with total carefree happiness. All I knew was that I was going to see my family and, of course, Laura. During these moments of pure joy and happiness, I let myself think about Laura. I thought, She was so beautiful, any man would want her. She was the loveliest person I had ever known. What if she didn't know that I was alive and well? What if she thought I had died years ago—on the march, on the ship, or maybe during the last days of fighting on Bataan? Then she might not have waited for me. I shook myself out of this train of thought. Then I talked myself into believing that whatever was to be, was to be and there was nothing I could do about it. In fact, that philosophy of not worrying about things I have no control over is still with me today. So, with that thought in mind, I concentrated on planning to get home as soon as possible.

The following day an American newspaperman by the name of George Weller, from the *Chicago Tribune*, entered our camp. We wondered how in the hell he got to our prison camp. We all started to ask him questions, but he beat us to the punch. He started telling us about everything involving the Japanese and our war with them. He explained the atomic bomb, how it was dropped, why it was dropped, and its devastating effects. Next, he wanted to interview a few men from Chicago, and I volunteered. Afterward I introduced him to Bob Martin and Jim Bashleban. During our conversation, he said U.S. airplanes had landed in Kanoya, but that it would be about a week or two before we would be released and put aboard a ship headed for home.

A few days later another B-29, the largest airplane in the world, flew over and dropped supplies. First out of the plane were clothes, then medical supplies, and last, more food. As one of the parachutes began its descent, the cases of food it was carrying broke loose and started to tumble to earth. One of my good friends who was on the field, waving to the pilots and yelling good tidings, thought they were coming down right on him, so he ran away. We watched as the cases that broke away from the parachute seemed to follow his every step. Then he screamed as a breakaway case hit him on the back of his leg, right below the knee. We rushed him to the hospital barracks, where Doc Hewlett began attending to his injuries.

That night while I was in the hospital ward, I overheard two of the medics talking with Doctor Hewlett in front of my room. "We should amputate tomorrow," said Doc. "He'll feel better when it's over with." Not me, I thought to myself, I'm not going to lose my arm now that the war was over. I'll just take my chances. About an hour later, Bob Martin came over to see me, to ask how my arm and shoulder were doing. I told him what I had overheard and said, "I'm getting out of here tomorrow morning. I'll find the Americans somehow. I won't stay here for them to cut my arm off. No way!"

Bob agreed with my decision and said he did not want to wait around any longer either. "So we'll both go and seek our release," he said.

We began making plans right then and there to head for Kanoya, where George Weller had told us the U.S. forces had landed. Where was Kanoya? How far away was it? How do we get there? How long will it take? We had a dozen questions in our mind but only one resolve: if we wanted freedom, we would have to find it.

# CHAPTER 17

# LOOKING FOR THE AMERICANS

Early in the morning of September 11, Bob Martin and I walked out of Camp 17 in search of the Americans. We each carried a small musette bag that contained the few personal possessions we had accumulated during the last three years. I had my bible (*Prayer Book for Jews in the Armed Forces of the United States*), my *Pocket Book of Verse*, an extra shirt, a pair of pants, some cigarettes, and a very primitive cigarette lighter. I had made it from a piece of flint, a three-inch piece of steel, and a four-inch piece of hollowed bamboo with some kapok stuffed down into its carved-out center. If I held the bamboo and the flint, which almost touched the kapok, in the same hand and then held the steel in my other hand and struck the steel against the piece of flint, I could cause a spark. When positioned properly, the spark would end up on top of the kapok-filled bamboo, and after blowing on it, the kapok would glow red-hot without a flame. I could then light a cigarette from this contraption.

Bob and I walked into the little town of Omuta and boarded a streetcar headed for the railroad station. Once we arrived, we asked directions to the train for Kanoya. We were two cocksure Americans without money and wearing Japanese-style prison clothes in Japan after the surrender to the U.S. forces. The humiliated Japanese had just admitted defeat in a war they thought they would surely win. Upon reflection, we were actually very dumb. Anything could have happened to us, from being murdered to being taken prisoner once again.

Some Japanese told us what train to take and warned us that we would have to transfer trains at the end of this run. We did not care; we just wanted to find our troops. The train arrived about an hour later. We boarded it and sat in a railroad car that was almost empty. Nobody bothered us all day long. Finally we came to the end of that train's scheduled trip. We got off the train, and the stationmaster escorted us into the terminal. There we were greeted with bows, smiles, and hot tea. The stationmaster insisted that we wait in his inner office, where inquisitive local citizens would not bother us. We did not argue. We were willing to do just about anything to get to Kanoya, never dreaming of the potential danger.

That evening the stationmaster informed us that the train we wanted was not leaving till the following morning. He generously brought us a home-cooked meal along with a large bottle of sake. At one point, two Japanese military officers came in. They bowed to us and took off their scabbards and swords. With a flourish, indicating defeat, they handed them to us.

A little later that night, the stationmaster brought us pillows and blankets. He promised that he would see to it that we were on the train to Kanoya the following morning. He bowed politely, took four steps backward, and then left us.

It was all so hard to believe. Here we were all alone in a small Japanese city, ten days after the Japanese surrendered, and being catered to by several Japanese people. It felt good and gave us a real emotional lift. By the time we finished eating and talking to the people who had gathered around us, we were so sleepy that we stretched out on the wooden benches in the stationmaster's office and fell sound asleep, without a worry in the world. What a difference a few weeks makes. We were free, and for the first time in three and a half years, we felt like it.

Just as promised, the following morning we woke up to find a train standing at the station with steam coming from its engine and a crowd of people milling around the closed train doors. The stationmaster came into the waiting room, where we had been sleeping and brought us breakfast. We had a small glass of sake, a bowl full of rice, two small pieces of fried fish, a cup of hot soup filled with vegetables, and, of course, a cup of tea. Bob just looked at me, and we both burst out laughing. Could this be real? Was it really happening? Only a few weeks ago I was being beaten to within an inch of my life, and today the Japanese could not do enough for us. I said to Bob, "Take advantage of everything offered. We don't know what tomorrow will bring."

After we finished eating and thanking the people who brought us the food, we went to board the train. We quickly saw that there was no room for us in any of the cars. The train was jam-packed with men, women, children of all ages, and a few soldiers. I saw a Japanese army officer standing on one of the car's steps, holding onto a railing. I moved closer to him and said in Japanese, "Give me your sword. We are the winners." Without a moment's hesitation he stepped off of the train steps, unbuckled his sword and belt, and handed both to me. He then bowed and in Japanese said, "We are sorry. Take this in friendship." With that he got back on the car steps and began to cry. I felt sorry for this soldier, but not enough to give him back his samurai sword.

With the train filled to capacity, the stationmaster led us to the engine of the train. There, he told us to climb aboard; we were going to ride in the engineer's and fireman's seats. We played engineer for the three-hour ride to Kanoya, while the fireman and engineer hung onto handles on the outside of the locomotive. I blew the whistle and rang the bell, proclaiming our victory and our freedom, all along the route. It felt good. Happiness like this may never come again, so I made the most of it.

The engineer and fireman were very polite to us. In fact, they even offered us the contents of their bento boxes for our lunch. We were so thrilled just to be there, however, that we refused their gracious offer. Then at about noon our train started to slow down as we approached what we thought was Kanoya. Within minutes our train came to a sudden stop. The engineer bowed and smiled, then he stood at attention and pointed to the east. "*Koko ni Kagoshima, Kanoya roku-bamme mariu*" (Here is the city of Kagoshima, Kanoya is six miles east, that way). "That way" meant we had to go the six miles in a boat, for Kanoya was across a small bay.

When we got off the train in Kagoshima, Bob and I were shocked to discover that on this train were five other American ex-POWs who had heard the same rumor that the Americans were in Kanoya. We had a good laugh about how all seven of us, from three different prisoner of war camps in Japan, were roaming around Japan, with little knowledge of the language and absolutely no money but with lots of guts, determination, and happiness.

Getting to the other side of the bay meant we had to commandeer a vessel of some kind that could safely make the trip and carry seven of us. We found three boats at the dock that we thought could make the trip. We chose one of them and went over to talk with the captain. We explained as best we could that we had to get to the other side of the bay to meet with the Americans who were there. We got excited because the skipper of the boat confirmed right away that Americans were on the other side of the bay in Kanoya.

When we asked to be taken across, the skipper replied, "*Ni-ju-bamme yen*" (twenty yen), stating his fee for the trip. We did not have any Japanese money, and I was the only one who had anything of value, about ten packages of cigarettes. In response to his fee, I pulled up on the sword I was carrying, took the ten packs of cigarettes from my pocket, and made a deal. I could tell by the way he looked at us that he did not like my terms, but realizing the position he was in, he agreed, "*Watashi wo kimasu*" (I will come). With that, we all boarded his thirty-five-foot fishing boat and were off to our final destination in this search for the U.S. Army Air Force.

While we traveled the six or seven miles across the bay, we sang and joked. We must have seemed mighty strange to the captain, because with a laughing gesture he put his hand to his head and slowly made a circular motion with his fingers, indicating "crazy." We did not care; we were free and happy. In just a short period of time, we knew we would find what we were looking for.

Finally the boat pulled in at a small dock, about twenty feet from shore. We grabbed our meager possessions and hurried onto the land. As I got off the boat, I screamed, "Free, free at last!" All seven of us walked to the road and then sat down and had a good cry or laugh, depending upon our emotional reaction. The area was out of a picture book, with lush green grass and bushes, flowers blooming in all the colors of the rainbow, and the water lapping at the shore. As we looked toward the mountain just south of our position, it was obvious to us that the Americans, if any, were going to be somewhere up the mountain. We decided just to wait until we found some form of transportation before venturing uphill.

We waited about twenty-five minutes, and all of a sudden we heard the sound of a motor straining up the hill. As the truck approached us, we stood in the center of the road and flagged it to a halt. We simply told the two Japanese men to get off the truck and rest, for we had decided to take the truck up the hill until we ran into an American someplace on the mountain.

I guess because of both my knowledge of Japanese and my personality, I took over as leader of this small contingent of ex-prisoners. I asked Bob to do the driving, and I sat in the seat next to him while the other guys piled into the bed of the truck. We were all as happy as could be. About a half hour later, at dusk, there in the middle of the road stood a man about six feet four inches tall in a military uniform and what appeared to be a German army helmet. In all the photographs I had seen prior to World War II, the German soldiers wore helmets that came down close to their ears. The helmets we wore were World War I vintage, known as "Dough-boy" helmets, or nothing more than a domed top with a brim about three inches deep.

The soldier we had come across stood in the middle of the road with his arms outstretched, signaling for us to stop. As we did so, I jumped out of the truck to look this guy over. I noticed he was wearing a dark blue arm-band with the initials MP emblazoned on it. Could he be an American military policeman? I walked up to him, made a fist, and hit him square in the stomach. The punch was sort of a "Hi ya" punch, not hard, just a friendly gesture. He did not even flinch. He just looked at me and the way I was dressed and demanded, "Who in the hell are you? Where the hell did you come from?"

All seven of us hollered at the same time, "It's about time! Where you guys been?"

I told the MP who we were, where we came from, and who we wanted to see—his commanding officer. He jumped on the running board of our truck and led us into the camp. Within minutes we were surrounded by army personnel, wondering who the hell we were. At last, the flight commander came over to our truck to welcome us on behalf of the U.S. Army Air Force and the United States of America. It was a thrill I never in my life will be able to forget. We really were free men now.

That evening we had dinner with all the men. The officers allowed us to order anything we wanted. And the first thing we said was, "All the rice we want, a steak, and to drink, milk." We ate whatever they gave us and drank whatever was put in front of us. We were like kids at a picnic, eating and eating until we could not hold any more. They told us that the following morning we would be flown to Okinawa aboard a B-24, a new bomber, so this evening we should do whatever we wanted. I asked for a hot shower, white sheets, and a real pillow. After talking to the men most of the evening, I finally went to the barracks assigned me for the night and fell sound asleep within minutes on a bare bunk without white sheets or a pillow.

At 7:00 in the morning, I heard the men starting up the airplanes' engines. I got out of my bunk, found the latrine, and had a good, old-fashioned bowel movement. I had not had anything like it for years, and all seven of us talked about our similar experience that morning over breakfast. It was not exactly table talk, but then again, no one knew us or our health problems the way we did. Our talking about it produced happy talk, talk that made us all laugh and, I might add, made all of the airmen in the mess hall laugh, too. At about 8:30, we boarded a B-24 bomber and took off for Okinawa. It flew smoothly like a bird in the sky—not a ripple, not a bounce, nothing to indicate that we were on a military aircraft.

# CHAPTER 18

# MEETING MY BROTHER

Our plane landed on the Okinawa airfield that was built by the U.S. Navy Construction Battalion, otherwise know as the Seabees. When our plane finally came to a stop and the stairs were lowered, allowing us to deplane, the seven of us just stood and stared out the door in total disbelief. There on the runway were hundreds of airplanes, all sizes and types. We had never seen anything like this in our whole lives.

As we walked down the plane's stairs, a group of U.S. Navy and Army Air Force people assisted us with our walking and with our minimal but precious personal possessions. As I handed my musette bag down the stairway, a voice called out, "Lester, Lester, you're here!" I was slowly able to identify this voice. It was that of my brother, Bunny. (Willard was his real name, and his shipmates called him Bill, but he was always Bunny to me.)

"Oh my God," I said, "is this for real?" With tears in my eyes and happiness in my heart, I ran as fast as my legs would carry me toward my brother. While I was trying to reach him, he was also running in my direction and reaching out to grab me. We touched hands, then hugged each other as best we could. We both cried tears of happiness. I just never expected anything like this to happen to me. I was so surprised to see my own brother here in Okinawa. Bunny was in the navy, a member of the construction battalion, and built airfields. I was so excited, I could not wait to start asking him questions about the folks back home and, of course, about Laura, my dearest Laura.

What had happened to make this meeting with my brother possible was another chance meeting my brother had had with a medic from Camp 17. A few days earlier the medical corpsman had come to Okinawa the same way I did. My brother had met him and asked if he happened to know me.

The medic exclaimed, "Oh, you mean Ten-Spot. Yeah, he's OK. You just wait a few days. I bet he'll come by—but be prepared for a sick-looking guy, with some medical problems." That was all my brother had to hear. Although Bunny had enough points to get out of the service and go home, he decided to wait a few more days, just to see if I came through. (Points were earned by such things as years of military service, overseas duty, marital status, one's number of children, and so on.) What a surprise for both of us when I showed up—we hugged, laughed, and just about went crazy walking away from the airplane. I was not sure who was the happiest, he for finding me or I for seeing him. Either way, Bunny had found his proverbial needle in the haystack.

The Red Cross had arranged for a photographer to record this happy occasion, but all I wanted was a few minutes alone with my brother to ask a few questions. Bunny told me that everyone was fine, even Bill, my athletic brother, the one I wanted most to imitate because he had always been able to do just about anything he wanted and do it well. "Yes, even Bill is OK now. He lost a leg during the war being a good Samaritan during a snowstorm in Cleveland. Everyone else is fine. Joe and Fay are still in Detroit. Harriet married Martin, and he's in the Navy. Lou and Edith are doing well; they have a new son, named him Richard. They're all doing fine."

Lou, hearing his name brought back memories. When I was thirteen years old, I decided I wanted to run away from home and go to California. I visited my brother Lou at his office in downtown Chicago, told him my plans, and waited for his offer of help. After all, I did not have any money for such a long trip, but I was sure Lou would help me out. Just as I had expected, he said, "Please write mom and dad every week to let them know how you're doing." Then he asked, "Do you have enough money?" That was just what I had been waiting for, so I answered by saying, "I don't have much. Can you help?" Without a moment's hesitation, he went to the cash box he kept in his desk drawer, pulled out twenty three-cent stamps, and said, "Here, at least you'll have stamps to send a letter home each week." I was devastated; that was not the offer I had expected. Without money I certainly had no place to go. I left my brother's office, boarded a street car, and headed back home. Funny how some memories never leave me.

It was good hearing about the family, I thought, and just mentioning their names gave me a chill. But why has Bunny not said anything about Laura? By now he had to know I was not interested in hearing only about everyone else. What is wrong? I wondered.

Just as I was about to interrupt, Bunny continued, "You know, Les, Laura was informed that you were missing in action, presumed dead. She waited three years; she's a wonderful girl. Les, Laura thought you were killed in action, and she didn't hear anything about you for, oh, so long. Les, Laura got married a few months ago."

My legs felt like rubber, and my face must have turned stone white. My body started to shake, then tears welled up in my eyes. Laura! I could not, or better still, did not want to believe it. How was I going to survive without her? All those days, weeks, months, years—all I ever dreamed of was coming home to my wife, Laura. Now my dream was shattered.

My brother was in tears. Obviously, he did not know how to handle what he told me. To make him feel better, I decided to deal with it. I rapidly regained my composure and said to my brother, in the best matter-of-fact-manner I could muster, "I expected it. I didn't think she would be able to wait this long." Then I said, "I'm a survivor, Bun. Everything will work out, you watch and see." Then I cried inside.

Still trying to hide my shock, I introduced Bunny to Bob Martin. After a few minutes of joking about how good we looked, my brother asked us to join him at his outfit's headquarters for dinner and a good night's sleep. He had informed his commanding officer about the possibility of my coming through Okinawa and was told that if I came through, I could be their guest.

Next, Bunny asked me why my arm was strapped to my side. I explained as best I could what had happened. He insisted that we go to his bivouac area so that I could see his company doctor and find out what could be done about the arm.

When we arrived at his company headquarters, Bob and I were introduced around to all of the officers and men. They asked what we would like to eat and what else could they do for us. After telling them that any good American chow was going to be a happy change, I then mentioned my dream of white sheets and fluffy pillows. The commanding officer, after hearing our requests, said, "You fellows can sleep in the hospital ward. It's the only place with clean white sheets and pillows just like you described."

Bob and I were then introduced to the doctor. After a cursory examination of my arm, he told me to remove the sling arrangement and to exercise my arm as much as possible. When he took the sling off, my arm was only about two inches in circumference. Until that moment, I had not given much thought to the problem since I had left Camp 17. So that I could exercise my arm, the doctor tied a rubber ball around my wrist and told me to squeeze the ball as often as I could. Then he told me that I would receive a thorough examination when I got back to the States. The doctor repeated his instructions: I needed to exercise the arm, get some meat on the bone, and restore some of the muscle.

Now that the examination was over, I said, "OK for that. Now, where's the chow line?" The doctor had me step onto the scale. Bunny gasped in disbelief as the doctor said, "A little shy of 101." I was surprised, for I knew I had weighed 185 pounds when I took my enlistment physical. Here I was now, truly just a shadow of myself.

At about that time, the cook said, "Come and get it! Chow time." All of the men made way for Bob and me to be first in line. Did we eat! We were told to take whatever and however much we wanted, the treat was on the Seabees. That night, after telling our story to dozens of men sitting around the mess hall, we went to the hospital ward and crawled into our beds between those clean white sheets we had dreamed about so often.

At first, I could not sleep. I kept thinking about Laura, my future, and what I was going to do now that my dream was crushed. Then I came to my senses and remembered how Laura had saved my life. She gave me the dream I needed, that something to hang onto. I had focused on her in my dream about the future, and without that dream, I felt I might have perished years ago. I realized that in her own way Laura had always been with me. It was because of her that I was in this comfortable, clean bed now. I told myself that the first thing to do was sleep, then afterward I could tackle the world.

# CHAPTER 19

# BACK TO THE PHILIPPINES

On the next day Okinawa airfield received a hurricane warning, so our flight to the Philippines had to be delayed. Bob and I did not mind the delay at all. We had already been eating, for about an hour, a breakfast with all the things we had dreamed about for so many years. We actually had all the bacon and eggs we wanted, plus hash brown potatoes, bread with butter and jam, and milk. We each had four glasses of milk before we were through.

At just about that time the storm hit the bivouac area, and the Quonset huts this group of sailors called home flew away. The hurricane lasted about two hours, and for a while Bob and I did not think we would ever get to the Philippines. During the worst part of the storm, all of us were herded into the only brick building within a twenty-five-mile radius. We were mighty lucky to have this building so near. In spite of the raging storm and the crowded conditions in the building, Bob and I talked of the events and challenges ahead. By afternoon the storm had subsided enough that we could leave the building. The first question I asked when we got out was, "When is lunch?" Once again the men in the kitchen gave us anything we wanted, and that was steak and milk.

That night I stayed up with my brother until dawn. We had a great deal of talking to do about people, places, and things. I wanted to know what my dad was doing now, how my mother had taken the past years, and whether any other family members were in the service. One question would lead to three others; one answer would elicit two more responses. I learned that Laura had received my monthly allotment for the past three and a half years.

Then when she decided to get married, she sent my parents a check for the whole amount. I tried to steer any conversation away from her. Although it was not easy, I had to do it if I hoped to maintain my composure.

Because of the storm's damage, we stayed in Okinawa another day. We were housed in a tent near the airfield, and a makeshift kitchen was set up just for the eighteen POWs who had come from various prison camps in Japan and through Kanoya. My brother stayed with me that day, and he was flabbergasted at the food the cooks prepared for us. I remember well the meals we had while in Okinawa. For breakfast the second day I had six fried eggs, half a pound of bacon, half a loaf of bread with a quarter pound of pure butter, a small steak with french fried potatoes, and a quart of milk.

Then by noon we were hungry again. We ate the same stupendous way four or five times a day, only stopping to rest, talk or go to the head (what the navy types called the latrine). At no time did anyone give us any medical guidance in our eating habits or our dietary needs. Eating everything and anything as often as I wanted seemed like the right thing to do then, but a few years later it proved to have severely damaged my stomach.

At last a B-24 was ready to take us to the Philippines. We were informed that we would be housed for a short period at the 29th Replacement Depot just on the outskirts of Manila. There the army would give us medical assistance and allow us to wire our families of our release and the status of our health.

The army could not have found a more cooperative and enthusiastic group of men anywhere. Everything the army wanted to do with us was OK. All we wanted was to go home. We only knew we were free men who were going to eat well. Most of us did not give a second thought to our health; it just was not that important at the time. We had too many other things to do or to think about. Being free was all that counted. We boarded the bomber as instructed and even had to wear parachutes. The army was not taking any chances with us, treating us sort of like special cargo. I had said my good-byes to my brother and told him I would see him back in Chicago real soon. I had reassured him that he should not worry about me, that I was a survivor, and that I would get over the anguish of losing Laura.

The three-hour trip to Manila was uneventful. The island was a sight to behold, with the lush green mountains, the blue ocean and the bay, and the island fortress of Corregidor. Over to the left was Bataan. I could not see much from the air, but I knew that I had to get over there to find my buried treasure. Finding it would make me rich, eliminate all worry, and buy me the finest of everything. This hunt is what I was waiting for, a chance to forget my troubles.

As the plane landed in Manila on September 7, all of us thought of a takeoff of General MacArthur's famous line, "I will return." We shouted in unison, "We have returned!" The plane taxied almost to where an old army truck was standing. When we got off the plane, about twenty Filipinos and fifteen U.S. servicemen were standing around the landing area. We walked down the stairs slowly and deliberately, not wanting to fall and get hurt. We still had on our old Japanese-issue work clothes—nowhere along the line did any of the military personnel we encountered try to put us into any other type of uniform—so I guess we looked out of place coming off that plane. All of the people on the ground just looked at us and stared without yelling, waving, or acknowledging us in any way. Nothing was said but we could feel the tension in the air. No one seemed to care whether we lived or died, came home or not. We felt like we were simply an annoying nuisance, something they had to deal with. It was a sad return and not at all what we had expected. I guessed that they felt that because we had surrendered, we did not deserve any welcome-home party.

We boarded the truck for the thirty-five-minute ride to the 29th Replacement Depot. As we pulled into the area, we saw dozens of tentlike buildings that were designed for sleeping and one very large tent structure that was obviously the mess hall. As we got off the truck, we were asked to fill out a sheet of paper that had spaces for our name, rank, serial number, home address, and three extra lines to put down any illnesses or injuries suffered during the past three and a half years. Three lines! The whole heart-wrenching experience had to be boiled down to three lines. Also on the sheet of paper was a number indicating our tent assignment. As we looked around, we noticed a lot of activity. There must have been three hundred to four hundred men milling around the tents, all neatly dressed in clean and well-pressed uniforms. When we got closer, we realized they were former POWs who had arrived here earlier.

Then I heard someone call out, "Hey, Ten-Spot!" I turned and saw, for the first time in more than three years, my good friend Lew Brittan. He was alive and well even though he looked like he had lost about seventy-five pounds from his prewar weight of 195 pounds. We shook hands and then hugged each other in a show of real friendship. Lew had been incarcerated in a POW camp in northern Japan, but he had made it. I knew he would.

Within a few hours, the army issued us new uniforms and boots, which made us acutely aware of how much we had changed. My new uniform was a size 34, with a waist of twenty-six inches. My original uniform when issued at the Maywood Armory was a size 44, with a thirty-six-inch waist. My shoes were still size ten and a half, but I needed a narrow width instead of the medium width I had worn before.

When I left Okinawa, my brother loaned me his camera, so I took pictures of all the survivors from Company B, 192d Tank Battalion, who were at the 29th Replacement Depot. I was able to locate only 12 of our original 164 men.

As we shared our experiences, the discussion finally got around to what happened to Willard Yeast of headquarters company, who had been a prisoner on Palawan. When I heard the story, I started to sweat profusely. Again I felt there but for the grace of God went I.

As the Allies got closer to winning the war, the most atrocious slaughter of Americans at the hands of the Japanese occurred at the Palawan prison camp in the Philippines around mid-December 1944. The Japanese began planning for this massacre about October 20, 1944, when the U.S. bombing of the area around Palawan began in earnest.

Each day more and more B-24s rained their bombs on Palawan. Each bomb made the Japanese fear they could possibly lose the war, and they wanted revenge for the destruction that the Americans poured onto them. During these air raids, prisoners would be beaten for no apparent reason, and if they fell to the ground, the Japanese kicked them continuously and often murdered them.

On December 14, the Japanese received word that U.S. troops were going to land on all the islands of the Philippines. The Japanese ordered all 150 inmates of the Palawan POW camp into three large and two smaller underground bomb shelters. When the men were safely inside, the Japanese soldiers barricaded the entrances and began systematically liquidating all the prisoners. The Japanese guards poured large containers of gasoline onto the roofs of the bomb shelters and then ignited them. The gasoline-soaked dried grass that covered the shelters went up in flames within seconds. As the blazes shot toward the sky, the heat from the fire became unbearable for the prisoners inside. Many of the men in the shelters were overcome by the fumes and heat. Some were trampled to death by their own buddies in their desperate attempts to find an exit. Others who tried to force their way out were met with rifle fire, bayonets, machine guns, and explosives. The Japanese did everything in their power to ensure that no one left the shelters alive. Of the 150 men who entered the makeshift crematoriums that infamous day, 139 died. Eleven of the group were able to escape, and they returned to freedom to tell their story of the Palawan massacre.

As it happened, in 1944 when we were instructed to build bomb shelters at Camp 17, I had misgivings about how they would be used. I knew the shelters, with only one way in and no other way out, would have been a good place to kill us. Then when the slaughter was over, a bulldozer could have just covered up the evidence by flattening out the shelter so that no one would ever know it had been there. I had been afraid that the Japanese might institute reprisals of this type in our camp.

As we later discovered, POW Camp 17 in Omuta had the reputation of being the worst camp in Japan. Our work in the mines was the most dangerous forced labor of any prisoner of war camp. In addition to our sadistic Japanese camp commander, the guards treated us American POWs more harshly than prisoners from other nations. For the beatings, starvation, and refusal to provide medical treatment, justice was ultimately served. At the end of the war, our Japanese camp commander was tried and convicted for crimes against humanity and was hanged.

So, when I arrived in Manila September 7, 1945, at the 29th Replacement Depot, I was not as shocked as many when I heard about the massacre at Palawan. I simply could not believe how lucky we were that the same thing was not done at Camp 17. Abundant evidence was available after the war to prove the atrocities committed in the Philippines were premeditated and based on orders from high-level superiors and not just the field officers. From all of the evidence regarding the Bataan Death March and the occupation of the islands, it appears that the Japanese had a hidden agenda not to allow any of the prisoners to live to tell their stories.

For the next few days, we compared experiences and exchanged information about friends—how they were or how they died. Once the sad commentary was over, we started again to act like repatriated soldiers. We ate whenever and whatever we wanted, however; and we came and went as we wished. We had no commander in charge, which was fortunate because we would not have accepted any restrictions on us at the time. In fact, on a few occasions when we went into Manila in the evening, if we did not have transportation and if we saw an empty, idle staff command car, we would just "borrow" it. At one point the Military Police stopped us for driving a vehicle that was reported stolen. They took us to MP headquarters and asked what unit we were in. When we responded, "29th Replacement Depot," the officer of the day merely said, "Let them go. They're MacArthur's boys; nothing we can do about it."

After a few days of eating all I wanted and of having as much fun as I could, I wanted to arrange a flight back to Bataan. I knew exactly where I had buried the money. That tree, those large roots, and the number of paces off the road at kilometer post number 167 were etched in my memory.

By the story I told and the tears I shed, I convinced an air force colonel to fly me back to Bataan in a small Piper Cub reconnaissance plane. A two-seater, it was good enough for me and the box of goodies that I was going to find. In only fifteen minutes, we flew across the bay to Bataan. The colonel landed and taxied to an area that had a few military vehicles. We headed for a jeep. A driver wearing corporal's stripes was just sitting there, sort of waiting for a fare. The colonel saluted the corporal, then we got into the jeep and told the driver to head for kilometer post 167.

Within ten minutes we arrived at our destination. I did not recognize anything near it. There were no trees or brush of any kind. I was devastated. Locating my hidden wealth was going to be impossible. With all of the landmarks gone, I slowly came to realize that the fighting, bombing, and shelling from Corregidor to Bataan had all taken its toll on the vegetation and terrain. Then, of course, forty-two months had passed, during which time the Filipinos must have scoured the area in search of food and firewood. In sum, I was licked. My dream of wealth came to an abrupt end.

I decided to tell the colonel the whole story; anyway, it was evident from my dismay that something was wrong. When I finished my account, he reared his head back and laughed uproariously. He told me that on the day of the surrender of Bataan, the serial numbers of all of the bills held in the Philippines, hidden or not, had been wired to Washington for cancellation. The colonel said to me, "If you had found the money, all you could have done with it was use it as wallpaper." (Or was it another kind of paper he mentioned?) We returned to the Piper Cub and made our way back to Manila. I had suffered another major disappointment, but one that I knew I could live with.

When I arrived at the 29th Replacement Depot, a medical table had been set up at the back of the mess hall. I was told to make arrangements to see the doctor and answer as many of his questions as possible. For the first time I realized that all of the soldiers' army records had been destroyed during the surrender of Bataan. The army had no files on any of our awards and special citations or our promotions. Our medical records of our sicknesses and injuries received at any time during our terms of service, especially those years spent at the hands of the Japanese, were gone.

When I got up to the medic's table, the doctor asked me if I had any problems I wanted to report. I said, "No, not now." He then asked me to describe any injuries or sicknesses I had had during the past four years. "You must be kidding," I said. "How in the hell am I supposed to remember all those beatings and tortures at a moment's notice?" All I wanted, all any of us wanted, was to get home. We had no time for silly questions and for standing in a long line with other POWs. At no time during our stay at the 29th Replacement Depot were we given a physical exam, and the doctors never advised us as to what we should or should not eat or how much we should eat at one time. We were only asked, "Any problems you want to report?" This charade of taking our medical histories was disgraceful. I felt these people were utterly incompetent in making this "examination and inquiry" of our health. In fact, only today have we begun to realize what a good medical exam would have disclosed and what prompt and proper treatment could have done to prevent many of our sicknesses, our premature mortality, and the constant pain and suffering many of us survivors still endure.

During the next week, we were still fed as if food was going out of style. Our mess hall was open to us twenty-four hours a day with all we could eat of anything we wanted. A typical dinner consisted of a whole fried chicken, potatoes, bread and butter, and milk followed by a steak with french fried potatoes. Then we enjoyed maybe two or three different desserts, which always included ice cream, one of our favorite snacks any time of the day or night. We also had fun during that week, dancing at local nightclubs, eating in small local restaurants, and dating a variety of girls.

Originally the doctors had told us that we could go home after we gained about twenty pounds. I was ready within ten days. Then the army wanted proof that my arm was better and that I did not need to be cared for on a hospital ship; otherwise, I would have to wait another two weeks. I told them I was fine, which was a little white lie but one I felt justified in telling. I wanted to go home, and I was not going to let my withered left arm deter me from my main goal. Dressed in my newly issued uniform and with my recently acquired samurai sword by my side, I was ready for the trip home. My dream was about to come true.

We military personnel and the civilians released from the University of Santo Tomás were excited at the prospect of going home. Finally, on October 8, 1945, we boarded the USAT (U.S. Army Transport) *Klipfontein*. We were all set to head out to sea when fate slipped a small monkey wrench into our early departure. Upon backing away from the pier, the ship hit something under water. The captain took the ship out in the bay, dropped the anchor, and to everyone's dismay, turned off the engines.

Within minutes I could hear the shouts from the men: "I want to go home, get this thing in gear!" "Are we going to eat Thanksgiving dinner aboard this ship anchored off Manila Bay?" We all sat and waited, one hour, then two hours, without knowing what was happening. At last the public address system assured all of us aboard that the following morning the captain would send some divers down to determine the seriousness of the damage to the hull since we were going to be traveling the high seas. That evening we ate dinner in the mess hall and slept in our assigned bunks.

At 3:05 P.M. the next day, a U.S. Navy barge drew alongside, and two frogmen, wearing air masks and fins, dived overboard to investigate the damage. Then, at exactly 3:33 P.M., they came up from their inspection and gave us a thumbs-up signal, assuring us of a safe and speedy journey. The captain decided not to waste any more time; he announced that we would get under way within minutes of the anchor being restored. At 5:25 P.M. that same day we set sail for home.

The next day the captain announced over the public address system that he needed a volunteer to assist in the radio room. Since I had completed Radio Operators' School at Fort Knox, Kentucky, I offered to help. When I arrived at the radio room, the captain told me that he needed someone to handle the entertainment and newspaper aboard the ship on our way to Seattle or San Francisco (the exact destination at this time was not known). Remembering the benefits I received in this same job on the way over to the Philippines, I readily agreed to do what I could. So I embarked on yet another amateur career in a long list of others: soldiering, coal mining, and producing and directing shows. I really was a "jack of all trades, but master of none."

The first thing I believed we passengers needed was news of the world's current events, so I formed an editorial staff to put out a daily newspaper. I became the editor, and after a vote of the newspaper staff, we named the paper *Frisco Lookout*. Circulation was handled by E. C. Canfield; art by G. H. Dee and W. G. Self; and typing and mimeographing by J. W. Emanuel, L. W. Van Liere, C. S. Kellogg, and J. B. Mathony. Our reporters were J. A. Leland, C. E. Shockley, and F. R. Ivins. The staff worked hard every day of the trip, getting the paper out every morning by eight o'clock. All seventeen hundred of the passengers looked forward to the paper and the news items we were able to glean from the radio waves.

As I had anticipated, being the editor of the paper and being in charge of the entertainment aboard ship conveyed some extra benefits. Most important, I had a stateroom all to myself that was great for entertaining some of the civilian women internees from Santo Tomás. I met some wonderful people aboard ship, many of whom were single women who enjoyed the company of a man. Of course, I was a man who wanted to enjoy the company of a woman. I no longer had a wife to be faithful to, so on this trip I did not have to go without a woman's love and affection. After being without female companionship for four years, I was not sure that I would know how to act in front of a woman, but as nature worked its wonders, I was able to overcome the problems associated with my poor health and my weakened physical condition.

On our twenty-first day out, the captain informed us that our final destination was going to be Seattle, for too many ships were going to the San Francisco port. Everything, we were assured, would be waiting for us in Seattle. Our overnight stay at an army base in Seattle, our trips to various hospitals, and our expedited transportation home would be handled for us.

Steaming from Manila to Seattle took twenty-eight days, and during that time I made many friends. The trip was like a dream come true. I ate all the good and well-prepared food I wanted; I slept in a real bed, with white sheets and soft pillows; and I even played the drums in a little band we formed aboard ship. I had to pinch myself just to make sure it was all real.

Except for the normal everyday activities associated with producing a daily newspaper and making sure that the ship's passengers had some type of entertainment four days a week, the trip was relaxing, not too exciting. I most enjoyed being able to talk to so many of the other released prisoners of war and the civilian internees, and finding out what went on in their camps. I would ask them how they were treated, what they did for entertainment and to eliminate their boredom, and how good the medical facilities were at their camp. I naturally evaluated everyone else's camp situation as compared to mine. I did not get all the answers I wanted because some of the people just wanted to forget the whole affair, to wipe it out of their minds as if it never happened. I could not do that. The war had been too much a part of my life, and I realized it would continue to have an important impact on my future. In fact, I know without a doubt that my experiences during those trying four years shaped my thinking, my philosophies, and attitudes about life for the next fifty years.

Sometime in the afternoon on November 7, 1945, we spotted land—Seattle. We all ran to the railing of the ship and watched as the ship approached the port. Within hours we got close enough to see the tall modern buildings that defined the downtown area. By dusk we had pulled into the dock, and in our excitement at being home at last, most of us jammed the passageways, just itching to get off the ship. We all wanted to call home, and some of us just wanted to kiss the ground as we got off the ship. Others had tears in their eyes; their happiness was more than they could stand. As for me, I wanted to make that phone call I had been dreaming about for years: "Hi, Mom and Dad. It's me, Les. I'm home." I had my speech all ready. All I needed was a phone, and I knew there was one down on the docks. As the ship tied up to its berth and the horn sounded its final blast, I cried—not tears of sorrow but tears of joy and hope. For an excited kid, this homecoming was an emotional experience.

We got the bad news over the loudspeaker: no one was allowed to go ashore that evening. Apparently, the officer of the day and the ship's captain were afraid some of the men and women who were too weak to make it on their own but too proud to seek help would get injured. When I heard this, I became quite upset. I was not going to let them keep me on board. I had to make my phone call. I walked down to the deck closest to the water, looked in both directions to make sure that no one would be able to stop me, and then jumped into the water. In just a few strokes, I reached the pier. An MP helped me out of the water. Without saying more than thank you to him, I then asked him if I could borrow a nickel, just for a few minutes. The MP looked at me in total astonishment, and as he reached in his pocket for the coin, he asked, "Who the hell are you?"

"God sent me," I replied. "Thanks." Then away I ran for the phone. I reached the telephone in my new GI-issue clothes, wet from head to toe and laughing. I was so happy I had tears in my eyes as I dialed the phone number I had remembered all these years. After a few rings I heard the operator ask whether my folks would accept a collect call from Seattle.

Before my dad was able to answer, I hollered into the phone, "It's me, Dad—Les! I'm home, here in Seattle." The operator, sensitive to the moment, just put my call through. Then there was no sound, nothing. I heard nothing. A few seconds later, I heard a loud sob. The crying lasted for about a minute or two, until my dad finally said, "Let me put Mom on." My mom got on the phone and said, as calmly as possible, "Well, it's about time." Mom always had a great positive attitude; Dad could not deal with adversity as well as she could. When I got home, I found out that my mother refused to display the gold-star flag she had received after they thought I was killed in prison camp. She told everyone, "I don't know when he's coming home, but he will come home." My mother was right as usual.

We talked for a few minutes. Then, Mom told me that Bunny was home, having been discharged from the navy, and that he and my brothers Joe and Lou were visiting my brother Bill. She asked if I would call them, too. Mom gave me the phone number, and after we said good-bye, I called Bill's home. Once again I heard the operator ask if the party would accept a collect call from Seattle. My brother Bill knew at once who was calling and agreed. Then my brother said to me, "Hello, punk, we've been expecting you." After a few minutes of conversation, he let me speak to each one of my brothers. What a joy, catching all my brothers in one place at the same time, and I was able to say hello to all of them.

My day was complete. I could not want anything more out of life this day. I admit it would have been nice to be able to say hello to Laura, too, but under the circumstances that was not advisable.

# CHAPTER 20

# HOME AT LAST

When I finished my phone calls to my family, I walked up to the MP, who was still standing near the gangplank, gave him his nickel back, and turned and walked aboard the ship as if I was expected. That night we all stayed aboard the ship and had one hell of a good time. After all, we were back in the United States, and all those days in prison camps were behind us. We did not even think about the war that evening. We just enjoyed talking, drinking a few beers, and dancing and singing with the few women on board. We partied almost till dawn, went to our bunks, and fell sound asleep. We were awakened by a loud blast of the ship's horn and a message over the loudspeaker: "We will be leaving the ship from the lower deck. Take all your possessions; you will not be coming back."

Within the hour, we began leaving the ship. We had expected some people on the dock, happy people waving at us, but no one was there. We only saw longshoremen, who were working to get the cargo off the ship, and these workers did not care who we were or why we were there. We were immediately loaded onto trucks and taken to a U.S. Army base in Seattle, where we ended up staying for the night.

Once again, we had a few beers together and talked a little. Then, we all grew quiet. What more could we say to each other? What other stories could we tell? By the end of the day we were depressed, and the only thing left for us was to go into town and have some fun. Lew Brittan and I went together, had a few drinks, enjoyed the company of a few women, and laughed all the way back to our barracks late that night. All we were able to think about the whole night long was, we were free. Freedom felt so wonderful.

The following morning a truck took us to the railroad station, where a train was waiting for us. We were told to board the train and sit anyplace we wanted. We would get instructions and find out where we were going once we got under way. Again, there was no one around to wave to, no one waiting for us. We started to realize we were not popular.

The train left the station, and about two hours out of Seattle, we were told our destinations. I was scheduled, along with two hundred other men, to go to Schick General Hospital in Clinton, Iowa. The army would have transportation waiting for us at the railroad station. Once at the hospital we would be examined, receive treatment if necessary, and then be discharged from the service. I could not wait. The word *discharge* sounded real good.

During our trip, everyone became quiet. It was hard to believe, especially with so many men on the train, but at one point, I could have heard a pin drop. Obviously, I was witnessing a mass depression; it seemed the reality of what was happening was sinking in. No doubt all of the men on that train were thinking about what they would find when they arrived home, what surprises were in store for them, what they were going to do with their lives, and how they would survive in this society that they had been away from for so long. We were all downcast. I sat in my seat, not saying a word, just staring out the window, and wondering, What's in store for me? What will I become?

We were also sad because after four years away from our country we had expected some type of welcome when we returned to the United States. We had thought maybe someone would give a speech saying how happy the people of the United States were for our safe return. Besides being ignored, we were also dejected because we had left so many of our friends behind.

The count was in. Of the seventy-two thousand Filipinos and Americans on the Bataan Death March only about seventy-five hundred survived— one in ten. Of the twelve thousand Americans, only about fifteen hundred came home. I viewed my survival as being given a little extra time to see if I could make the most of it. I learned that life has great value. No single day can be wasted or thrown away.

A traumatic demonstration of our sinking self-esteem occurred when our train pulled into the St. Louis, Missouri, train station. It was a large and noisy place, with thousands of people roaming around on the platform. Because of our feelings of inferiority, most of us quickly pulled down the shades on the windows of our Pullman car. Sadly, we were embarrassed, and we did not want anyone to see us, the losers who had surrendered.

As we found out later, the American people did not find out about the horrors of the Bataan Death March for more than a year after the fall of Bataan. A few of the servicemen on the march had escaped and eventually found their way back via submarine to the United States. When they arrived, the escapees told our government leaders what had happened and about the atrocities, the starvation, the murders of our fighting men. Our leaders in Washington decided not to make this tragic news public, because the Japanese might take reprisals on those men still prisoners. An interview in a Chicago newspaper, a year after the event itself, brought the horrors of the death march to light. Still much of the whole truth was held back from the public, because, as was said, "the American people can't deal with such disturbing facts at this time."

When we survivors returned, therefore, the impact on the public of what had happened had long been lost. It seemed that the war in Europe was more important, and when it came to an end on V-E Day, the Americans at home felt the war was over. At that point they wanted to get on with their lives while we were held captive for three more months.

Maybe, if we had fought to the last man, like at the Alamo, then we would have commanded a little respect. The respect we sought was not for us; after all, we returned. Respect was reserved for those who gave their lives in the defense of their country. That same country, however, did not, or could not, send us more food, more ammunition, more equipment, more men, or respond more quickly to our prime military questions. Any one of these requests, if fulfilled then, would have saved Americans lives.

None of us wanted to be seen in uniform now. It was a very humiliating situation. We did not know what to do or how to handle it. If we could have crawled into a hole and pulled it in after us, I think we would have. Instead, we pulled down the shades of our train windows.

Many hours later we arrived at the Clinton railroad station. Without any fanfare, we got off the train, said our good-byes to friends we did not expect to see ever again, and climbed aboard the waiting trucks. An hour later we arrived at Schick General Hospital. We did not see any banners or any acknowledgment that we had returned after being gone for four years. We figured the people wanted to welcome winners, not losers.

When I checked into the hospital, I was given a room on the third floor and told to go upstairs, where I would be taken care of. So, I took the elevator up to the third floor, and as I got off the elevator, I turned. Then I saw them. First, my brother Bill, all six feet of him, beaming at me. After he was sure I had seen him, he bent down, put his cane on the slick marble floor, and with one mighty shove, pushed it toward me. I guessed Bunny had told him about my poor physical condition and my sorrow over what had happened with Laura. By turning the cane over to me even though he was disabled and needed the cane for himself, Bill showed me he was willing to help me overcome my problems.

Standing to Bill's left was my brother Lou. Lou stood about two inches taller than Bill and as straight as an arrow. He was crying, not little tears, but big sobs. Just as in my dreams, my family was not embarrassed or bitter about my surrendering to the Japanese. They were here to comfort me and to show me they cared.

Then I spotted them, standing in the hallway next to my brothers—my mother and father. They looked about the same as I remembered them; maybe their hair was a little grayer, but they looked real good. The tears welled up in my eyes as I ran as fast as I could into their arms. Both of them were beaming and smiling, and their eyes were brimming with tears of happiness. After a few minutes of hugging, we pushed back from each other. I looked at them and thought, Is this real? while they were looking at me and saying, "It's really you." We were incredibly happy people at that moment. They told me that because of gasoline rationing, only one car could make the trip from Chicago. Bunny was waiting for me at home, and Joe was working.

After our reunion I checked in with the floor nurse. She informed me that I was going to have a private room and that the doctors would be in shortly for the first exam. They would determine if I could get a pass and go home for a week so that I could get acclimated to normal life. In half an hour a group of doctors came into my room. After examining my shoulder, my hip, my back, and my nose, they gave me permission to check out for a week, but they warned me to come back for treatment, or else my condition could deteriorate beyond repair.

I hurriedly dressed and left the hospital. My family helped me down the stairs and into the car. I was on my way home. How can I describe my happiness? I was all smiles. I wanted to ask so many questions but was afraid of opening bad wounds. I wanted to ask about Laura and why she did not wait for me, but I just could not do it. I was certain it would break my mom's and dad's hearts if they knew I was still carrying a torch for her. I did the best I could all the way home. Finally we arrived in Chicago. When I got out of the car in front of our apartment building, a group of my parents' friends was waiting for me. They all just wanted to say, "Welcome home. It's good having you back." It felt good to be home.

That week I had to take care of a few things before I returned to the hospital. First on my list was to talk to Laura. I called her that evening, and she cried. She then began to explain what had happened. She had been notified that I was missing in action and, under the circumstances, presumed dead. Then, after waiting for three years for some word from the government regarding my status, the pressure I had feared from her family took hold. At about this time, her father told her younger sister, who was in love and wanted to get married, that in accordance with Jewish religious law she could not marry before the oldest daughter. That meant Laura must marry first.

Poor Laura. First, I had kept the legal papers the justice of the peace had given us because I knew neither of us wanted Laura's father to find out about our affair and ultimate elopement, and second, she had no idea where in Kentucky we had been married. So, when the time came to show her father evidence of our marriage, she was unable to produce a marriage certificate. Maybe seeing the actual allotment checks I had authorized for her would have convinced her father otherwise, but the fact is he did not want to believe it.

Laura explained the total confusion of not knowing what had happened to me and not wanting to hurt her sister. Her family and friends had advised her to get on with her life. She had been seeing a man who had proposed to her many times and she felt she could love him, so she took the easiest way out at the time. She agreed to marry him. She did it not only for her own sake, but so that her sister could get married, too. At that time, she told me, her husband was in the Philippines and not expected home for a number of months. And, she continued, she was pregnant. Then, she sobbed and asked for my understanding.

As we continued to talk, I could sense the guilt she was feeling. I did not want that for her; after all, I loved her. I did not want her to be unhappy, so I lied to her. I told her I understood why she did what she did. I explained that even though the marriage certificate had been lost with all my other possessions when the Japanese bombed our base at Fort Stotsenburg, if I had to, I would go back to Kentucky and drive all over the state to find that little town with the small general store and the justice of the peace. But, I went on, if no one knew about this except us and if I did not make an issue out of it, why bother? We could have the marriage annulled. She agreed with that solution and thanked me for being so considerate. Considerate, hell! I was devastated, and I wondered how she really felt.

We talked a few minutes more, and she mentioned that many of our friends from the south side of Chicago wanted to have a welcome-home party for me the following Saturday night. Would I come? I did not want to do anything that was going to involve Laura, but not wanting to show my grief, I said I would be pleased to go. I arranged to pick her up, which would give me an opportunity of seeing her family for the last time.

Saturday night came very quickly. I worried about how I would handle this situation and what I should say and do. I had to keep from showing any animosity toward her family for its insistence that Laura was not legally married. Here I was, a full 123 pounds, with my left arm partially paralyzed and my right leg so weak I could hardly walk on it, and I was going to meet the family while pretending to be so happy. I drove over to her home that night, said hello to her parents, and put on a good act of being nonchalant. Then Laura and I left for the party. I understood why Laura's parents were none too happy with my coming over and picking up their married and pregnant daughter. After all, I had been away for more than four years, and they worried that I may have changed.

Soon we arrived in front of the home where the party was being held. I got out of the car, walked around to the passenger side, and opened the door to help Laura out. In a split second, without thinking of the consequences, I held Laura close to me and kissed her on the lips. As I did I said, "I still love you." Before I could stop kissing her, she fainted dead away. She actually fell down on the sidewalk, out cold.

What in the world could I do now? I thought. I was too weak to lift her, did not have enough strength in my one good hand to hold her, and was unable to run and get help. I was devastated. I had caused this, and I should have known better. I just wanted to have the opportunity to see her one last time, but I did not think this through clearly, allowing my emotions to rule my good sense. Now here I was, helplessly standing by someone else's pregnant wife who was lying on a street curb, passed out. Just about the time that I was becoming truly concerned, another friend and party guest stopped nearby, saw the problem, and helped Laura to her feet. Laura was herself again, and we went into the party.

I do not remember much else about that night, but I do remember leaving the party early, taking Laura home, and walking her to the door. We looked each other in the eyes and said, almost in unison, "Good luck, and good-bye."

For me, it was truly the end of a dream that had helped me get home alive. Despite my heartbreak, I realized that the dream of being with her was one of the reasons that I never gave up and never stopped believing that one day I would return. For that I was eternally grateful, but our relationship was over, and there was no sense in crying about it any longer. I wondered then, and still wonder today, if she had told me the whole truth or if she had tried to ease my pain by telling me something that she felt I would rather hear. Did she give up on me because she fell in love with another man? Or was it my prolonged absence and the uncertain future that caused her to give up waiting? I guess I will never know.

The following Saturday night my folks rented a hall and put on a welcome-home party for my brother Bunny and me. I left the hospital on a weekend pass. When I arrived at the party, the hall was full of people: my folks' friends, my brother's friends, neighbors, a few of my old girlfriends, and a few of my old buddies who were classified as 4F, or unfit for military service due to poor health. Many of my healthier old friends were still in the service and overseas. The girls whom I had dated were all married, and most of them were pregnant. Consequently, I did not have many young friends around when I came home. The party was great, nevertheless, especially because no one asked me about my wartime experiences. I do not know how I would have responded at that time.

We took pictures of everyone there. Relatives from Detroit—my niece Harriet, her husband Martin, my brother Joe, his wife Fay, and my niece Shirley—and, of course, my family from Chicago including Lou, his wife Edith, Bill, and his wife Evelyn, all welcomed Bunny and me home. Even my best friend, Lew Brittan, was there. It was a glorious feeling to know we had been missed and to know we were wanted.

By the first of the week I had to get back to reality, which meant going back to Schick General Hospital. The doctors recommended two operations—one on my shoulder and one on my hip. Meanwhile, I also had to submit a report to the quartermaster listing the personal items I lost when the war broke out. As I understood it, I was allowed to have my belongings over in the Philippines during peacetime, and the U.S. government assumed responsibility for any personal items I lost due to the outbreak of war.

The bombing of Clark Field destroyed everything in my foot locker and duffel bag. Of all the items I lost, the one I really cared for the most was my marriage certificate. On later reflection, I was relieved that I never found it. After all, I did not want to hurt Laura, and if I had found it, I may have done or said something I would have regretted later.

Before I went in to apply for reimbursement for my lost possessions, all my friends warned me that the officer in charge was cutting the requested amounts in half and that I should take that into consideration when submitting my claim. Armed with that advice, I applied the full stateside replacement value to the items. When the officer asked for the value of my loss, I quickly said, "Seven hundred dollars, sir." The officer just looked at me, read my list of items, and smiled. Then he said, "Fine. Just sign this form."

I could not believe it. I had enough money to replace all the items I lost and then some. After all, when I left the United States for the Philippines, seven hundred dollars would buy a 1940 Buick convertible. While in prison camp, I daydreamed about owning that car, so I decided to use the money I received from the government to satisfy yet another long-awaited dream. The 1940 Buick convertible was going to be mine.

Before I left the hospital on my second weekend pass, I went to the paymaster and asked for my paycheck, all four years of it, and cashed my government reimbursement check. It only took about ten minutes for the clerk to verify and agree with me as to the amount of money I had coming. He processed my request for my back pay, and as they were preparing to issue me a check, I asked if they would object to giving me the amount in cash. We counted the money out together, all forty-seven hundred dollars, in tens and twenties. I had to go into the post exchange (PX) and buy a suitcase just to carry it all. I felt like a millionaire.

When I got home my first order of business was to find a 1940 Buick convertible. Bill explained that no new cars had been produced since the 1941 model, and all the car dealers sold and displayed used cars. He suggested I go to the nearest Buick dealer to see what he could do for me. When I arrived at the local Buick dealership, I saw a pair of what appeared to be shining new convertibles on the showroom floor. I walked in, pointed to the black one, and said, "That's the one I want. Wrap it up." The salesman looked at me and offered, "Why not take both of them? I can give you a real good buy." "For God's sake," I said, "what would I do with two of them?" He looked at me and replied, "You're a dealer, aren't you?" Did I look like a car dealer, in my Army uniform? I laughed and said, "No, thanks. I'll take just one."

Almost as an afterthought, I asked how much the car was. When he said the price was $3,750, I almost fainted. The salesman said, "It has very low mileage and is really a very good buy considering there won't be any new cars produced for at least another year. Where have you been? Don't you know the price of cars?" No, I was afraid I did not know the price of cars, and I did not think he really wanted to know where I had been. So, I just smiled, turned around, and walked out of the showroom. I decided I did not need a car at this time, especially not $3,750 worth. Besides, I was still in the hospital and did not have any idea how long I would be there. I decided to wait a while before buying my first car.

At first when I looked around the city, I did not see any changes. Everything seemed to be just about the same as when I left. After all, all of the country's resources had been channeled into the war effort and little was left for local consumption or construction. The changes were more subtle. On my first day at home, for example, when my mother asked me what I wanted for dinner, I said a big, thick, juicy steak. My mother immediately went to her purse and, after pulling out a little booklet, said, "I don't know if I have enough coupons for meat this month." I did not know what she was talking about. Not enough coupons? Then she explained the government rationed such products as toothpaste, meat, sugar, shoes, canned goods, gas, and other items we could have bought just four years ago without any limitation.

I also heard about the illicit trading on the "black market," in which rationed goods could be purchased without using government-issued ration coupons. Of course, the marketeers sold these products at prices significantly higher prices than regular established prices. Some businesses were run almost exclusively to sell items at black market prices, and I was shocked to find legitimate businesses selling products without the required ration coupons and, of course, at inflated prices. I could not believe some of the stories I heard. I wondered, is this what I was going to have to deal with now that I was home?

Another change since I had left four years ago was in women's hair styles. The girls stopped wearing the pageboy and adopted Veronica Lake's style of long, flowing hair. Right away I also noticed the girls were donning shorter skirts. The new hemlines saved material, they told me, but they did not need an excuse as far as I was concerned. I was all in favor of the new style of showing off a girl's legs, and I liked the pin-up of Betty Grable. Another cultural change was reflected in the movies. They all seemed to have a war theme, and of course the United States always won every battle. At times I would become irritated at the constant glorification of winning. Only the cowardly enemy was ever shown to surrender.

New songs like "Rosie the Riveter" surprised me only because I never thought of women doing such dangerous jobs. In fact, what astonished me when I returned from the Pacific was seeing women doing what in the past had been only men's jobs. Women were working as draftsmen, mechanics, machine operators, and gas station attendants. Seeing women in army and navy uniforms was a complete shock.

The most amazing thing to me, however, was when I learned that Congress had passed a bill that would pay the tuition for returning veterans who wished to go to college. Better still, the veteran would receive a monthly stipend while attending school. It was something to consider.

While in my hospital bed, I had me plenty of time to think. My mind wandered to those awful days on the Bataan Death March and what had kept me going. Was it luck that I survived the ordeal while so many others succumbed, or was it part of a broader plan? I seriously evaluated this. If I could determine what it was that brought me back, then I could use the same philosophy for making the most of the rest of my life. Then I realized that those friends of mine who survived all had a positive attitude. Like me, they had believed they would come home, and they worked hard at making their dream a reality.

At last I found the answer of why I returned. I always had a positive attitude, from the day we surrendered Bataan through the sixty-eight excruciating miles of the march to the years in prison camp and in the coal mine. I kept saying, "You can't have a dream come true if you don't have a dream to start with." Hope sees the invisible, feels the intangible, and achieves the impossible. I always filled my mind with dreams, and I always had a goal. Now I could start putting my life in order.

I figured out I had unconsciously followed a sort of five-point plan of survival. As I looked back, I realized there was more to it than just my having a positive attitude. Although it was definitely the first and most important part of my plan, I found I also had to have a strong commitment to survive in the face of adversity. I had to abandon all negative thoughts, all pessimism. It was no longer a question of whether I could survive but a determination to do it. "I know I can," I would say to myself.

Second, I had established for myself long-term goals, such as getting home, being reunited with my loved ones, and surviving each ordeal, and short-term goals, such as making it to a bend in the road or to that herd of carabao on the march. The short-term goals had to be realistic and achievable, whereas the long-term goals were my dreams. I had to believe that if I wanted something bad enough, I could get it. The survivors of the death march were ordinary people who had extraordinary determination.

My third point of survival was keeping as healthy as I could. I knew that eating was an important part of living. I watched scores of men die because they said they could not eat another bowl of rice, they just could not swallow it. Some died only a few days after trading their rice for cigarettes or simply giving their rice away.

Once when I was deep in thought about what my life was like back in those dark days in prison camp, I started to laugh as I remembered the time when the Japanese carted into camp a load of dogs, all barking and whining. We were told they were going to be our treat at our next meal. We did not get a very big piece of meat in our soup that day, but whatever it was, I ate it. Then I recalled the day we were served a fat and rubbery undigestible stomach of a whale. It took an agonizing effort to consume this so-called piece of meat, which was so bad that the following day almost half of the men came down with the runs. Of course, we could not get time off from work just because of that, so we had to make the best of a bad situation. Once inside the mine, I spent just as much time shoveling over my runny bowels as I did shoveling coal. The fact was I knew I had to eat to stay alive, so I ate whatever was put in front of me.

Another way of staying healthy was to keep mentally active. I developed friendships with those men who could hold an intelligent conversation and who had experiences to relate and share. Keeping my mind active meant taking time away from sleeping and joining with others in a discussion group. One of our group's most lively discussions involved developing breakfast, lunch, and dinner menus, including recipes for all of the main dishes. By the end of the war, we had meals planned for more than 350 days. The men who wanted to keep mentally alert were also the ones who had a positive attitude toward life. Those negative men who had refused to exercise their minds had to be left to their own little world. I could not afford the time or energy to be with them.

In recounting my survival plan, the fourth step was the need to develop "survival smarts." It was important to have a "feel" for the situation at hand. Having the smarts meant paying attention to a wide variety of telltale events and individual traits to gauge how to act. For example, knowing when to get into line first and when being last would be better saved me from beatings. Many times rushing to get in line first would have given the guards a longer period of time to harass or beat me. Also, sometimes being first meant that I better understood what they wanted me to do, helping me to avoid abuse. Of course, being last was no assurance of better treatment, for the guards would hit me if they thought I was deliberately taking my time.

Finally, in looking back, I determined the fifth step of the survival plan was the most important: I had to know when to apply the other four steps.

On those days when the doctors or nurses had plans for me, they would pull and push me all over the hospital from the X-ray room to the examining room and to the operating room. Everything they did was in an attempt to give me a life without constant pain and at the same time allow me the full use of my arms and legs.

After three months of operations, treatments, and soul searching, I finally asked when I could be discharged. I just wanted to go home, to start my formal education, and to get on with my life. The chief of staff looked at me and said, "You want to be discharged? Why didn't you say so? How about tomorrow?" I smiled. Tomorrow would do.

On June 30, 1946, I was honorably discharged from the service and was ready to start my new life as a civilian. My goal was to practice what I preached: enjoy today and look forward to tomorrow, and establish priorities, with happiness as the top priority.

# CHAPTER 21

# JAPAN REVISITED

In the decades after my return, hundreds of people have asked me what brought me home. I sensed that what they really wanted to know was whether some POWs survived because their overall health was better than others', or they followed a particular lifestyle, or they had positive attitudes. Certainly luck—being in the right place at the right time and not being in the wrong place at the wrong time—played an important role in my survival. In general, however, I realized that much of the luck I had, I had to make myself. My positive attitude, my dreams, and my goals all combined to enable me to endure and ultimately to survive.

People have also asked me how I currently feel about the Japanese. In the mid-1990s, it has been fifty years since those heinous days I spent as a prisoner of war. Back then I hated the Japanese who beat me. I despised the guards on the march. They were inhumane barbarians, one and all; but I was never able to hate just for the sake of hating. I had to have a reason. Thus, I did not then and do not now detest the Japanese as a people.

In 1988, I had the opportunity to visit Japan, which was a wonderful experience for someone with my background. In 1968, when my wife and I were living in San Diego, a mix-up in housing occurred for a transfer student from Japan. I agreed to let the young man stay with us just for the weekend, but the weekend lasted for ninety-five days. We had dozens of unusual experiences. When we first met, for example, I greeted him in his language. He smiled and asked where I had learned Japanese. When I told him I was a guest of the Japanese army for almost four years during World War II, his face turned pale. Then with a quick smile, he said, "I wonder how I'll sleep tonight?" Then he quickly said to my wife, "Don't learn Japanese from him. He speaks gutter Japanese, learned from the poorly educated men in the coal mine." Our whole family became close friends with our newfound, extroverted Japanese boy.

After our Japanese student returned home, we corresponded regularly for the next twenty years. Then one day in 1988, I received a phone call from Japan from our good friend, Toru Tasaka San. He was going to get married and asked if my wife and I would be his guests at the wedding. We immediately accepted.

So, back I went to Japan, where the soldiers had killed my friends and tortured me and where I was held prisoner in inhumane conditions for three and a half years. Memories and emotions flooded over me. My wife and I were more than a little apprehensive of both what my reaction would be and how we would be received by the Japanese. Our fears, however, were soon put to rest. Toru met us at the airplane and, with tears in his eyes, said, "Welcome to Japan, my American mama and papa."

Toru took us by cab to a hotel in Tokyo, where he had reserved a room for us. The following morning he arrived at the hotel with his fiancée and his mother. None of his wedding party—his family, his bride's family, or his bride—spoke English. After the formal introductions were made his mother, who was about four feet six inches tall, bowed politely to us and gave us a bag full of gifts. She then said in Japanese, which Toru interpreted for us, "Thank you for taking my son into your house and making him a part of your family." I returned the bow and said in Japanese, "Arigato goraimasu" (thank you so kindly). I shook from happiness. I was glad that I could greet a Japanese person without feeling hatred or wishing for revenge.

Later that day the religious Shinto wedding ceremony took place, and we were the only Caucasians present. We felt quite honored when we found out that only family members are invited to the formal wedding. After the pictures were taken, we went into the ballroom for the wedding banquet. There were about eighty-five guests, seventy of which were men, and once again, we were the only non-Asians. During the dinner, Toru asked me if I would say a few words to the guests. I spoke hesitantly in the language I had learned from the Japanese who had been the guards in camp and laborers in the coal mine. I knew I did not say the words perfectly, but my spirit was apparent. I said it was time to forget the past and focus on the future, and today we could start. As I concluded I said, "Anatawa tomodachi, yeroshi" (you are my friends, I am happy, very good). All the guests stood and applauded. Over the sound of the applause, I heard many of the men say, "Yeroshi do." It gave me chills to realize that we were able to see each other as friends, despite our different experiences during World War II.

Later that night we were invited to a party with the bride and groom and all of their young friends. First, we went to one nightclub for drinks, dancing, and of course karaoke, and then after about two hours, we moved along to another night spot. The young people, having been told of my experiences in Japan during the war, asked me to say something. By this time I was feeling quite good, so I told a few stories about Toru in the United States. In one anecdote, I told them how I gave Toru a haircut, and he said he could not believe he was allowing an ex-POW to hold a pair of long, sharp scissors against his neck. We all laughed, and when I was through, they all stood up, applauded, and hollered, "Yeroshi!"

The following day, the bride and groom informed us that we were going to accompany them on their honeymoon. This came as a bit of a surprise, but my wife and I went along. The four of us spent two weeks driving all over Japan, staying in traditional Japanese inns, and seeing the country as if we were royalty. Every night after our "honeymoon bath," which consisted of each couple going into their own bathing room, then washing ourselves with soap, and then rinsing with hot water taken from the tub. Only then would we enter the hot tub and soak in the 107-degree water. After soaking for about fifteen minutes, we would then dry off, put a robe around us, and return to our sleeping room. It was then that Toru and his wife would come into our room and give us a Japanese massage, he with me, and his wife with my wife.

After two weeks of vacationing all over Japan, the memorable honeymoon finally was over. Every day I would offer to pay for the room, the food, or the gasoline, but Toru would only say, "Later." When we finally had to say good-bye, I once again tried to pay our share of the expenses. Toru refused to accept one cent. This trip, he said, was his way of repaying us for our kindness to him when he was in the United States. I felt that, somehow, my painful war wounds and memories had truly begun to vanish.

Another often asked question concern my feelings about the use of atomic bombs at Hiroshima and Nagasaki. I can only say that one horror of war is that not only soldiers get killed, but many times innocent civilians become casualties. In this case, although not all the people of Japan wanted war, they all had to live under the wartime rules. As for me, the atomic bomb surely saved my life, as I do not believe I could have survived working in the coal mine much longer. More important, most experts from both the United States and Japan agree that had the war continued, it would have taken at least another million lives on both sides. Dropping the atomic bombs ended this long, terrible war. In the long run, I believe using the bomb was the best thing to do for the most people and for that particular period of time.

I was not aware of harboring any animosity against the Japanese all these past years, but when I put together my notes and stirred up my memories to write this manuscript, I felt the hot flush of hatred come over me once again. With each page I wrote, I recalled events that made my eyes blur with tears and caused me to have nightmares once again. I often could not control my emotions, but I soon realized that I was not angry with all Japanese people, only those who deprived me of my dignity and of my health.

My life today is a reflection of what I learned through my experiences as a prisoner of war. I have a positive attitude, and I set goals, goals that are attainable, about life. Moreover, if I want something badly enough, I know I can achieve it by trying hard enough. After many fulfilling years of work in the business world and as an academician, I still look forward to each day, and I still plan for my tomorrows.

On February 19, 1945, as Gen. Douglas MacArthur fought to liberate the Philippines, he made the following statement to the press:

> Bataan, along with Corregidor, the citadel of its external defense, made possible all that has happened here today. History, I am sure, will record it as one of the decisive battles of the world. Its long, protracted struggle enabled the United Nations to gather strength to resist in the Pacific. Had it not held out, Australia would have fallen with incalculable results.
>
> Our triumphs of today belong equally to that dead army. Its heroism and sacrifice have been fully acclaimed but the great strategic results of that mighty defense are only now becoming fully apparent. The Bataan garrison was destroyed due to its dreadful handicaps, but no army in history more thoroughly accomplished its mission. Let no man henceforth speak of it other than as a magnificent victory.

My positive attitude has enabled me to accept these words and to exorcise the demons of despair that once distressed me. I am now able to live with myself, knowing that, although I once surrendered, I did not fail my country.

# APPENDIX

MEMBERS OF COMPANY B AND THOSE ATTACHED TO
HEADQUARTERS COMPANY OF THE 192d TANK BATTALION
WHO DID NOT RETURN

From December 7, 1941, to September 15, 1945
Based on the records of Lt. Jacques V. Merrifield, aide-de-camp, and the
U. S. War Department

*(I apologize for any name unintentionally omitted or listed in error.)*

| | |
|---|---|
| Allison, E. A. | Died in Cabanatuan, January 29, 1942, of beriberi |
| Bainbridge, James A. | Died in Cabanatuan, September 23, 1942, of malaria |
| Ball, John E. | Died in Cabanatuan, July 3, 1942, of malaria |
| Bennett, Charles | Died aboard prison ship to Japan, October 24, 1944 |
| Black, Bertrum | Died in Fukuoka, Japan, February 2, 1945, of dysentery |
| Bloomfield, Kenneth | Died on the march, April 13, 1942, of exhaustion |
| Boni, Daniel J. | Died aboard prison ship, October 22, 1944 |
| Bronge, Robert | Died in Cabanatuan, July 31, 1942, of dysentery |
| Brown, Laprade D. | Died in Bilibid Prison, Manila, February 10, 1945, of TB |
| Brown, W. L. | Died on a work detail in the Philippines, 1942 |
| Bruni, Fred T. | Burned alive in prison camp on Palawan, Philippines, 1945 |
| Burholt, Arthur V. | Died aboard prison ship, January 27, 1945 |
| Burns, William E. | Died on work detail in Philippines, 1942, of dysentery |

KIA—Killed in action     MIA—Missing in action

| | |
|---|---|
| Bushaw, John F. A. | Died in Cabanatuan, August 3, 1942, of malaria |
| Byars, Frank | KIA, January 1, 1942 |
| Cahill, James A. | KIA, February 9, 1942 |
| Cambell, Willard | Died in Camp O'Donnell, June 3, 1942, of dysentery |
| Cigoi, Walter F. | Died on Formosa, November 3, 1942, of dysentery |
| Colter, Harley W. | Died in Japan, January 29, 1945, of colitis |
| Corr, Charles | Died in Cabanatuan, June 9, 1942, of dysentery |
| Danca, Richard E. | Died in Takao, Formosa, November 13, 1942 |
| Deckert, Henry J. | KIA at Agoo, December 22, 1941 |
| Dettmer, Donald A. | Died on work detail in the Philippines, May 14, 1942 |
| Edwards, Al | Died aboard prison ship, October 22, 1944 |
| Ehrhardt, Clyde D. | Died aboard prison ship, October 24, 1944 |
| Eldridge, D. J. | Died in Cabanatuan, July 21, 1942, of dysentery |
| Ellis, Ralph | Unknown |
| Flores, Felix | Died in Camp 17, Japan, January 22, 1943, of pneumonia |
| Garr, C. E. | Died in Cabanatuan, November 9, 1942, of dysentery |
| Gorr, Alex | Died aboard prison ship, October 24, 1944 |
| Graff, R. W. | KIA, February 3, 1942 |
| Griffin, James | Killed at Bilibid Prison, July 3, 1944 |
| Griswald, Jack | Died in Tenagawa, Japan, December 4, 1942, of dysentery |
| Hanes, Donald | Died in Fukuoka, Camp 1, Japan, February 5, 1945, of dysentery |
| Hay, John | Died in Cabanatuan, October 18, 1942, of dysentery |
| Heilig, Roger J. | Died aboard prison ship, October 24, 1944 |
| Hepburn, Andrew | Died in Bilibid Prison, December 18, 1943, of pneumonia |
| Heuill, Charles | KIA, February 3, 1942 |
| Hildebrandt, Warren | Died aboard prison ship, October 24, 1944 |
| Holland, Arthur A. | Died aboard prison ship, October 24, 1944 |
| Humphries, Quincy | MIA |
| Hurd, Willie S. | Died aboard prison ship, October 24, 1944 |
| Jannisch, Fred | Died in Cabanatuan, October 14, 1942, of dysentery |
| Jendrysik, Frank | Died in Cabanatuan, July 3, 1942, of malaria |
| Jennings, Harvey V. | Died in Cabanatuan, December 1, 1942, of malaria |
| Jennings, Willard | Died in Camp O'Donnell, June 12, 1942, of dysentery |
| Johnson, Robert | Died aboard prison ship, December 15, 1944 |

| | |
|---|---|
| King, Harry | Died at Camp O'Donnell, June 2, 1942, of liver failure |
| King, Ronald J. | Died in Cabanatuan, September 14, 1942, of dysentery |
| Kolbe, Lyle | Died in Cabanatuan, July 16, 1942, of malaria |
| Kwiatkowski, Joseph | Died in McKinley Hospital, January 14, 1945, of TB |
| Lovering, Fred | Died in Cabanatuan, July 3, 1942, of dysentery |
| McArthur, Albert C. | Died, September 23, 1942, of diphtheria and malaria |
| Mahr, Walter J. | Died in Cabanatuan of dysentery |
| Mason, Raymond | KIA at Tarlac, Philippines, December 29, 1941 |
| Massey, Howard I. | Died aboard prison ship, January 15, 1945 |
| Massie, Charles | Died in hospital from battle wounds, March 2, 1942 |
| Meueller, Alexander | Died in Cabanatuan, August 12, 1942, of dysentery |
| Miller, Robert | Died in Bilibid Prison, December 18, 1942 |
| Moody, August | Died aboard prison ship, September 4, 1944 |
| Peppers, Clemmath | KIA, February 3, 1942 |
| Peterson, Charles | Died in Cabanatuan, August 9, 1942, of dysentery |
| Reed, William | KIA, December 29, 1941 |
| Schwass, Reuben | Died in ZenSgi, Japan, April 6, 1943, of starvation |
| Singletery, E. R. | Died in Camp Olivias, Philippines, May 25, 1942, of dysentery |
| Sorensen, Robert | Died in Osaka, Japan, June 22, 1943, of dysentery |
| Spencer, Norman | Died in Cabanatuan, November 12, 1942, of malaria |
| Squires, E. E. | Died in Cabanatuan, August 17, 1942, of malaria |
| Swartz, Michael | Died in Camp O'Donnell, May 1, 1942, of dysentery |
| Swift, William | Died in Cabanatuan, October 28, 1942, of dysentery |
| Swinehamer, Jack D. | Unknown |
| Taylor, Ralph | Died in Cabanatuan, November 28, 1942, of dysentery |
| Thorman, Russell T. | Died aboard prison ship, January 25, 1945 |
| VanArsdall, George A. | Died aboard prison ship, January 12, 1945 |
| Van Pelt, A. | Died aboard prison ship, October 10, 1944 |
| Vonbergen, Willard | Died in Cabanatuan, August 11, 1942, of dysentery |
| Winger, Edward G. | Died in Bataan Hospital, February 7, 1942, of wounds |
| Wisnieski, Joseph | Died in Cabanatuan, October 17, 1942, of dysentery |
| Write, Walter | KIA, December 24, 1941, by exploding land mine |
| Yeast, Willard | Burned alive by the Japanese guards on Palawan, Philippines, December 14, 1944 |

# INDEX

# ABOUT THE AUTHOR

Dr. Lester Tenney is a survivor of the infamous Bataan Death March. For a total of three and a half years, he was a prisoner of war of the Japanese, first in the Philippines and then in Japan. Tenney spent the first eighteen months after returning home in and out of army hospitals, where he underwent numerous operations on his shoulder and hip, both war- and prison camp–related injuries.

Tenney obtained his bachelor's degree in business from the University of Miami in 1949 and taught at Miami Senior High School in 1950–51. Then Tenney entered the insurance business, in which he enjoyed seventeen successful years. He next received a master's degree in business from San Diego State University. After teaching insurance, finance, and accounting at San Diego State, Dr. Tenney got his doctorate in finance and insurance from the University of Southern California.

Later Tenney worked with the Arizona state legislature in developing a retirement and insurance program for all Arizona State employees. Dr. Tenney is now a professor emeritus of insurance and finance from Arizona State University and continues to lead seminars dealing with retirement and financial issues.

Tenney's many publications include the nationally acclaimed pre-retirement series "Planning for the Years Ahead" and a series of five booklets on financial planning entitled "Your Financial Education Series." His most recent book, *Your Financial Survival Under the Medicaid System*, has won acclaim from the insurance and finance industry. *My Hitch in Hell* was really fifty-four years in the making. He maintains he spent four years researching the book and fifty years in writing it.

Dr. Tenney has one son, Glenn, and two grandsons, Aaron and Micah. His wife of thirty-four years, Betty, has two sons, Donald and Ed Levi, and three grandchildren, David, Aaron, and Crystal.